1982

Planning for Services to Handicapped Persons

Planning for Services to Handicapped Persons
Community, Education, Health

Edited by

Phyllis R. Magrab, Ph.D.
Associate Professor of Pediatrics, Georgetown University;
Director, Georgetown University Child Development Center;
Chief Pediatric Psychologist, Georgetown University Hospital,
Washington, D.C.
and

Jerry O. Elder, M.A.
Assistant Professor, Crippled Children's Division;
Director, Interagency Collaboration Project,
Crippled Children's Division,
Child Development and Rehabilitation Center,
University of Oregon Health Sciences Center,
Portland

·PAUL·H·
BROOKES
PUBLISHERS

Baltimore • London

Paul H. Brookes, Publishers
Post Office Box 10624
Baltimore, Maryland 21204

Typeset by The Composing Room of Michigan, Inc. (Grand Rapids)
Manufactured in the United States of America by The Maple Press Company
(York, Pennsylvania)

Library of Congress Cataloging in Publication Data
Main entry under title:

Planning for services to handicapped persons.

 Includes index.
 1. Developmentally disabled services—Planning—
United States—Addresses, essays, lectures.
I. Magrab, Phyllis R. II. Elder, Jerry O.
HV3001.A4P57   362.4'0973   79-21474
ISBN 0-933716-04-4

Contents

Contributors vii

Preface ix

Dedication xv

Chapter 1 Community Service Planning / *Anderson Pollard, Howard
           Hall & Charles Keeran* 1

Chapter 2 Educational Planning / *Ronald Wiegerink & John Pelosi* . . 41

Chapter 3 Perspectives on Planning for Prevention of Mental
           Retardation / *Andrew E. Lorincz* 77

Chapter 4 Community Health Planning / *Herbert J. Cohen* 91

Chapter 5 Health Planning for Handicapped Persons in Residential
           Settings / *Philip Ziring* 121

Chapter 6 Rehabilitation Planning / *William Kiernan* 137

Chapter 7 Advocacy / *Marianne Bennett & Robert P. McNeill* 173

Chapter 8 Coordination of Service Delivery Systems / *Jerry O. Elder* 193

Chapter 9 Case Study for Planning Coordinated Services / *Elynor
           Kazuk, Lorna Greene & Phyllis R. Magrab* 211

Index 247

Contributors

Marianne Bennett, J.D., COMSERV Center for Legal Representation, Los Lunas, New Mexico (87031)

Herbert J. Cohen, M.D., Director, Bronx Developmental Services, University Affiliated Facility; Professor of Pediatrics, Albert Einstein College of Medicine, Yeshiva University, Bronx, New York (10461)

Jerry O. Elder, M.A., Assistant Professor, Crippled Children's Division; Director, Interagency Collaborative Project, Crippled Children's Division, Child Development and Rehabilitation Center, University of Oregon Health Sciences Center, Portland (97207)

Lorna Greene, Consultant, Head Start Feasibility Project, John F. Kennedy Child Development Center; Coordinator, Interagency Project, John F. Kennedy Child Development Center, University of Colorado Medical Center, Denver (80220)

Howard Hall, D.S.W., Community Liaison, University Affiliated Facility, Neuropsychiatric Institute, University of California, Los Angeles (90024)

Elynor Kazuk, M.A., Assistant to the Director, John F. Kennedy Child Development Center; Coordinator, Head Start Feasibility Project, John F. Kennedy Child Development Center; Acting Director of Community Affairs, John F. Kennedy Child Development Center, University of Colorado Medical Center, Denver (80220)

Charles Keeran, M.S.W., Director of Administration, Neuropsychiatric Institute, University of California, Los Angeles (90024)

William E. Kiernan, Ph.D., Director of Rehabilitation, Developmental Evaluation Clinic, The Children's Hospital Medical Center, Boston, Massachusetts (02115)

Andrew E. Lorincz, M.D., Director, Center for Developmental and Learning Disorders; Professor of Pediatrics, The Medical Center, The University of Alabama, Birmingham (35294)

Phyllis R. Magrab, Ph.D., Associate Professor of Pediatrics, Georgetown University; Director, Georgetown University Child Development Center; Chief Pediatric Psychologist, Georgetown University Hospital, Washington, D.C. (20007)

Robert P. McNeill, J.D., COMSERV Center for Legal Representation; Consultant, American Association of University Affiliated Programs for the Developmentally Disabled; private practice, Western Bank Building, Albuquerque, New Mexico (87102)

John Pelosi, Ph.D., Associate Director for Planning and Evaluation, Developmental Disabilities Technical Assistance System; Associate Professor, Division of Special Education, University of North Carolina, Chapel Hill (27514)

Anderson Pollard, M.S.W., Community Liaison, Neuropsychiatric Institute, University of California, Los Angeles (90024)

Ronald Wiegerink, Ph.D., Director, Developmental Disabilities Technical Assistance System, Frank Porter Graham Child Development Center, Chapel Hill; Professor, Division of Special Education, University of North Carolina, Chapel Hill (27514)

Philip R. Ziring, M.D., Associate Clinical Professor of Pediatrics, Columbia University, College of Physicians and Surgeons; Associate Attending Pediatrician, Presbyterian Hospital; Deputy Director, Staten Island Development Center, Staten Island, New York (10314)

Preface

Handicapped citizens in this country represent a unique challenge to our society to provide for them a supportive environment that will optimize all aspects of their lives. This is a time of social change where we as a society have become more willing to accept our moral and ethical obligations to these individuals. Until the passage of legislation giving handicapped citizens the right to an equal education, and the implementation of other rights guaranteed in the constitution of due process and equal protection of the laws, they, by and large, have been treated as second class citizens. Recent landmark court cases in New York, Pennsylvania, and other states have resulted in a diversity of new services. On the one hand this represents a positive step toward meeting the needs of handicapped individuals; on the other hand, there has been little or no effort to adequately plan for the orderly implementation of these services. This has resulted in duplicative, fragmented, and, in many cases, chaotic multiple service delivery systems. The necessity for planning for coordinated comprehensive services is a significant problem and serves as the focus of this book.

Services to handicapped persons transgress the traditional boundaries of the community and social field, the educational system, the health delivery system, and the vocational rehabilitation system. All of these service delivery areas must be considered in planning for services to handicapped persons. Most handicapping conditions require the services of two, three, or all four of these human service delivery systems. Importantly, there is a need to look at how these services relate to and affect each other. Because they are handicapped, this segment of our population cannot easily pick and choose the appropriate services required.

The challenge of the Seventies has been one of providing equal services for handicapped individuals that have traditionally been a right of the non-handicapped population. The challenge of the Eighties, however, will be to provide a plan for a coordinated, collaborative human service delivery system that will enable the handicapped to receive services in an expeditious and coordinated fashion. This book will provide some insight into how this might be accomplished.

Because numerous books and articles have been written about methods and techniques on planning in the health, educational, vocational, community, and social field, this book does not address the planning process itself. Instead each of these service delivery systems is examined as a sound foundation for developing a planning process. Once this understanding is achieved, planning processes already in existence can be applied to the development of a coordinated, multi-faceted human service delivery system to handicapped individuals.

IDENTIFYING HANDICAPPED PERSONS

One of the problems in planning for services to handicapped individuals is the lack of an agreed upon definition. Various public efforts currently exist to define the handicapped population, but there continues to be controversy between those who prefer a functional approach to definition as in the new Rehabilitation Comprehensive Services and Developmental Disabilities Amendment of 1978 (PL 95-602) and those who prefer a more categorical approach as in the Education for All Handicapped Children Act of 1975 (PL 94-142). The basis of this controversy rests on such issues as utility, labeling, and planning for needs.

For the purposes of this book, we have adopted a definition for handicapped individuals similar to the one put forward in PL 94-142. At this point in time this appears to be the most broadly accepted, comprehensive definition; nonetheless, we strongly acknowledge the virtues of a functional approach to planning for services of these handicapped individuals. The term *handicapped persons* will include the mentally retarded and those with related neurological handicaps; the orthopedically impaired; the multiply handicapped; deaf and blind; and the severely learning disabled who, because of these impairments, require special services at all ages.

In answering the question "who are handicapped persons," it is also important to have a sense of the magnitude of this problem. Throughout this volume, the question of identification of the handicapped population and how to obtain accurate incidence and prevalence statistics recurs. The health, educational, and social systems have not been able to develop sufficient methodologies to answer these questions. Through a better coordinated system of services, we may be able to work toward more accurate needs assessments and to better estimates of the handicapped population requiring services.

SERVICE DELIVERY SYSTEM

The service delivery system for the handicapped in the United States is really a series of fragmented service delivery systems in the areas of community and social services, education, vocational rehabilitation, and health delivery. Each of these systems was developed independently in response to needs within each of these areas over the past decades. For example, in the health care delivery system, health service for the handicapped was based in the early part of the century almost entirely on an institutionalized population. All of the programs which were developed related to institutional needs and, until recently, little attention was given to health services for the handicapped in local communities outside of the large state and private institutions. Similar changes in focus and direction can be cited in each of the major human service delivery systems.

Overlapping Legislation

A major factor contributing to the current fragmented human service delivery system is overlapping legislation at the federal level. For example, the Federal Programs Information and Assistance Project (1978), in their document "Guide to Federal Resources for the Developmentally Disabled," identified 165 different federal programs or services which can potentially assist developmentally disabled persons. Numerous programs have been developed in response to meeting the needs of handicapped individuals as a result of recent court action. New programs have been developed and existing ones expanded in federal agencies such as the Administration for Children, Youth and Families; Rehabilitation Services Administration; Health Services Administration; National Institutes of Health; Alcohol, Drug Abuse and Mental Health Administration; Health Care Financing Administration; Social Security Administration; and the Office of Education. Unfortunately, with few exceptions, most of these programs were developed independently, with little apparent concern for potential overlap in programs among these various agencies. Another confusing factor is the differing definitions of what constitutes a handicap under the various federal programs. However, the federal government has recognized the lack of planning in the past and some steps are being taken to correct this oversight. These issues are addressed throughout this book with concluding chapters on coordination of service delivery systems.

Multiple Funding

Another contributing factor to the fragmentation of the human service delivery system is multiple funding that exists for the provision of services to the handicapped. Most of the financing available for services to the handicapped is in the form of yearly budgets from various federal, state, and local governmental programs. Again, since there is little coordination of effort to plan for these programs, the funding of these programs also naturally lacks the needed coordination of financing. Because the federal government provides the major funding for most programs and services to the handicapped, it is able to influence the policy and direction of these programs heavily. This is not an undesirable situation as long as the federal government listens to the input of local planning agencies and special interest groups concerned with the needs of the handicapped and as long as it maintains the commitment to continued funding of programs for the handicapped.

For health services to the handicapped, a portion of income for health services is derived from private third party insurance coverage. This is only true, however, for handicapped children of parents who are employed and carry third party coverage or for handicapped adults who are employed and also covered by a third party group insurance policy. The largest share of health and related services for the handicapped comes from Title XIX coverage under the Social Security Act.

Another source of financing for services to the handicapped comes from handicapped individuals themselves. Because of the high cost of specialized services for the handicapped, however, financing of these services from the clients themselves is very limited, except for the very wealthy members of our society. Private foundations and organizations generate a considerable amount of funding through contributions. They fund various educational and service and demonstration projects.

Unfortunately, there is very little effort to coordinate these multiple funding sources. This results in an overlap of funding in some areas and creates gaps in other areas. Again, this problem is raised in several chapters and the final chapters of this book discuss suggested solutions to this problem.

Multiple Planning Bodies

Most of the planning done to date in developing services to the handicapped has been carried out by special interest groups organized around major disease categories. For example, services to the mentally retarded have been a concern of the President's Committee on Mental Retardation and various private organizations with a special interest in mental retardation. Planning for services to individuals with epilepsy has been a concern of the National Epilepsy League. For those affiliated with cerebral palsy, the United Cerebral Palsy Association has championed these individual's rights. With the expanded functional definition of developmental disabilities under the 1978 amendments to the Developmental Disabilities Services and Facilities Construction Act, a large percentage of the handicapped within the United States will fall under this functional definition. However, there are still individuals who do not fall within this definition for whom planning is still carried on by special interest groups. These include children with severe learning disabilities, disease categories of hemophilia, arthritis, leukemia, the deaf and blind, and others. Little coordination of planning efforts exists among these special interest groups and the Developmental Disabilities Councils.

There also is little coordination of effort between the Health Systems Agencies who are concerned with the health needs of handicapped individuals and other planning bodies, such as the Developmental Disabilities Councils, who are looking at more than just health needs. Therefore, multiple planning bodies only contribute to the fragmentation of the overall service delivery system for handicapped individuals.

Different Models of Service Delivery

Another contributing factor to the fragmentation of the service delivery system is the existence of different models of service delivery. Different models have developed over the years because of the severity and complexity of handicapping conditions. Those in the education field consider their "education model," which concentrates on the educational and behavioral aspects of the handicapped individual, to be the most appropriate mechanism for providing services to the handicapped. At the same time, those in the health field argue that the "medical model," which concentrates on the health problems of the handicapped individual and the physician's role in meeting these needs, is the most appropriate service delivery model. Others in the social service and rehabilitation fields consider their models of service delivery to be more appropriate.

Each of these service delivery systems has a place and role in providing services to the handicapped, and each model can and should work harmoniously together. For example, in the early childhood years of a physically handicapped individual, the medical model of service delivery might be the most appropriate service delivery mechanism. Once this child becomes school age, the educational model may be more appropriate. As the child matures, becomes an adult, and is ready to go into gainful employment, certain aspects of the vocational and service delivery systems may be more appropriate in dealing with the needs of this individual.

This book examines these various models of service delivery so that the reader may examine the complexity of each of the major service delivery systems. The concluding chapters address how each of these models can operate in a coordinated service delivery system for handicapped individuals.

We would like to express our deepest appreciation to Jean Marie Murphy for her dedicated assistance with the preparation of this manuscript.

Phyllis R. Magrab

Jerry O. Elder

Dedication

To our families
　Kylee, Brendan, and Ryan
　Janice, Susan, Molly, Jimmy, Scott, Steven, and Shawn

Planning for Services to Handicapped Persons

Chapter 1
Community Service Planning

Anderson Pollard, Howard Hall & Charles Keeran

This chapter is concerned with the encompassing and complex concept called community service planning. Within this context, the basic concept of community is broad and often ambiguous. It may be used to refer to a variety of social, political, or geographic areas as well as to a variety of special interest groups within a given area. Community may be defined as the territorial organization of peoples, goods, services, and commitments. It is usually seen as an important subsystem of the larger society and one in which locally relevant functions are carried out. With such diverse characteristics it can readily be seen why purposeful and disciplined planning is needed for development of human services delivery systems on a community level.

This picture is further complicated by the fact that community service planning often involves the coordination of many other subservice systems such as health, education, and welfare (to be dealt with in more detail in later chapters). Community service planning, thus, becomes the umbrella under which other more direct service delivery systems are developed and function. As such, it needs to be set on a firm foundation in order to provide the best possible climate for the myriad of services which fall under it.

The need for community service planning is taking on a new urgency with the present national policy and commitment to the deinstitutionalization of handicapped persons, particularly mentally ill and mentally retarded persons. This is causing planners to contemplate designs for new concepts of community-oriented programs. Planning for community-based services is creating new alliances between urban planners and planners of human service systems.

This chapter begins with a discussion of the goal and purpose of planning—the creation of community-level service delivery systems. The main thrust of the chapter is the presentation of a new planning model, one which has sufficient specificity so as to be applicable to particular service delivery systems and sufficient flexibility so as to be appropriate to a given

1

community at given points in time, or to a variety of communities. This is followed with an examination of the importance of the interplay between the private and public service sectors, particularly as it relates to this model for community planning. It continues with some general observations on the planning process, particularly the more traditional approaches to planning. The chapter concludes with a discussion of such impinging factors as legislation and social trends and of how they influence the application of the model.

SERVICE DELIVERY SYSTEMS FOR HANDICAPPED PERSONS

A delivery system is seen here as a general strategy for the mobilization and organization of all appropriate resources to provide for the prevention, intervention, and rehabilitation of human problems. At present, the human service system is actually a number of separate systems, including health, education, welfare, rehabilitation, recreation, employment, and housing. However, none of these systems separately can solve the multiple problems of handicapped persons and, therefore, there is a need for cooperation, coordination, and collaboration among these subsystems.

Characteristics of a Delivery System

Human service delivery systems occur at three stages of consumer need: prevention (the attempt to avoid crisis), crisis intervention, and rehabilitation. Although it is generally recognized that it is simpler, more economical, and more humane to prevent human crisis than to provide crisis intervention services, the problem of delivering services to an individual or community at the prevention stage is largely one of mobilizing and organizing the community when problems and dangers are still potential and not yet real. Most communities, however, are reactive in that they tend to do nothing about their problems until something goes wrong. Therefore, there is minimal planning for human service systems at this stage. As a consequence, most delivery systems are created to meet the needs of consumers in their intervention and/or rehabilitation stages. Ideally, systems for these stages should have five primary characteristics:

1. Intervention and rehabilitation should be immediately available, accessible, and affordable.
2. Intervention and rehabilitation should be flexible enough to meet the special needs of individual consumers while dealing with broad categories of problem areas.
3. Intervention and rehabilitation should take place within a person's own social milieu where he is firmly linked to family and friends.
4. Intervention and rehabilitation should be aimed at reducing the risk of institutionalization and disenfranchisement from the community.

5. Intervention and rehabilitation should be coordinated so that delivery systems make the most effective and efficient use of existing and emerging community resources.

Attitudes, Beliefs, and Values: Basis for Service Delivery Systems

Planning for human services is an outgrowth of a community's beliefs, values, mores, and cultural norms. The resulting service systems involve such value judgments. The question is not whether planning will reflect politics, but whose politics will it reflect (Long, 1959). What values and whose values will planners seek to implement? McGee and Hitzing (1976), in their article "Current Residential Services: A Critical Analysis," state that all human services are based on belief systems, either conscious or unconscious, that shape the quality and type of services to citizens who are disabled or handicapped.

Traditional belief systems have resulted in designing and developing human service systems that are in segregated settings and environments. We have usually assumed that people with special needs require separate and special services, including separate places in which to live. Our beliefs have been translated into environmental terms: old people belong in nursing homes or "old folks' homes," retarded and mentally ill people belong in institutions, and people with other handicapping conditions such as leprosy and tuberculosis should live in segregated colonies or villages. Sadly, this institutional orientation is a reflection of our society's beliefs and values for a devalued segment of our population—the disabled and the aged.

A glimpse into the history of primary service provision systems—prisons, health, welfare, and education—reflects societal attitudes, beliefs, and values at given points in time and how these values shaped the service delivery systems of those times. For example, at one time in the history of the Western world, to be poor or to be a debtor often led to imprisonment (prison system) and at a later point in time, poverty led to confinement in county almshouses or "poor farms" (welfare system). Because of the high correlation between poverty and handicapping conditions, the service delivery system for disabled persons was often the jail or the almshouse in earlier days. Although greatly improved, contemporary community attitudes toward the disabled, the dependent, and the poor still tend to be punitive.

Much of our attitudinal change towards handicapped persons has been influenced by a sequence of events that have reshaped American social policies. The atrocities of World War II, culminating in the Nuremberg trials, helped us to think in more humane terms; the Civil Rights Era of the 1950's and 1960's pushed us in the direction of today's focus on full human and legal rights for all persons; the concept of normalization, which was first advocated in the Scandinavian countries and spread to the United States, created a climate of accepting mentally handicapped persons back into the mainstream of society.

The concept of "normalization" emerged in the United States at a time when reliance on institutional care was diminishing and the development and utilization of community programs was considered as the best way to proceed. It is based on the assumption that more benefits can be obtained by the handicapped person through focusing on his/her normal aspects than through the remediation of his/her deficits. It recognizes the value of providing services to the handicapped person in as normal a setting as possible and, therefore, averting some of the secondary handicapping conditions resulting from living in an institution: isolation from the normal ebb and flow of the communities, the reduced contact with normal others who can serve as role models, and limitation of opportunity for individualized lifestyle and decision-making.

Most present community-oriented systems of services are built on the foundation of such value-based principles as:

1. "Normalization"
2. The "least-restrictive alternative" or more positively stated, "the most appropriate alternative" (the handicapped person should have the opportunity to live in the most independent setting possible)
3. The "developmental model" (full recognition that the handicapped person, regardless of the severity of his/her disability, is capable of growing emotionally, socially, physically, and intellectually)
4. Handicapped persons are entitled to the same human and legal rights as any other citizen
5. "Mainstreaming" (integration of handicapped persons into the normal activities of the community to the maximum extent possible)

The courts have been a major force in reshaping practices that were previous traditions in the care and treatment of handicapped persons. Court decisions have been translated into federal and state legislation that implement new social policy prohibiting discrimination, the demeaning practices, and the injustices that were heaped upon the nation's 35 million handicapped citizens.

The evolution of attitudes, beliefs, and values within the field of education has created a swing from an original belief that education was a "privilege" reserved exclusively for the wealthy, to the present-day concept that education is the right of all people regardless of class or socioeconomic circumstances. Furthermore, the United States supreme court's landmark decision in 1954 ruled that education is a "right" which must be available to all on an equal basis. Such a decision set the direction for shaping our present-day educational system for handicapped children and adults.

Public education programs for handicapped children have proceeded through a cycle of 1) complete exclusion from public schools, to 2) participation of a few categories of children in regular classes, to 3) the development of special education classes, and to 4) the current reintegration of handicapped students into regular classes to the maximum extent possible—the concept and practice of "mainstreaming."

Today, Public Law 94-142, Education for All Handicapped Children Act, is the law of the land—a social policy influenced by attitudes and beliefs of our contemporary society. It reflects society's beliefs and values that handicapped children need to be integrated from an early age into regular classroom programs whenever appropriate. It further reflects the attitude that handicapped children are individuals, with unique problems and needs that must be addressed on an individual basis.

Although social policy becomes legitimatized and operational through adoption into law and regulations, this by no means creates an attitudinal climate of full acceptance. In reference to Public Law 94-142, there are attitudes on the part of teachers, parents, the general public, and the students themselves (both handicapped and nonhandicapped) that oppose this new educational direction.

Attitudes, beliefs, and values affect the handicapped person in the occupational field. A front page article in the *Wall Street Journal* of January 27, 1976, pointed out that the major barriers to the employment of 8 million disabled persons are attitudinal.

Against a backdrop of American history that is deeply embedded in the Puritan work ethic and a high respect for competition, it has been a difficult task to influence changes in attitudes in the area of employing handicapped persons.

As individuals, employers harbor a wide range of attitudes and beliefs towards handicapped persons. On one side, there is the belief that "hiring the handicapped is good business." Employers subscribing to this belief recognize that handicapped persons have lower rates of tardiness and absenteeism, and turnover costs are lower. On the other hand, it is believed that hiring the handicapped person is not good business because of the notion that there are extra costs and risks.

Over the years, beliefs and values have influenced the policy guidelines and practices of our federal and state rehabilitation agencies. Until recently, vocational training programs carried out by these agencies concentrated their training efforts on those handicapped persons who showed promise of being successful in competitive industry. Today, there is an attitudinal shift and a new policy direction within the field of vocational habilitation and rehabilitation which provide improved opportunities in the world of work to severely handicapped persons.

The impact that community attitudes, beliefs, and values have had in shaping human service programs at different points in time has likewise affected the evolution of our health delivery system. Paralleling the history of education, the health system has proceeded over time from a concept that health care was originally a privilege for the wealthy to the present day social policy which states the right of all citizens to comprehensive health services which are accessible and available. However, the affordability of health services, particularly by middle-class citizens, continues to be a major barrier to the achievement of the goal of quality health services for all citizens.

The public attitude towards the provision of health services to mentally handicapped persons has never been on the same positive level as the public attitude towards serving physically handicapped persons.

Crocetti, Spiro, and Siassi (1974) in their book, *Contemporary Attitudes Toward Mental Illness,* state:

> Illness constitutes a universal phenomenon. Every rational person is aware of the possibility that illness or a handicapping condition, may at any moment strike him or her or those held dear. This awareness plays perhaps the most significant role in the universal compassion for the sick and handicapped, the privileges attached to the sick role, and the tolerance for the deviant behavior of the ill person.
>
> However, mentally handicapped persons tend to be viewed differently from the physically handicapped person. Some researchers suggest that the two views are radically different.

As an example, in the field of mental retardation, we have seen an evolution of programs ranging from early efforts to educate the mentally retarded individual and to make him/her socially competent ("Era of Optimism," 1850 to 1915), to an era typified by programs to identify, segregate, and sterilize every "feebleminded" person as a menace to social decency—to the end that they shall not reproduce their kind.

Society's prejudice toward mentally handicapped persons manifested itself in social barriers and social distance leading to the development of isolated state institutions as the primary mode of service for this population.

It took a series of landmark court cases during the early 1970's to create dramatic changes in the care and treatment of mentally retarded persons. These cases directed us to the social policy of today—"the right to treatment of all persons."

Problems in Creating Service Delivery Systems

The primary objective of a service delivery system for handicapped or disabled persons is the maintenance and support of the "client," "consumer," or "patient" (recipient of services) so that each individual is able to achieve a maximum level of functioning.

There are a number of problems that stand in the way of reaching a "utopia" type of human service delivery system within communities. Unfortunately, in spite of substantial advances made during the past two decades, no community can pride itself on having a full array of essential services for its handicapped population. For instance, public transportation to accommodate physically handicapped persons may be lacking in some communities; early intervention programs for infants and children at high risk of becoming physically or mentally handicapped have only slowly begun to emerge in other communities; and services for the handicapped geriatric population are sorely needed in most communities.

In today's mobile culture, many families have not established adequate resources and social networks (relatives and friends) to provide necessary support to meet vital life problems; therefore, a formal community-based intervention system is necessary.

Since handicapped persons may have a variety of problems that cut across social, vocational, educational, and health areas, it is not possible for a single agency or discipline to serve the total needs of an individual or an individual's family, nor should any agency or discipline claim primacy in providing needed services. Effective access to services requires each agency in the service delivery system to serve as a resource to the individual and the family, and to provide linkage to all other services within the system. A high degree of communication, cooperation, and coordination is therefore required among all the elements of the service delivery system.

The problem of interdisciplinary communication and mutual respect in the broad field of handicapping conditions raises a major barrier to needed cooperation. Terminology, one aspect of the process of communication, illustrates the difficulties involved in coordination planning. For example, the terms "mentally handicapped," "slow learner," "educable retarded," or "severely retarded" may have different meanings to the pediatrician, the psychiatrist, and the educator. Clarification of contradictory terminology alone would be a major factor in bridging the interdisciplinary gulf.

As a major step in achieving interdisciplinary understanding, the University Affiliated Facility (UAF) program has been most notable in developing and spreading, through the educational establishment, an interdisciplinary approach to education in the field of developmental disabilities. The UAF interdisciplinary process promotes the development and use of a basic language, a core body of knowledge, relevant skills, and an understanding of the attitudes, values, and methods of participating disciplines.

The most striking feature of the human service field is its nonsystem character: the lack of coordination of various service elements. The barriers against the coordination of services are indeed formidable because of such factors as:

1. The competitiveness of long established institutions
2. The lack of an organizational structure that brings agencies together around areas of mutual interest
3. The parochial interests of agencies and organizations that make them myopic to the needs of a broader community
4. The lack of experience in the techniques of coordinated planning

5. Awkwardness in interdisciplinary communication and lack of respect among the many professional groups whose skills are needed by the handicapped
6. Failure to recognize that programs for handicapped persons are co-equally a major responsibility of several government agencies at the federal, state, and local levels: *e.g.*, Health, Education and Welfare as well as Mental Health, Rehabilitation, Housing and Employment
7. The temptation of system delivery designers to become so preoccupied and fixated on the "system design" that they lose sight of the functional role of the system and of the individual agencies working to meet the service needs of handicapped persons

A relatively recent development in the efforts to solve some of these problems has been the establishing of multiservice structures; one-stop centers designed to meet a multiplicity of client needs, In 1966, President Lyndon B. Johnson initiated a national program to establish 14 multiservice centers across the country with the combined efforts and funds of five federal agencies. Before that, the Office of Economic Opportunity supported neighborhood service centers on a smaller scale in communities throughout the nation. Currently, the federal government is playing a key role in bringing about the integration of services by mandating such coordination as a condition for funding in order to ensure a comprehensive range of services.

Coordinated planning, whether at the federal, state, or local level, requires a sophisticated approach to the planning process, a high degree of communication and cooperation among relatively independent agencies, public and private, and a real commitment to interdisciplinary teamwork. The concept of interagency, coordinated planning in services to handicapped persons is not an easy one to implement, partly because we are accustomed to a compartmentalized administrative structure. This coordination of effort constitutes a major challenge to the field of community organization which may well serve as a prototype for further efforts in planning for human services.

DEVELOPING A CYCLICAL MODEL FOR PLANNING

It is generally assumed that knowledge, skills, and resulting services grow in a linear or logically progressive manner. For example, it is assumed that there was a more knowledgeable base and sounder practice of medicine 50 years ago than 150 years ago. It is assumed that a higher level of social enlightenment and more humane social policy exists in the present than in the Twelfth Century. It is also assumed that the potential for a better lifestyle for human beings has existed during the industrial and atomic age than during the many centuries of agrarian life.

An uncritical acceptance of these assumptions, however, denies us access to some of history's most valuable lessons. To act on the unquestioning belief that "new" is necessarily "better" and that "change" is the equivalent of "progress" is to miss the delightful irony of the truism: "The more things change, the more they stay the same." A review of history shows that we have repeated most of our major experiments many times, frequently modifying the "new" and "different" with the "tried" and "true" of the past. This repetition of and building on time-tested models gives us a cyclical pattern which utilizes the past in planning for the future.

To be an instrument of value, the cyclical model must be applicable to current and future service planning in a manner which is supplementary and complementary to the traditional elements of planning. Traditional models place initial emphasis upon defining population bases, identification of service needs, clarification of resources, program design, service implementation, and evaluation of services. Although clarification of statistical data, potential funding resources, and program priorities are important, such a focus substantially ignores the broader social and environmental elements which impinge upon the planning process.

The cyclical model places initial emphasis upon the interrelated social variable which influences the mechanized elements of traditional service implementation. Secondly, the cyclical model provides a method of exploring the continually shifting relationship between the cultural and social variables which affect service delivery or, ultimately, fulfillment of needs. Prior examination of such variables could lead to patterns of meeting needs of handicapped persons not envisioned through previous methodologies.

Defining the Cyclical Model

The cyclical model is built upon the following premises:

1. There is value in building upon the knowledge gained through experience and history.
2. Planning and service systems are responsive to current and emerging social values emanating from both the public and private sectors.
3. Although dominant social systems and values are not always compatible with a progressive pattern of service development, effective planning must be responsive to such variables.
4. As the repetitious cycles of history evolve, they tend to pick up service patterns developed in the past, extract elements thereof, and generate a new service pattern through inclusion of current innovations and methodologies.
5. Through the cyclical pattern of short and long term history, the progressive patterns of today may trigger the regressive patterns of tomorrow as well as the progress of patterns in years to come.
6. Individuals and societies often proclaim the extremes of the value system in order to witness its inception and implementation.

7.   There are certain boundaries for planning inherent in the current values and structure of society.

8.   Although ideal planning models can never be achieved, the most applicable planning models emerge through an understanding of the current society-related systems and the capacity for adaptation or consolidation.

9.   Planning is part of a complex exchange between the public and private sectors of society which contribute at different points of the planning and service development process.

10. Significant contributors to the planning process will operate from different points of a value spectrum at a given place and at a given point in time.

11. Loss, rediscovery, and repetition can be positive forces in the planning process when applied with an appreciation for both past experience and current application.

The cyclical model is illustrated in Figure 1. The variety of elements, among others, emanating from the public and private sectors which influence the character of service planning and implementation are represented at the base of the figure. Such variables perpetually intertwine in irritation or support of emerging or disintegrating service patterns. A positive or negative contribution of each variable is relevant to complex circumstances at any point in time. A variety of continua reflecting planning variables are represented on either side of the central core of the figure. These continua, among others, pertain to: 1) social attitudes toward handicapped persons; 2) values placed on services, and 3) how services are planned and delivered. The vertical placement of each continuum has no significance, as their values are clearly interrelated. However, the placement does reflect the potential for a culture, an organization, or an individual to occupy any point on a specific continuum and different points on various continua at any specified time.

The spiral pattern climbing up the central core of Figure 1 represents time and the potential for recycling values, service patterns, skills, and knowledge in a manner which will make a positive or a negative contribution to current service patterns. These cycles, which could cover the width of the page, also represent the perpetual shifting in time of societies, organizations, and individuals along the continua of the planning variables when an attempt is made to promote or demote specific attitudes, policies, or services.

Application of the Model

At any point in time, a society may be represented on different points of the continuum relevant to different variables. For example, during the last 20 years, the United States has reflected a relatively humanistic value system related to handicapped individuals, consequently placing itself on the left-hand side of the humanistic/dehumanizing continuum. During the early part of

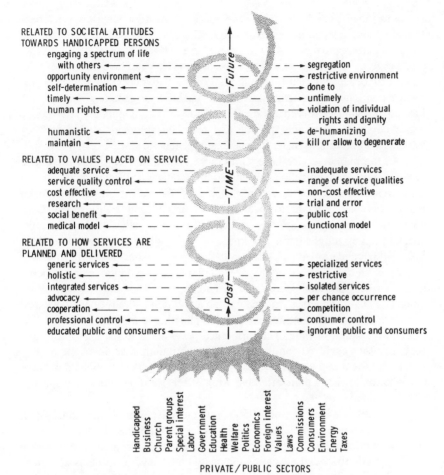

Figure 1. Continuum of planning variables.

this period, the country tended to segregate developmentally disabled individuals from contact with the broader spectrum of the culture, consequently placing itself on the right-hand side of the continuum at the top of the figure. To further illustrate the movement in relation to time, during the early 1960's private parent groups and organizations piloted many specialized services for developmentally disabled and other handicapped individuals, while the public system gave these individuals only limited access to generic services. During the middle and later 1960's, the public sector increased its role in provision of specialized services, while the private sector began to envision and formulate a model relevant to a generic service base. As such concepts as "mainstreaming" and "least-restrictive alternative" became popular, the public sector began to move away from specialized services toward a generic service base through those institutions which traditionally had provided services for the handicapped population. At this point, the private sector began to de-emphasize its role in direct services and assumed greater responsibilities relevant to advocacy, thus shifting to the left of the "advocacy/per chance occurrence" continuum to generate a wider service base for generic systems which had not previously served handicapped individuals. Eventually, the public sector began to adopt this attitude and formulate protection and advocacy systems within various states as mandated by federal law.

As the public service base shifts more toward delivery through generic systems with maximization of engaging handicapped individuals in the mainstream of community activity, some of the values which were once highly cherished in the more specialized training programs will be lost. Consequently, there may be a move on the part of the private sector to reinstitute special training programs for a segment of the handicapped population which they will have identified as "lost" in the more impersonal and nonresponsive generic system. As it is demonstrated that this population gains benefits through surrogated and specialized programs, other populations will be included. Thus, planners participate in an evolutionary movement back and forth along various continua of service-planning variables while cycling through the spiral of time. The difference is reflected in the probability that each time they cycle to a familiar point of a continuum or a value system, they bring with them knowledge, values, and skills that generally make a positive contribution toward a more effective array of service programs at that specific point in time.

In another example, the 1950's reflected a generic education system through which most handicapped persons received services in regular classes. In modern terminology, they were "mainstreamed." During the 1960's, there was a growth of special education classes with a range of teachers and other professionals trained to provide specialized services for developmentally disabled and other handicapped individuals. The late 1970's are witnessing a rapid movement of handicapped individuals from special classes back to generic education within the regular classroom. The return to the regular classroom should be accompanied by the skills and knowledge contributed by professionals trained during the period in which segregated education was promoted. Consequently, although planners may rapidly fluctuate in the values and methodologies through which services are provided, society will probably distill the better qualities of this previous experience in the future.

Frequently, concepts are overdramatized or overmarketed in an attempt to establish programs which are responsive to values on an extreme end of the continuum. "Normalization" has been marketed to contradict "special classes." The "least-restrictive alternative" is frequently marketed in a manner which would negate the value of "institutional care." Innovation is frequently valued as a goal in itself. New values and program concepts have an emotional appeal which tends to draw people from previously established programs. Most such activities are based upon false premises, inasmuch as the components of many "innovative" programs are the remnants of past service patterns. Tremendous amounts of time, energy, and finances are consumed in this basic process while planners "reinvent" what they have already experienced.

Implementation of Cyclical Model

Although a society can be approximately placed on a series of continuums with reference to a specific period of time, there is also value in placing subelements of the society on the continuum for the purpose of comparative analysis. It is also important to identify discrepancies between the professed and the operational values of a society (or societal subelements) on a continuum at the same moment in time.

The extremities of a continuum are only reference points for the direction in which a society or elements of a society are moving within a specified time. Cultures tend to profess values and lofty goals as a rallying point to influence service policy and direction. This is the traditional pattern. The strategies and timing of such efforts would be better served through an appreciation for the position and movement of a host of elements within the public and private sectors on continua with impact on the service delivery system.

Regardless of the values and merits surrounding a proposed program, it may be critical to examine issues such as the following with reference to the present time and to a projected period of time:

Is this a time for program demonstration, replication, or consolidation?
Is this a period in which the private element of the service sector should demonstrate innovative programs or advocate assumption of program responsibilities by the public service sector?
Is the public attitude and, consequently, the tax dollar receptive to expanded or restrictive programming?
Should emphasis be placed upon program expansion, quality control, or fiscal responsibility?
What is the current tone of public response to handicapped persons?
Are we currently overemphasizing or underemphasizing structure and procedure in serving handicapped persons?
What elements of our current technological patterns will help or hinder program development?

These and other significant questions can be partially answered by examining major societal and subcultural trends. To do so, two factors must be identified. First, the societal or subcultural target of concern must be identified, *e.g.:* public attitude among the politically influential, public or private

service agencies, parents, professionals, consumers, churches, private industry, and educational institutions, among other variables. Second, specific
continua must be identified as applicable to the addressed concern, *e.g.*:
*social benefit/public cost, medical model/functional model, professional
control/consumer control, cooperation/competition, self-determination/
"done to," program emphasis/procedure emphasis.*

The problem is in not allowing our personal values and goals to influence
our identification and view in selecting the social target groups, the continua
on which they will be placed, or the position and direction of their interrelationship. If an individual could objectively examine the relative position and
direction of target groups on various continua, collective analysis could
provide direction regarding the nature, timeliness, and direction of elements
within the service system for handicapped persons. Such analysis should
precede program planning, implementation, or expansion.

Several value-latent continua are presented in the remainder of this section. The intent is to illustrate the movement patterns of different cultural
target groups on such continua and their relative influence on public policy.
Although the illustrations primarily focus upon public attitudes and broader
social variables as targets, specific subcultural targets, such as those specified
above, should also be analyzed on various continua in a similar manner. The
aggregate result of analyzing the interrelationships between cultural targets
and continua, both individually and collectively, will provide substantial data
for program planning and implementation.

Continuum: Engaging Life with Others/Segregation   Our society has
witnessed rapid cycles and shifts on the integration/segregation continuum in
response to many subcultures such as American Indians, blacks, chronically
ill persons, and handicapped individuals. During the first half of the Twen-
tieth Century, integration was more a function of lack of alternatives than
design. Later patterns of segregation from the community was lead by expanded institutionalization and segregated patterns in education.

Currently, such terms as "mainstreaming," "normalization," and
"least-restrictive alternative" have lead us toward a more integrative,
philosophical stance. The fact remains that most of our resources are still
focused on a segregation pattern of service. Also, the public attitudinal climate is still biased toward segregation of developmentally disabled persons.
At best, public attitudes shift slowly. However, such a shift may be further
impaired by factors related to the following continuum.

Continuum: Humanism/Self-Survival   Our democracy was based and
built upon many humanistic values underpinned by creeds of individual self-
worth and self-determination. The "Puritan work ethic" underscored the
mandate for individual motivation, whereas the religious base in which it was
rooted also embraced broad humanistic principles. This dual heritage has
allowed the culture and cultural subelements an uncanny ease and comfort in

shifting along a humanistic/self-survival continuum. The Civil Rights Movement of the 1960's and the consciousness-raising which flowed into the 1970's carried similar legislative and advocacy benefits for the developmentally disabled and other handicapped persons.

However, although legal, organizational, and procedural avenues on behalf of this population may be strengthened, another variable may override the broader base of public acceptance. There is increased documentation that current inflation and economic pressures are causing the American public to shift from humanistic toward self-survival concerns and priorities. As this pattern continues, planners can expect a hardening of attitudes toward the underprivileged and less influential members of society. This shift will be signalled by a disproportionate tightening of public and private monies or programs related to the developmentally disabled. There are already signs of increased procedural and regulatory requirements under the guise of tighter auditing, advocacy, and increased program quality; however, funds to support such procedural and administrative requirements have not been forthcoming. The aggregate result is higher ideals, glorious proclamations, increased structure—and decreased services.

Continuum: Self-Determination/"Done To" Philosophically, our culture is shifting from the "done to" toward the "self-determination" side of this continuum in anticipation that developmentally disabled and other handicapped persons may take greater responsibility for their own lives. However, an interesting phenomenon is occurring. We are rapidly structuring such professionally defined concepts as "normalization," "mainstreaming," and "least-restrictive alternative" to the point where the original intents have little meaning. Professional, organizational, and regulatory procedures have nearly reisolated the handicapped consumer from the process. What was intended to generate "self-determination" is rapidly becoming a legally mandated and bureaucratically enforced structure for "done to" or "others-determination."

State advocacy programs have been designed to oversee and override local advocacy activities which are closer to the client and service base. Class action suits and other legal procedures may reinforce the principle of human rights while compounding the difficulties of the individual in weaving through the increasingly complex process. In essence, professional intervention, legal gymnastics, and the resultant increase in procedural barriers may often impair the individual's opportunity for self-determination.

Continuum: Individual Responsibility/Legal Mandate This culture has moved toward increased reliance upon regulatory procedures which, in turn, often impinge upon the freedoms of persons whom they were intended to help. This results from the shift of the culture from an individually motivated base of responsibility, as evidenced by the value bases of previous generations, toward increased reliance on legal and regulatory structure to mandate certain behavior which was previously envisioned as morally imperative. Family responsibilities have been replaced by mandates for public education which far exceed basic responsibility for provision of educational opportunity and growth. Countless laws and regulatory procedures have been developed as social mandates for values which were previously envisioned as within the capacity, prerogatives, and moral judgment of individual responsibility.

Although this trend may be defended through efforts to extend civil rights or increase human equity, the decrease of individual responsibility and moral imperatives may have negative side effects such as desensitization to the needs of fellow beings and lessening of interpersonal reaction. Perhaps we cannot legislate morality or the capacity and structure for interface between handicapped and nonhandicapped persons. Self-determination and human exchange requires a deeper individual and moral commitment than the mandates of law and regulatory structure permit.

Continuum: Social Benefit/Public Cost   The former continua illustrate the range of social values which collectively define the quality and style of interface between persons in our society. The issue of cost-effectiveness is closely tied to such values and serves many purposes. During the past decade, society was not particularly concerned with cost-effectiveness. Emphasis was placed upon program innovation and replication. Private programs received substantial public subsidies as pilot demonstrations. In their infant structure, public programs generally did not have the capacity to meet the loftier ideals of public mandates, and monies were frequently reinvested to be rerooted in "special projects" or "projects of national significance."

The inflated economy and resultant public anxiety has triggered a rapid move toward concern for efficiency of public services and cost-effectiveness. To assure congruency with our professed humanistic values, budget "slashing" is handled under the guise of cost-effectiveness. Cost-effectiveness is tied to quality control which, in turn, triggers the rationale for more structure and procedures for monitoring and auditing. In general, greater emphasis appears to have been placed on fiscal audit than on program audit. Professional or service-oriented department heads are being replaced by fiscal luminaries. Administrators with knowledge related to people and services are being replaced by persons with expertise in accounting, systems, and basic management.

Although dehumanizing in nature, this process may produce some benefits beyond cost-effectiveness. When coupled with the experiences of the past decade, this period may introduce an opportunity to evaluate and identify the most effective types of services and methods of delivery. In addition, the austerity economy may force planners to explore alternative methods of service delivery or resolution of need. Perhaps the term "service" is outdated as a dominant concept. Planners may be forced to explore the options for handicapped persons within the private enterprise market. "Patients," who are now beginning to be called "consumers," may soon be seen as "customers," along with others negotiating within the free enterprise system. That would be a large step toward the favored concepts of "self-determination" and "normalization" without the heavy burden of surveillance.

Continuum: Self Regulation/Procedural Regulation Several references to the nature and cause of increased government structure and regulatory procedures have been made within this chapter. This continuum is presented to illustrate the close tie between the broader public attitudes and service planning. This society is passing through an era of sharply increased official regulatory requirements with a surveillance system related to service delivery. There is increased evidence of public dismay at this trend. An increasing volume of public service is being diverted through contracts to the private sector. If this pattern continues, a shift in trends may also be indicated for conceptualization of methods for meeting needs of handicapped persons.

Continuum: Low Technology/High Technology The technology explosion of recent years has great implications for services to handicapped people. Advanced audio and video technology combined with satellite systems provides an international potential still unrealized. Groups of practitioners, parents, and consumers are able to address each other face to face without the time, convenience, and dollar demands of travel which are unrealistic for many organizations and handicapped persons. This expanded technology provides an opportunity for exchange of ideas, evaluation, education, and replication of programs in a manner and at a rate which remain unimaginable to most people. Such exchange will require the discarding of dated methodologies and an openness of exchange with decreased emphasis on authorship.

The potential cost savings and expanded services through use of new technology may trigger the shift in attitudes and adventuresome spirit essential for such advances. Consequently, it is evident that the negatives evidenced in a shift on one continuum may underpin the positive shifts on another continuum. Such foresight is an essential element of planning services for handicapped persons.

COMMUNITY PLANNING: PUBLIC AND PRIVATE SECTORS

Heterogeneous Character and Function

The public and private sectors, as noted, play a repetitious and interwoven function in planning, developing, redefining, and redirecting services in a cyclical pattern through time. In order to see the flow and specific character in this interrelationship, it is important to envision these terms with a more generic application than is generally assumed. The public and private sectors with an impact on community planning for handicapped persons are inclusive of, but not limited to, the agencies and parent groups which have made substantial contributions to planning and implementing the services for this population. Both the public and private sectors must be envisioned with relevance to the power basis from which they emanate.

The public sector encompasses the local, county, state, regional, and federal official bureaucracies, organizations, committees, individuals, and interrelated systems which implement the service delivery *vis-à-vis* the elective, executive and judicial processes. The private sector encompasses consumers, parents, private advocates, planning and service agencies, parent groups, lobbying organizations, and the broad cross section of "public" with its complex range of special interest values and attitudes which define the basic receptivity to handicapped persons and attendant services. With changes in the source and characteristics of funding, a sizable number of private entrepreneurs have become service providers. These have included owners and operators of small group homes, intermediate care facilities, and skilled nursing facilities. These providers have been inclined to band together into associations. They have, in turn, become politically active to attempt to bring about legislation, regulations, and practices that would be favorable to their industry. These groups have and will continue to be yet another important voice in the planning and public policy decision-making process.

Although planners frequently tend to credit both the private and public sectors with exclusive and relatively unique organizational styles and functioning, it is important to note that the participants in both sectors emanate from a broad cross section of the citizenry. Consequently, although special interest and service groups within both sectors may reflect a concentrated interest in services for the handicapped, the basic values and attitudes, measured in terms of the support base for services at any one time, originate from the same cross section of persons who comprise the "public" sector.

While viewing the unique power basis of both sectors in terms of their potential impact on planning, it is important to recognize two basic phenomena. First, the power basis within both the public and private sectors is heterogeneous in nature and, more often than not, in a state of conflict. Second, individual interests are not homogeneous in nature. The desire of a private agency to develop a needed service through paraprofessional personnel may be contradicted by the political interest of a private professional organization. For example, the desire of a parent group to establish a recreational site for handicapped individuals may be counterbalanced by the desire of an industry to establish a waste disposal plant at the same site. Where objectives are in greater accord, the willingness of a company to establish a training program for handicapped individuals may carry restrictive conditions for purposes of tax benefit which could pressure a compromise in values and objectives of an advocacy group seeking options for a training program. The interest of the unity in a public health department in establishing an early identification and prevention program may be overshadowed by the transfer of funds to another service; the interest of congressional representatives in supporting a stronger bill for handicapped persons may be compromised by tradeoff interest in diverting money to the aerospace program.

Because individual interests are not homogeneous in nature, parents or consumers who have devoted many years to enriching services for handicapped individuals may effectively cancel much of that progress by voting for a politician or a proposition which would severely curtail funds to the services of greatest benefit. Conversely, an individual who may hold negative values related to handicapped individuals might be instrumental in fighting for a broad principle of the civil rights which could ultimately have an impact on services to this group.

Contributions of the Private Sector

Both the private and public sectors make distinctive contributions to community planning for the delivery of services. The spearhead of the private sector is substantially represented by parent groups, private agencies, and other special interest groups or individuals exerting energies on behalf of developmentally disabled, handicapped, or other less privileged persons. Although there is occasionally a "halo effect" around their efforts which affects populations with similar characteristics, the interest of these groups tends to be focused upon specific subgroups of the handicapped population such as persons affected by mental retardation, cerebral palsy, muscular dystrophy, Tay-Sachs disease, and deafness and blindness, among other debilitating conditions. Interest in developing coalitions among these groups has been sporadic and generally disfavored because of the highly focused interest of participants and a general reluctance to be identified with additional areas of deficiency. Even when the funding base is broadly defined such as in the current National Rehabilitation Act, special interest groups tend to avoid the types of coalitions which could have greater political impact in an attempt to maintain the funding and high public visibility of specific handicapping conditions.

Elements of the private sector which are further from the center of the special interest sphere are substantially less active in influencing planning for handicapped individuals. The interest of these industries, organizations, or individuals is generally of a broader nature and emanates from different motivation. For example, an industry may develop training or employment programs for handicapped individuals to take advantage of potential for tax reductions or to obtain earmarked public monies. A church may respond to service needs of handicapped persons in response to a moral mandate or in recognition of potential pressure for utilization of their space for an enterprise which would be less favored by the membership. Moving further out in the sphere of public influence, the interest and motivations for planning for handicapped individuals are frequently intertwined beyond recognition in the maze of subgroup and individual values, motivations, and interests. It is at this level that one captures such thoughts and slogans as "the enlightened society." "humanism," and a variety of expressions which tend to crystallize a philosophical direction in which the nation moves.

However, although philosophically in accordance with a higher ideal, functional realities, personal priorities, and trade-offs among the varied needs of a society generally overshadow such slogans. Even during periods of national wealth, prestige, and high ideals, the interest of persons with the least power, least influence, and greatest need is occasionally verbalized but seldom responded to by the complex range of individuals and organizations within the private sector of our society. Consequently, the generic service systems emanating from the private sector seldom respond to developmentally disabled and other handicapped individuals. Insurance companies consistently fail to respond to the needs of this group. The efforts of private industry are token at best. Even basic access would seldom be gained without the impact of public law. Smaller segments of the private sector relating to such areas as real estate, restaurants, and transportation frequently give a negative response to the needs of handicapped individuals.

Contributions of the Public Sector

Financing is the most basic contribution of the public sector to developing and expanding services for the handicapped persons. During the last two decades, the extent of public expenditure on behalf of this population has grown so rapidly that private expenditures are insignificant in comparison. Also, the public sector has performed a significant service in generating a national focus review and response to service needs in this area. Although national regulations, standards, and procedures often seem to exceed their purpose, the unifying effects of such public mandates have led toward higher and more consistent levels of service. This pattern has also facilitated links between program stands for handicapped persons and other state and federal laws in such areas as civil rights.

The public sphere has also generated an expanded knowledge base through extensive funding of research, replication, and dissemination of research, clinical, and programmatic findings. Essentially, the public sector has become the rapidly widening mainstream of educational and service activities for developmentally disabled and other handicapped persons. Public money has funded private research and service resources which have created the potential for replication within other service activities.

Through state and federal mandates, the public sector has established a spectrum of systems for planning, implementation, delivery, and monitoring services for this population. A gradual integration of parents and consumers into this process has generated increased congruency between the public and private sectors, their goals, and their products. Subcycle patterns within this relationship lead to congruencies and incongruencies which result in role exchanges between the public and private sectors on some occasions and direct conflict at other times. For example, the public sector has absorbed much of the service base previously provided by the private sector. More recently, the public sector established nationwide and heavily funded advocacy programs operated through state and regional systems, Currently, the private sector, partially in quest of activities to replace previous functions, is making a strong bid to regain its dominance in the advocacy process. Its primary target has been the more visible and definable public system, which is already providing the vast majority of services, rather than the private open market with its broader range of services. Ironically, this pattern is in conflict with the widely professed value of guiding developmentally disabled and other handicapped persons toward the "mainstream" of American life.

Public and Private Sectors and the Cyclical Model

Given the diversified interests and attitudes of these sectors, how do they affect the cyclical pattern of community planning for handicapped individuals? Recognizing that either sector can have a positive or negative influence on this process, the impact potential of the private sector takes several forms. Perhaps the most permeating but least definable impact of the private sector is reflected in the attitude of the public toward handicapped individuals at a specific point of time. Ultimately, through the elective process and the direction of private resources, public attitudes are translated into enhanced or diminished program levels for this population. When public values and attitudes are concentrated on wars, economic crises, or international prestige (such as the aerospace movement), the needs of the developmentally disabled and other handicapped individuals are substantially diminished first among private and, ultimately, public priorities.

Again, moving toward the special interest areas, the attitudes emanating from the private sector are more focused, positive, and consistent when translated into efforts on behalf of handicapped persons. Although such interests are generally not powerful enough to counterbalance the broader thrust of the public sector, they do shift the emphasis and direction in accordance with the realities of that moment in time. The eventual shift in values of the private sector and priorities funded through the public sector places the special interest groups in a continual stance of adaptation and innovation.

The innovative demands placed upon private agencies and interest groups serving handicapped individuals result in their greatest contributions to the planning process. Traditionally, the private sector has initiated most of the basic pilot efforts in new programs and new methodologies for service. Most of the early education programs, vocational training programs, preschool programs, and infant development programs, among others, were developed through private agencies and interest groups. They were operated, refined, and demonstrated at a level that generated visiblity and public interest in replication through the public service systems. Proud, energetic parents generated organizations and programs through which their youngsters could be better served. They then advocated replication of such efforts through public systems under the general conviction that ''we are in business to go out of business.''

With the arrival of the mid-1960's, the public systems began to replicate many programs developed for school-aged handicapped children through private organizations. As public education systems were mandated to implement special education programs for the trainable mentally retarded, the educable mentally retarded, and other handicapped individuals, they rapidly absorbed children from the private programs that had traditionally served this population. Elements of the private sector initially responded with a sense of panic. For many parents, it was emotionally less demanding to wave the flag for public services and keep their children in the private school than to face the consequence of transferring children to these substantially enriched programs offered through the public sector. Many private agencies cringed at the reality of their potential demise. However, after the initial shock, the private sector assumed the primary role for which it is historically noted; namely, it shifted its priorities to meet the challenges of unmet needs. Gradually, private agencies began to explore innovative methods of developing preschool and postschool programs related to such areas as infant development and vocational training. This pattern strengthened the diminishing lifeline of the private system as these organizations began to draw upon the strengths of new parents and the older parents whose children were beyond school age. It also gave them access to a new and relatively unrecognized support group, the adult consumer.

In the 1970's, advocacy efforts by and on behalf of the pre- and postschool population again attracted public attention and response. As the public sector began to expand programming related to the pre- and postschool populations, the private sector was again forced to examine its priorities for purposes of justification and survival. Since the public sector was assuming greater responsibility in the complete spectrum of the service continuum, the private sector had to look in other directions for its innovative and survival efforts. The answer was advocacy. During recent years, the private sector has begun to devalue its role in direct services and establish a foothold on the platform of advocacy as the conscious prober, monitor, and evaluator of public services. As specialized public services begin to meet the needs of a larger number of handicapped services, the advocacy efforts of the private sector, including the recently established state Developmental Disabilities Councils, have shifted toward pressures upon generic systems to provide greater services for this population.

The advocacy efforts of the private sector have focused primarily upon generating, expanding, and refining programs within the public sector. To date, relatively little energy from the private sector has been devoted to encouraging other elements of the private sector (*e.g.,* insurance companies, manufacturing firms, housing industry) to initiate basic avenues for including handicapped persons within their services or sphere of influence. The next decade may witness a decrease in the dichotomy of the public and private sector as the energies of both spheres are increasingly directed toward the private sector, as evidenced in the Scandinavian countries during recent years.

The effect of the direct lobbying function of the private sphere and the local, state, and federal systems should not be minimized. Historically, the most notable product of private lobbying for handicapped persons has resulted in the extensive array of services for disabled veterans. The veterans' movement, supported by one of the nation's most powerful private lobbies, has resulted in the development of a medical and rehabilitative service system which proved to be a testing ground for many concepts and procedures that were later translated into both state and federally funded health programs. A substantial array of categorical services for the blind have been developed through powerful private lobby groups working on behalf of this handicapped population. In examining the public and official receptivity to their claims, it should be noted that both lobbies represent a group for which the American public has generated a high level of identification, guilt, and sympathy. The American public sent its veterans to war. Most individuals readily identify with blindness and experience some level of fear of its potential for personal impact. Also, disabled veterans and blind persons are frequently seen in public, a constant triggering process for individual feelings and response. It is reasonable to assume that a lobbying process of this dimension and effectiveness could not be marshalled for other forms of handicapping conditions with which the public has less identity. Consequently, these are lucid examples of the public's adaptation of values and functional responses to probing conscious awareness emanating from the private sector.

SOME GENERAL OBSERVATIONS OF THE PLANNING PROCESS

Planning Process

In simplistic terms, "planning" may be defined as "the process of designing a course of action to achieve ends." To plan human services effectively for any community, the planner must take into consideration four basic elements of planning: geography, population, services, and delivery system.

Geography The service area or territory to be served must be identified discretely since the specified geographic or planning boundaries provide a "building block" upon which further planning may be developed. Within the specified area, planners need to be able to determine the land mass, the distance between various points, the key market places, the natural boundaries, the topographical barriers, rural and urban areas, and the routes of travel. They need to be able to locate services in accordance with specified mandates and good planning principles such as the requirement of the Community Mental Health Centers Act that provides for a population base catchment area of 75,000 to 200,000 people and a provision for clients to be within 2 hours' traveling distance from the nearest center.

The same concept was adopted by the Office of Economic Opportunity for Neighborhood Health Centers, but with smaller areas and populations. Similarly, California's regional centers for developmentally disabled people are established within a statewide network of 21 regional centers, with each center serving a population base of approximately 1 million persons.

The designated service area should contain a population that is large enough to support a full array of essential services but small enough to make it possible to coordinate those services and organize them into a delivery system. Also, the area should be small enough so that services are physically accessible and the population is discrete.

Population The population to receive services may be estimated in a number of ways, including field surveys, agency surveys, and statistical data based on incidence and/or prevalence rates for various handicapped populations. It is essential to know the characteristics of the target population. Ideally, the number, percentage, and location of handicapped persons in the population should be available through the Census Bureau. The 1970 census did not include identification of handicapped persons except as a handicapping condition relates to working or not working. Unfortunately, the Census Bureau has failed to include an item which would provide this information on the number and location of disabled persons by census tract in the 1980 census form. Planning services for the estimated 35 to 40 million disabled persons in the United States could be done more efficiently and effectively if there were census data identifying this population, not only in terms of location, but also in terms of the type and degree of disability, housing needs, vocational needs, transportation needs, and social service needs.

Services An inventory of services is needed to identify the quantity and quality of existing services, the agencies and individuals providing services, and the location of services. A mapping system, constantly updated, would provide the location of all services, as well as the location of persons waiting for such services. Such a bank of information would offer a basis for realistic planning by reflecting areas of service duplication and service gaps.

Service Delivery System The bringing of people and services together should be accomplished within a network of specialized and generic service components organized into a system. The system should be concerned with the coordination and comprehensiveness of services, as well as their availability and accessibility. The system should have capability of carrying out a systematic method of collecting data useful for planning and coordinating activities. Additionally, the system should have provisions for an ongoing public information and community education program. Ideally, a service delivery system should have a fixed point of entry into the spectrum of services and a fixed point of return when those services break down or when new or additional services are needed.

In spite of the problems noted in this description of the basic community planning elements, the planning process has, nevertheless, been made to sound deceptively simple. However, community planning in the human service field is far from a simple process. In the absence of clearly defined goals and policies, planning on a national, state, and local level has tended to lack comprehensiveness, has sought to fill service vacuums in haphazard fashion, and has tended to disrupt order at the local or community level. Such piecemeal planning efforts have tended to focus on a short term balance between needs and resources and on achieving decisions and actions necessary to distribute scarce resources.

Also, as these decision-making processes become more individualized, the planning process results in service delivery systems that are in tune with the needs of a given community; nevertheless, the same individualizing process produces differences from one community to the next in the service delivery system. This difference needs to be recognized and understood, as planners too often think of a service delivery system as homogeneous activity.

In his classic book on community organization, Murray Ross (1976) describes the planning process as including the logical steps of the corporate planning model. However, as his major theme, he emphasizes citizen participation in the process. Through this involvement, consumer groups gain cohesiveness and strength; their bargaining position is improved and their demands more clearly defined.

The Step-Down Process of Planning

In spite of the complexity that they add to the process, communities need to get involved in the planning of human services. To try to decide at the federal, or even the state level, what the service needs are in a particular community or geographic area is impractical and merely reinforces people's belief that governmental systems are unresponsive. People at the local level—agencies, providers, professionals, citizens, and consumers—should make the decisions. At higher jurisdictional levels, such as the federal government, planning is necessarily broad and related to the planning concessions that must be made to the political processes. As planning is then implemented at the state level of government or for smaller areas within corporate structure, the planning becomes more specific. In this process of becoming more specific, planning relates to the unique characteristics or needs of the state. In larger states, planning goes through an intermediate level of counties. In smaller states, it is not atypical for planning to go virtually from the state to the community level.

Ralph Littlestone (1973), in his writings on "Planning Mental Health Services," states that planning today might be conceptualized as the merger of two branches of planning experience—business or corporate planning, on the one hand, and community organization planning on the other. These branches developed in settings that produced fundamentally different planning approaches.

In the world of business, there is corporate planning with a focus on the production and marketing of goods. The corporate planning process is one which sets objectives and assesses resources. Within this corporate process, alternate ways of using resources most effectively and economically to achieve objectives are analyzed. The course of action is decided, the action plan is carried out, and the outcome is assessed. Then, if the first choice is not effective, necessary changes are made or an alternative is adopted. Community organization planning is less precise, to the extent that it is concerned with people and their problems and is an attempt to reach decisions systematically and implement actions through community participation. Involvement of the community in the planning process has become widely accepted, at least in principle (Feldman, 1973).

Planning Considerations for Manpower

The federal government carries a responsibility to insure adequate manpower resources which will deliver the various services funded through federal legislation. This role and responsibility is best illustrated in the planning for a national network of Community Mental Health Centers as promulgated by Public Law 88-164 (Mental Retardation Facilities and Community Mental Health Centers Construction Act of 1963). Initial planning focused basically on a "brick and mortar" approach, calling for the construction of community-based facilities. Subsequent federal legislation, Public Law 94-63 (Community Mental Health Centers—Staffing and Construction Act), recognized the need to provide financial support for skilled professional and paraprofessionals to carry out the complex services of this growing crop of Community Mental Health Centers. Unfortunately, since 1976, the number of staffing grants, as well as the amount of each grant, has declined significantly, resulting in some serious losses and setbacks to this plan for a national network of Community Mental Health Centers (CMHC).

Planning for human service manpower needs must certainly consider the distribution of skilled professionals and paraprofessionals. National, state, and local government studies and surveys by professional graduate schools and professional associations reflect a well known fact—the maldistribution of manpower. The underserved and often unserved geographic areas, such as rural communities and inner city minority neighborhoods, are woefully lacking in the number of skilled practitioners necessary to provide the multiple services needed by handicapped persons.

At the national level, there has emerged a semblance of effort to correct this inequity of manpower distribution through the National Health Corps Program and through the Assistant to the Primary Care Physician Training Program, a program aimed at training paraprofessionals, who are being encouraged to serve in rural and inner city areas.

Planning: Data Sources

Comprehensive planning for community services for handicapped persons must be supported by more than assurances of good intentions. Baseline information essential to decision-making is basic to the effective planning process. Without correct and sufficient data, intelligent planning cannot take place. In his welcoming address to the 1964 Conference on Data Collection and Utilization in Institutions for the Mentally Retarded, Dr. George Tarjan expressed the belief that in the fields of mental illness and mental retardation, the lack of epidemiological information represents a major roadblock in program planning.

In attempting to focus on the numbers, types, and functioning levels of handicapped persons who present a wide variety of special needs, planners are faced with the realization that there are only gross estimates on the prevalence of handicapped persons in this country. No hard data are available. This is due, in part, to the lack of a systematic method or plan for gathering essential epidemiologic information.

With the advent of automated data collection systems, planners are provided with the technical capability of handling a great mass of information. The benefits of computer technology are manifold, particularly from the standpoint of providing program planners with more information to help them make decisions that are based on fact rather than hunches. However, there are not always advantages to gathering mass data in a "shotgun" approach, inasmuch as data that is indiscriminantly collected may have no relevance to the specific program under consideration. In order to make efficient use of a data collection system, program planners must give extremely careful thought to the specific items of information they need for planning purposes.

The advantages of a data processing system are many if the system is used with proper discretion as well as with imagination. It can help estimate program needs on a quantitative and qualitative basis. It can help isolate a myriad of client characteristics that can be used in predicting progress or lack of progress in specific programs. It can identify areas of need, match populations of clients to such needs areas and, consequently, determine whether needed resources and programs are available and accessible to the target population. Having information available leads to building mathematical models and making predictions regarding the present or future status of specific groups of handicapped persons. Finally, it is highly important to planners and program administrators who must keep up with trends so that they may make timely and relevant program changes.

There are, of course, roadblocks to an adequate data processing system. There are resistive attitudes on the part of professionals who fear that their clients will be "turned into statistics," as well as resistance to the idea of a central registry of handicapped persons by the general public. However, such registries have been developed in other countries such as England and the Scandinavian countries where there is highly efficient planning of services for handicapped persons. Implied in data gathering is the issue of losing the human touch when planners start putting data into the computer system. Unfortunately, the rapidly developing technology which now allows planners to develop such sophisticated data systems may also create blind spots and set traps for them. In the fascination with the efficiency by which they handle the volume needed for ever-growing systems, they may lose sight of the structure that needs to be an integral part of planning.

EFFECT OF LEGISLATION ON PLANNING SERVICES

Influences of the Public and Private Sectors on Legislation

Over the years, state and federal legislation that has been promulgated to serve the interests and needs of handicapped persons has been spurred on by a variety of influences. Persons, in many instances parents, who were dissatisfied with inequities generated by the service systems organized into such power groups as the Association for Retarded Citizens, United Cerebral Palsy, the Epilepsy Foundation, the National Association for Mental Health, and the National Foundation-March of Dimes to advocate for essential service programs for their respective constituencies.

As cited earlier in this chapter, other influences that have led to new legislation and several policies benefiting handicapped persons stemmed from court mandates establishing equal rights for handicapped persons. The Civil Rights Movement of the 1960's set the stage for the later development of full citizenship for all handicapped persons and the leadership of the executive branch of the federal government resulted in the White House Conference on the Handicapped of 1977. This conference, in itself, led to the initiation of several important pieces of legislation aimed at enhancing the quality of life for all handicapped persons.

The list of legislative accomplishments that have significantly influenced the delivery of services to handicapped persons is too long to be covered here; therefore, this will be only a brief look at some of the most recent significant legislation which has affected present planning considerations.

The federal government has taken a leading role in the last 20 years in providing resources directly as well as through the states to advance solutions to the problems of the handicapped population. The states, themselves, have made substantial progress in the planning and development of services and in providing increasing funds for their support. Local communities, usually at the county level, have been the scene of increasing activity in service delivery as programs of deinstitutionalization have been developed, particularly for mentally handicapped persons. Fiscally, the heaviest burden has been borne by the states; however, the federal contribution has amounted to a substantial annual sum when support of services and income maintenance are combined.

Many of the key concepts and terms used earlier in this chapter, including "comprehensiveness and continuity of services" and "accessibility, availability and affordability of services," were developed and woven into the Community Mental Health Centers Act. In the field of developmental disabilities, federal legislation has shaped the system through the infusion of such concepts as "deinstitutionalization," "normalization," "least-restrictive alternative," and "client rights." The concept and growing practice of "advocacy" is attributable to the requirements of federal legislation (PL 94-142, PL 94-103, and PL 95-602).

Federal legislation in the field of education, particularly PL 94-142 (Education for All Handicapped Children Act of 1975) sets the stage for integrating or "mainstreaming" handicapped children into normal classroom programs to the maximum extent possible. This act further calls for parental involvement in developing an educational plan for their handicapped child, as well as providing the parents an avenue of appeals if they are not satisfied with their child's plan or progress.

"Rent subsidization" for handicapped persons is yet another program made possible through federal government initiative and funds [Housing and Urban Development (HUD), Section 8 of the Housing Assistance and Community Development Act]. Acquisition of "full citizenship" is a goal that is central to all federal legislation concerning handicapped persons and is the major focus of Section 504 of the Rehabilitation Act of 1973. All of these key terms reflect the philosophies and principles which serve as a basis for the present-day planning for handicapped persons.

Federal Health Care Legislation

By the late 1950's, it was becoming clear that initiative and planning in mental health care must take place at a national level. The beginning of new, major health care legislation occurred in 1963 with President John F. Kennedy signing into law the Maternal and Child Health and Mental Retardation Planning Amendments of 1963 (PL 88-156), one of two highly significant pieces of legislation formulated to prevent and combat mental retardation. The complementary piece of legislation was PL 88-164, the Mental Retardation Facilities and Community Mental Health Centers Construction Act of 1963.

The planning amendments were designed to provide states with federal funds to develop comprehensive plans that would provide a means of coordination for the many state services available to mentally retarded persons. This was the pioneering effort and forerunner of today's state plans for Developmental Disabilities Councils, as required by PL 94-103 (The Developmental Disabilities Services and Facilities Construction Act of 1975), a.k.a. Developmental Disabilities Assistance and Bill of Rights Act.

It was the intent of the Mental Retardation Branch of the Public Health Service (which administered the planning grant program) and the Office of the Secretary of Health, Education and Welfare to optimize the use of the planning monies and bring about effective programs in service, training, and research in all states.

PL 88-164 (Mental Retardation Facilities and Mental Health Centers Construction Act) PL 88-164 was based on the philosophy of developing comprehensive services for mentally retarded and mentally ill persons at the community level where these services would be easily accessible to consumers and their families. This act, which provided federal funds for the construction of community-based facilities, was basically directed toward the redistribution of the care of mentally retarded and mentally ill persons from large state custodial institutions to the local community and the coordination of human services needed in the care of these persons. The act combined funding resources with program mandates, and recognized that the primary responsibility for planning services and facilities for mentally retarded and mentally ill persons should be vested in a state agency (inasmuch as the individual states, rather than the federal government, would be more acutely aware of and knowledgeable about specific needs and problems). It further acknowledged that states should delegate planning to the local level.

The planning of mental health services provides a good example of the extent to which traditional patterns of government responsibility have been altered in recent decades and the extent to which public programs involve all levels of government as well as the private sector. In this and other areas, federal government initiative and financial capacity have been brought to bear increasingly on what were once viewed as primarily, if not exclusively, state functions. In many states, funding of community mental health centers is based on legislation enacted specifically for that purpose. A number of states allocate funds to counties or county boards which, in turn, allot funds to centers within their jurisdictions. Centers typically operate under contract with these units of government. This new focus on a community-based care model has led to the growing realization that the public has a responsibility for mental health services in their community, from both a financial and decision-making standpoint.

Housing for Handicapped Persons The signing into law on August 4, 1976, of the Housing Authorization Act (PL 94-375) presented new opportunities to handicapped and disabled persons to achieve a greater degree of self-direction, self-expression, and self-realization through the provision of a basic need—housing. Housing to the handicapped person is more than shelter, since special needs, such as barrier-free accessibility, must be addressed. Appropriate housing must therefore be considered as an essential service for handicapped persons. Under the Housing Authorization Act, a whole range of housing and living arrangements for handicapped persons is available, including single family homes, shared homes, individual or shared apartments, groups of individual apartments, dwellings in new apartment buildings specifically designed for handicapped persons, elderly housing projects, congregate housing, residential hotels, group homes, boarding homes, hostels, and foster homes.

There are several sections of the HUD-administered housing program that directly benefit handicapped persons. Probably the most important financing program for rental housing for the handicapped is Section 202. The congressional intent for the Section 202 program is that it serve as the primary vehicle for the production of housing for elderly or handicapped persons by private, nonprofit sponsors and developers. Recommended for Section 202 housing is a range of support services, including health, continuing education, welfare, information, recreation, homemaker, counseling, referral, and transportation. Section 202 does not have asset limits as it concerns the determination of rent-paying ability. Section 8 of the Housing Assistance Payments Program, Housing and Community Development Act of 1974, provides a rental subsidy to low and middle income families and permits such families to pay rents equalling no more than 25 percent of their income.

Section 504 of the Rehabilitation Act of 1973 Joseph A. Califano, Jr., Secretary, Department of Health, Education and Welfare, made the following statement on April 28, 1977:

> The 504 regulation attacks the discrimination, the demeaning practices and the injustices that have afflicted the Nation's handicapped citizens. It will usher in a new era of equality for handicapped individuals in which unfair barriers to self-sufficiency and decent treatment will begin to fall before the force of law.

Under the provisions of Title V, Section 504, of the Rehabilitation Act of 1973 (PL 93-112), a physically or mentally disabled person has the same right as anyone else to education, employment, health care, senior citizen activities, welfare, and any other public or private service that federal dollars help to support.

For planners of health, education, employment, and welfare services, the guiding principle of Section 504 is to consider the delivery of services to all persons, handicapped and nonhandicapped, in such a way as to provide equal opportunity to all. This means a departure from previous styles of architecture and building construction that restricted the admission of handicapped persons to educational, recreational, and employment opportunities. It means developing innovative and flexible means of integrating, to the maximum extent possible, handicapped persons in all levels of educational programs. Most important, it means the need for planners to be sensitive to any and all facets that may impose barriers and embarrassment to handicapped persons who are attempting to achieve or live a lifestyle as close to normal as possible.

1978 Amendments to the Rehabilitation Act of 1973, entitled the Independent Living Program, further reflected a national policy to the effect that all persons, regardless of the severity of their handicapping condition, have a right to the opportunity to develop to their maximum potential. The amendments provide comprehensive services for independent living designed to meet the current and future needs of individuals whose disabilities are so severe that they do not presently have the potential for employment but may benefit from vocational rehabilitation services that will enable them to live and function independently. This is a major shift in national social policy, which discards previous notions that rehabilitation funds should be spent solely on those disabled persons who show the potential to eventually be producers in the world of work. This program makes it clear that no individual should be denied services because the vocational potential is not there.

Education for All Handicapped Children Act (PL 94-142) The most far-reaching federal legislation ever proposed for providing educational opportunities for all handicapped children was passed overwhelmingly by Congress and signed by President Gerald R. Ford in 1975. Known as PL 94-142, it is entitled the Education for All Handicapped Children Act of 1975. It stipulates that all handicapped children must have access to a free and appropriate public education, with special education and related services available as needed. The act is supported by massive infusions of federal dollars which are channeled through the Department of Health, Education and Welfare, Office of Education to states and to local school districts. Commencing in September 1978, education must be provided to all handicapped children ages 3 to 18, and by September 1980, all such children ages 3 to 21 must be served. The intent of the federal funding is to absorb the additional costs of educating a handicapped child.

Significantly, the law is also a civil rights act, which provides for several individual protections for handicapped children and their families, including prior notice of school actions regarding placement of children; nondiscriminatory testing based on more than a "single instrument"; and an impartial due-process hearing by a hearing officer not employed by the school district. The parents are entitled to legal representatives, various rights of appeal, prior examination of evidence, and independent evaluations of the child by outside professional persons. The law contains extensive provisions for in-service education by school districts, expecially regular classroom teachers. The cornerstone of the act is its provision for a written, individualized education program for each child, which is developed by professional persons as well as parents (and by the child, if appropriate). Parents will have continued access to the plan and to the child's record of progress.

It is too early to determine the full impact of this act. Despite the optimism that mainstreaming may lead to better education for handicapped childeren, certain difficulties loom very large. Teacher organizations have taken steps to prevent the inclusion of severely handicapped children into regular classrooms. In Michigan, teacher organizations went on record stating the presence of children with behavior disorders or physical or intellectual handicaps would impede the educational progress of the entire class. The authors of the act were, indeed farsighted by including provisions for teacher in-service training. Perhaps one of the greatest barriers that stands in the way of smooth implementation of this program is attitudinal—manifested by teacher resistance.

PL 94-103 (Developmental Disabilities Assistance and Bill of Rights Act On October 30, 1970, the first federal developmental disabilities legislation was signed into law (PL 91-517) by President Richard Nixon. Known as the Developmental Disabilities Services and Facilities Construction Act, this legislation brought under one legislative unbrella three major disability groups (mental retardation, cerebral palsy, and epilepsy) and, theoretically, others which share common service needs. The original act (PL 91-517) was amended in 1975 with the passage of the Developmentally Disabled Assistance and Bill of Rights Act (PL 94-103).

This legislation aims at coordinating a wide range of diversified program activities by placing an emphasis on comprehensive state planning. The amendments of 1975 introduced a unique provision entitled Protection and Advocacy of Individuals' Rights (Section 113). The act focuses on the rights of developmentally disabled persons and delineates the human and legal rights to which developmentally disabled persons are entitled. Furthermore, it establishes a formal mechanism for the protection and enforcement of these rights. The act also provides for an infusion of federal funds to each of the states through the awarding of formula grants, as well as funds for Special Projects and Projects of National Significance, in which the aim is to develop and improve the quality and quantity of services for developmentally disabled persons. Other important features of the act include the establishment in each state of a Developmental Disabilities Planning Council to advocate for developmentally disabled individuals, the designation of state administering agencies to be fiscally responsible for all funds awarded to the states through the program, and finally, the provision for a national network of University Affiliated Facilities to train the manpower needed in the field of developmental disabilities.

PL 95-602 (Rehabilitation, Comprehensive Services, and Developmental Disabilities Amendments of 1978) The 95th Congress passed this act. Essentially, it extends two existing laws: the Rehabilitation Act of 1973, and the Developmental Disabilities Services and Facilities Construction Act.

In extending the Rehabilitation Act of 1973, PL 95-602 provided new Comprehensive Services for Independent Living. This new category is designed to meet the needs of severely handicapped individuals who do not currently have the potential for gainful employment, but who can benefit from services which will enable them to live independently.

The developmental disabilities portion of the new law alters the definition of a "developmental disability" by changing it from one based on categorical definition to one based on the individual's ability to function in society.

This law continues to stress advocacy as a vital function of the state Developmental Disabilities Planning Councils and it further changes the composition of the councils so that developmentally disabled persons, or their parents or guardians, make up at least one-half of the membership of the councils.

Other important features of this omnibus act include the abolishment of the National Advisory Council on Services and Facilities for Developmental Disabilities and the creation of a National Council on the Handicapped; the designation of four priority areas of service for developmentally disabled persons which must be addressed in the state plan (case management, child development, alternative community living arrangements, and nonvocational social development services); and the development of a plan for the training of essential personnel in the field of developmental disabilities.

THE IMPACT OF SOCIAL FACTORS ON PLANNING

A considerable volume of literature pertaining to community organization, organizational structure, and systems analysis reflects upon procedures for development and implementation of services to handicapped persons. Although such methodologies are readily applicable to the traditional models of service delivery, they fall short when implemented without consideration of the changing cultural and social variables which so frequently underscore the success or failure of a program at the community level. Even when implementing pilot programs within a limited geography, it is difficult to assess significant social or cultural variables which will determine the success or failure of the proposed service. For example, the high value placed upon the family and church within a Mexican-American community may be the key factor in generating a broad base of volunteer support for an emergency program which is designed for and by that community. In contrast, the high value placed upon privacy related to family matters within an Oriental community may negate efforts for group and community involvement in the planning and service delivery process. The wide range of professional or technical expertise, knowledge of group process, leadership skills, and relevant affluency within a white, middle class community may appear to provide the ideal base for development and organization of high quality community-based services. However, the desire of this subgroup to overly engage in process, blue ribbon committees, seek federal support, and generally avoid direct contact activities may significantly impair planning for implementation of a significant service program.

Although social and cultural variables are most readily identified and applied at the local level, it is extremely difficult to generalize such application when replicating services on a county, state, or national basis. Service modules which are appropriate for an urban area are not necessarily applicable to the rural area. Priorities and needs within one part of a state are not necessarily represented in another area. Timing, charismatic leadership, and accessibility of clients, among other variables, establish different patterns for service planning and implementation which tend to negate replications based solely upon procedural guidelines or official regulations.

Another factor which is affecting planning is the shift in the current definition for developmental disabilities from medical to functional terms. This trend is in keeping with the service pattern which has shifted from a medical toward a developmental model; these share points on a common continuum. Interestingly, the definition of "developmental disabilities" in the legislation is remarkably similar to the definition for "handicapped persons" in the same legislation. The similarity is so striking that the term developmental disabilities may fall out of popular usage in federal legislation in the coming years. This trend could cause a serious impairment of the ability of special interest groups to influence federal service trends without forming coalitions and, thus, sacrificing some of their specific identity.

During the postwar years, society shifted its planning emphasis from the volunteer or private to the public sphere. Time-honored concepts such as individual responsibility, Puritan work ethic, and related moral values have yielded to a movement toward government responsibility, depersonalization, and the valuing of standardization rather than uniqueness. As the service responsibilities shifted from private to public domains, large scale replication led to the current demands for continual auditing and accountability. As the knowledge base related to people and services erodes at the top administrative levels, the continuum shifts toward management by regulatory procedure. This pattern reflects a shift in national values from the long-valued moral responsibility of the individual to responsibility as defined by law.

Such dramatic shifts in social values, priorities, and procedures have a strong impact on the community planning process. We are emerging from a period of "demonstration" into a period of "replication" through government funds and bureaucracies on a national basis. We have shifted from moralistic toward legalistic bases for implementation. Procedural issues frequently dominate or precede issues related to service content or quality. In addition, a looming potential for national economic crisis further underscores the power shift from human service professionals toward accountants and other fiscal management personnel. Values, knowledge, and techniques related to the production and marketing of sewing machines are now being applied to the design and marketing of human services.

A major shift in such social, cultural, and procedural variables must be engaged in as part of the planning process if successful program implementation or modification is to be realized. As the economy begins to restabilize and dissatisfactions are recognized within current or forthcoming service patterns, we may again move from the mechanistic toward the humanistic end of the human service delivery continuum. It is predictable that the public trend will be preceded by direct recognition and active engagement of small groups in this process. However, it is far easier to destroy than to create broad-based cultural values with deep individual humanistic and moralistic fibers.

From a community planning point of view, it is important to recognize not only the social, institutional, and cultural variables which have an impact on planning, but to recognize which groups or individuals must be engaged in the planning process and where they stand on a particular value continuum. It is as faulty to assume that a national trend is applicable to all circumstances as it is to attribute the values of a subculture to the total society. Consequently, one needs to consider the scope and target for planning as well as the nature of the system through which one is trying to generate changes in patterns of service delivery.

SUMMARY

Although designation of community geographic boundaries, incidence of handicap tabulations, measurement of units of service deficits, and similarly measurable variables contribute to the identification of need, they provide little guidance toward the implementation of planning for services to the handicapped population. Although couched in the security of hard numbers derived from mathematical formulas and affirmative jargon, their accuracy is only as valid as the assumptions on which the basic formula was based. An examination of the interrelationship of social and organizational trends, although subjective in nature, appears to give more viable direction and perhaps new innovation to the community planning process. These phenomena may be plotted along numerous continua to be examined before drawing collective direction for service planning. This approach has been called the Cyclical Service Planning Model.

Through examining the trends and interactions between continua of opposing values, two patterns are evidenced. First, the cyclical or repetitive nature of events, priorities, and practices are identified. As such planning and service patterns recycle, an opportunity is presented for building innovatively upon previous experience through interplay of currently available tools, trends, and options. Second, innovative and timely planning options can be identified. For example, the following options might be considered on the basis of such identification:

1. Movement toward self-determination through greater involvement of consumers in the planning process and reduction of official regulatory barriers
2. Stimulation of public recognition of the capacities of handicapped persons
3. Greater collaboration between the private and public service sectors in stimulating the larger free enterprise system to develop markets for the handicapped individuals
4. Greater collaboration between the private and public sectors in developing effective and efficient use of audiovisual and other technologies on behalf of this population
5. More efficient structuring, administration, and documentation of service programs to maximize qualitative and quantitative effectiveness as well as to increase cost-effectiveness
6. Generation of higher responsibility, trust, and reliance on consumer judgment in identification and utilization of service and free market options to fulfill needs
7. Expansion of ability to look beyond traditional professional, agency, and service systems as the vehicles for response to needs of handicapped persons
8. Development of broader based coalitions among consumers and providers to maintain a service base during a period of restricted private and public expenditure

This list could be expanded through examination of additional continua and interrelated trends. Nevertheless, even this abbreviated illustration of the cyclical model, when linked with traditional planning methodologies, illustrates several principles.

Basically, most planning models are too rigid for self-contained application. The social sciences are often too eager to generate models which are applied as formulas which give the illusion of the precise application methodologies of the natural sciences. In quest for such identity, we may be discarding unique characteristics of individuals, cultures, and the infinite patterns of interaction toward social change. Incidence data and related information may appear as definitive answers when derived from sophisticated formulas and printed on bona fide computer paper. Unfortunately, such formulated procedures frequently lull us into a rigid, dehumanized form of planning which provides an artificial sense of reality. Adding well intended slogans such as "consider ethnicity" or "poverty is different," although sparking legitimate concerns, gives little direction to the planning process. Institutionalization of professional jargon generally stimulates more hope and inspiration than direction. "Least-restrictive alternative," "normalization," and "dignity-of-risk" will soon join such heralded slogans of yesteryear as "grass roots," "change agents," and "social planning."

The cyclical model is presented not as a formula, but as a lightly structured approach to stimulating a creative thought process in planning service for handicapped persons. This flexible model may jar us from rigid and sometimes dated assumptions and procedures. It is a guide to the recognition and incorporation of current or projected societal trends, values, and lifestyles in the planning process. Through analysis of such interrelated variables, planners can better relate the service needs of handicapped persons to the social climate, timeliness, and applicable modalities for service implementation. Service needs are intimately related to the society and subculture in which the individual resides. Thus, problems and needs of the handicapped persons should no longer be identified as isolated factors. It is misleading to define either needs or optional responses in isolation from the environment in which the individual resides or wishes to reside.

Furthermore, there is greater potential benefit in planning with appreciation of current flaws and inhibiting factors within a society than to pursue idealistic slogans which have little connection with the realities encountered by handicapped persons. Slogans and false hopes wrapped in current jargon do not alter the limiting realities encountered in a given time and space. By recognizing the shortcomings while integrating the opportunities and strengths of a specific milieu, we may be able to engage more innovative and realistic approaches toward effective lifestyles for developmentally disabled and other handicapped individuals.

REFERENCES

Crocetti, M., Spiro, H., and Siassi, I. 1974. Contemporary Attitudes toward Mental Illness. University of Pittsburgh Press, Pittsburgh.

Feldman, S. 1973. Administration of Mental Health Services. National Institutes of Health, Springfield, VA.

Littlestone, R. 1973. Planning mental health services. In S. Feldman (ed.), Administration of Mental Health Services. National Institutes of Health, Springfield, VA.

Long, N. E. November 1959. Planning and politics in urban development. J. Amer. Inst. Planners p. 168.

Lublin, J. S. January 27, 1976. Lowering barriers: Pressured companies decide the disabled can handle more jobs. *Wall Street Journal*.

McGee, J. and Hitzing, W. 1976. Current residential services: A critical analysis.

Unpublished paper, Center for the Development of Community Alternative Service Systems, Omaha, NE.

Ross, M. 1976. Community Organizations: Theory in Principles. Harper & Row, New York.

Tarjan, G. 1964. Data collection and utilization on institutions for the mentally retarded. Address to Conference, Pacific State Hospital, Pomona, CA.

Chapter 2

Educational Planning

Ronald Wiegerink & John Pelosi

Effective planning of educational services for handicapped children has at its base an understanding of the rights and needs of handicapped persons. It is also dependent on the use of an effective planning process which responds to those rights and needs. Presently within the educational services system for handicapped children planning occurs at two levels: the individual and the programmatic. In addition to being conceptually and programmatically sound, these two levels of planning are mandated by federal and, in most states, state law. This chapter outlines a process for planning and presents a context that integrates these two levels of planning.

The context of planning includes legal, social, and educational factors that influence the process and outcome of planning. This context is currently governed by the Education for All Handicapped Children Act (PL 94-142) and the zeitgeist of mainstreaming and normalization. These, however, are often in conflict with current practice in the educational system. Therefore, planning also must concern itself with what has been and is. Effective planning is needed to reconcile these two worlds of special education into an integrated system of services.

Next, the inputs necessary to produce a data-based planning effort are considered. The inputs required are the needs assessments of children to be served, and an assessment of resources and manpower. The process of planning is based on the development of individualized educational programs required by PL 94-142 and strategies for integrating these program plans. The products of planning are based on an effective evaluation of the outputs of the system, *i.e.* an assessment of the impact of the educational systems on handicapped children and their families.

This chapter attempts to provide an integrated discussion of both the planning process and the planning content. In the final analysis it is the interaction of these two which produces effective action planning and results in a plan that can be a roadmap to the future rather than simply a description of what exists.

THE CONTEXT OF SPECIAL EDUCATION PLANNING

The effort to provide full educational services for persons with special needs takes place in a larger context. Part of this context is that special education is provided within the system of general education. A practical assumption is that the majority of school-aged children do not need special education. A corollary is that only a small percentage of children needing special help receive it outside the general education system. Most receive help within general education programming in the regular classroom. This includes both those with special needs who are not identified and those who are consciously placed or left there with or without auxillary support.

Historical Overview

A review of the history of special education for handicapped children in general and mentally retarded children specifically is helpful in an understanding of the current status and trends that are developing in the field. Three fairly distinct periods can be identified: 1896 to 1936, 1936 to 1948, and 1948 to 1970 (Wiegerink and Simeonsson, 1975).

The first school for backward children was established in Providence, Rhode Island, in 1896 as an outgrowth of a school originally designed for children who presented special discipline problems. Ten years later 13 other school systems had established special classes for children who appeared to be mentally retarded. By 1922, when the Office of Education began their record keeping, there were 23,252 children in 23 states who were enrolled in special classes for the mentally handicapped. The records for 1936 reveal that special education was a well established practice in this country with 43 states enrolling 99,621 children in special classes for the retarded.

Several factors have been identified to account for the interest in, and the rapid growth of, special education programs for the mentally retarded. The early work of Jean Marc Gaspard Itard and Edward Sequin in methods of special education for mentally defective individuals pointed the way to the educational potential of children who had heretofore been considered uneducable. In this country, Samuel Gridley Howe was an early advocate for the right to education of the retarded and the responsibility of the state to provide such education. Alfred Binet's mental age scales were brought to this country about 1914 and the translations and adaptations of these scales comprised the beginnings of the testing movement which became very popular for identification and classification purposes in special education. However, his notions of educability of intelligence received scant attention and were, in fact, contradictory to the current trend at the time in this country of pessimism towards the training of intelligence.

Perhaps as a result of this kind of thinking, the philosophy of special education was reflected in the idea that retarded children would be happier if they were grouped with their mental equals. If a child's intelligence quotient did change, it was held that the original finding of retardation was incorrect. We see this notion of grouping for the happiness of the child today in the idea of better self-concept and improved social adjustments advocated by the proponents of special classes.

As the population of cities grew, more children who were classified as mentally retarded or slow learners were found within an individual city school system. It became economically feasible to consider the possibility of special education classes or, in some cases, one school in the system. The growth of special education programs was much slower in rural and county systems because of the problems of transportation of retarded children into a special class and the probable lack of demand for such services.

Parent groups and professional organizations were mobilizing as effective lobbying forces with state legislatures during this period. Perhaps the greatest impetus to the establishment of special education was the development of state laws and special subsidies for special education. Eleven states enacted permissive or mandatory special education statutes in the period from 1911 to 1921. There was usually a subsidy for partial or complete support of special education in addition to statutes.

There appeared to be a shift away from the rapid growth of special education during the period from 1936 to 1948. In 1948, there were 87,179 children enrolled in special classes for the mentally retarded compared to 99,621 in 1936. There was also a decrease in enrollment in special education classes associated with 7 percent decrease in total school enrollment over these years. Decreased enrollment was due in part to the relative expense of special education programs during the years of the Depression and World War II.

In addition to these population and economic factors, there was also a disenchantment on the part of superintendents and other administrative personnel with the general quality and effectiveness of special education programs. Relatively little thought had been given to curriculum for these special classes. There were few personnel available who were trained to serve as special education teachers. The first college training program for teachers of retarded children was not organized until about 1920, and by 1949, there were only 22 colleges or universities that had developed some teacher preparation programs for the special education of the mentally retarded. Most of these programs offered only a 9- to 12-semester hour sequence in the specialty. These programs were not based on research or experimental data. Training was based on the experimental activities of teachers who had some teaching experience with the retarded.

The total school enrollment rapidly increased after World War II as the economy expanded. There was again a dramatic increase in special education for the retarded. The late 1940's saw the beginnings of inclusion of the moderately retarded or trainable mentally retarded (TMR) in public school education. The National Association of Retarded Children had, as one of its main objectives in the 1950's, the support of TMR programs by public educational units. In 1948, 4,509 or 7 percent of moderately retarded pupils were enrolled in special classes in local school systems. By 1963, 30,022 or 27 percent of TMR pupils had been enrolled. By the early 1970's it was estimated that at least 50 percent of moderately retarded pupils would receive their education in local public school facilities.

The totals for all special education classes for the retarded increased from 109,000 in 1953, to 207,000 in 1958, to 361,000 in 1963, and 649,000 in 1968. Much of this growth during the late 1950's and early 1960's was due to the impact of federal legislation of 1957 that allocated two-thirds of a million dollars for the retarded; in 1958 grants were made available for training leadership personnel in education of the retarded; Elementary and Secondary Education Act Title funds became available for handicapped children in 1967 and 1968; and new monies became available for training and research in mental retardation in 1967.

The monies for training greatly increased the number of programs offering preparation in education of the mentally retarded. By 1964, 221 colleges and universities requested funds for the support of special education programs.

Concomitantly, with the growth of special education for the retarded, many types of exceptionalities have received attention and the variety of special classes has expanded.

The question still remained as to whether the public school was effectively dealing with the problem of educating the handicapped child. There also was concern about what resources public schools had to develop appropriate programs, which litigation had made a reality, for increasingly disabled children. These questions have generated dilemmas involving comparisons of cost and benefit for the exceptional child. Although a variety of terms has been used to describe these dilemmas, they focus on the relative value of academic achievement versus social adjustment, normative experiences versus individualization, and the use or abuse of behavioral technology in modifying behavior.

The problem of public education for the retarded has been debated more frequently with regard to the role of the special class than any other topic. Although research is fragmented and of limited availability, there is no lack of critical reviews and proposals for new models. Bruininks and Rynders (1971), in a discussion of alternatives for special class placement for the educably mentally retarded (EMR) child, stated that the special class came into being at the turn of the century and accounted for approximately 90 percent of retarded children by the mid-1960's. In the latter 1960's, beginning with Dunn (1968), critical reviews began to emerge regarding special class placement, emphasizing possible misplacement and its sequelae for borderline, minority, or disadvantaged populations. Similar positions have been taken by Lilly (1970) and Christoplos and Renz (1969), who argued for the inclusion of the handicapped in regular classrooms to expand social adaptation of the handicapped and to enhance the attitudes of the nonretarded. They further proposed additional research on the effects of including a variety of exceptional children in regular classrooms. MacMillan (1971) provided a thorough review of research on special class placement for the mildly retarded and concluded that special education was a complex problem and could not be met with a dichotomous discussion of integrated or segregated placement. He recommended exploration of how a wider range of individual differences could be accommodated and adapted to regular class placement. Miller and Schoenfelder (1969) and Harvey (1969) also provided critical reviews and restated the need for public education to meet the special needs of handicapped students through a variety of diagnostic and prescriptive methods. In their comprehensive review of the literature, Bruininks and Rynders (1971) stated that the assumptions of homogeneous grouping, unique curriculum, and specially trained teachers as factors of optimizing education for retarded children have not been adequately tested. Summarizing basic positions of many of the earlier cited, critical articles for or against special classes, they conclude that available evidence is equivocal and essentially uninterpretable. Bruininks and Rynders (1971) proposed several alternatives to special class placement for EMR children which incorporate the principles of normalization and individualization.

Valletutti (1969) deplored the integration-segregation argument in special education from a somewhat different perspective. He suggested that aside from specific considerations of efficacy, legitimate criteria can be invoked for segregating the handicapped child to reduce negative consequences on teachers and children in regular classrooms. Furthermore, Valletutti felt that a crucial issue in the successful educational placement of handicapped children is the role of teacher attitude and expectancy. The values and attitudes of teachers would become an important consideration both in teacher training as well as in the programs and placements of handicapped children. The reality of severely and profoundly handicapped children attending public schools led Smith and Arkans (1974) to present a list of important considerations. These focus on the unique physical needs of severely and profoundly retarded children, the inability of a large regular classroom to meet these needs, and the lack of emphasis in regular classes to adequately incorporate appropriate education and training. Efficacy studies for trainable level children are fewer and even less definitive than for the less handicapped, educable-level children. Some of the studies, however, have indicated substantial capabilities of trainable children to respond to instruction.

In summary, it seems clear that many questions concerning public education of handicapped children have yet to be resolved. There has been little substantive research on the issues, and that research has been open to equivocal interpretation. There has not been a lack of critical debate and model building. Continued debate and model building without adequate empirical evidence can only contribute to further confusion and premature action. In approaching public education's responsibility to handicapped children, consideration must be given to the academic, social, and personal needs of the child. Consideration also must be given to the interactive components of this need with physical settings, teacher qualifications, attitudes and values, as well as peer and parent involvement. Clearly, a variety of interactive permutations is possible in equations of accountability. Some alternatives elaborated by Bruininks and Rynders (1971) and the special education contract model proposed by Gallagher (1972) are representative of approaches which would take into account some of these interactive variables. Implementation of effective programs for the mentally retarded in public schools should be based, now more than ever, on the execution of comprehensive planned services.

Litigation

A sudden proliferation of lawsuits involving public education and mental health accompanied the advent of the 1970's. Predominantly class-action in nature, this litigation focused on three main issues: the right to education, the right to treatment, and the use of inappropriate procedures for the classification and placement of children with special needs.

Although the impetus for each action has been supplied by diverse issues and concerns, the legal basis for the litigation has most often been in response to an apparent violation of the Due Process Clause of the Fifth and Fourteenth Amendments and the Equal Protection Clause of the Fourteenth Amendment of the United States Constitution. Under the cloak of due process, legal proceedings must be followed in accordance with the rules established by the jurisprudence system. A generally accepted interpretation of the latter clause is that "equal protection . . . shall be given to all under the circumstances in his life, his liberty, and his property, and in the pursuit of happiness, and in the exemption from any greater burdens and charges than are equally imposed upon all others under like circumstances." (Sovereign Camp)

Right to Education The *Pennsylvania Association for Retarded Children* v. *Commonwealth of Pennsylvania* (filed in January 1971) is recognized as the landmark right to education case. It was in the Pennsylvania Association for Retarded Children (PARC) consent agreement that the responsibility of the public schools to comply with due process procedures was first established. The case involved 14 mentally retarded children who had been denied a public education through state statutes. They sought free access to public educational opportunities for themselves and all mentally retarded children in

Pennsylvania via this class-action suit. Among the principles established by the resultant injunction are that:

1. Every mentally retarded child must be provided "... access to a free program of education and training" by public schools.
2. All due process procedural protections must be applied before imposing a label such as "mentally retarded" on a child.
3. "All mentally retarded persons are capable of benefiting from a program of education and training; ... that a mentally retarded person can benefit *at any point in his life* (author's emphasis) and development from a program of education." (President's Committee on Mental Retardation, 1974)

The decision for the plaintiffs in *Mills* v. *Board of Education of District of Columbia* (1972) expanded the holding of the PARC case to include all handicapped children. In addition, the court declared that insufficient funds were not an excuse for noncompliance when Federal Judge Joseph C. Waddy stated, "the inadequacies of the District of Columbia public school system, whether occasioned by insufficient funding or administrative inefficiency, certainly cannot be permitted to bear more heavily on the exceptional or handicapped child than on the normal child." (Mills case, 1972).

Further clarification of the right to education was established in *Maryland Association for Retarded Children* v. *State of Maryland* (1974). This included the decree that the educational program provided for a child must be an *appropriate* (authors' emphasis) program, meeting the individual special needs of that child. By stating that such programs must be made available to all children, "... no matter how seriously or extensively they are retarded" (MARC case, 1974), the court eliminated the severity of a child's disability as justification for nondelivery of services. Finally, the order affirmed that because Maryland statutes provide for education for each child at no expense to the child, his parents, or guardians, the practice of sending children to non-public schools without full funding is unlawful. To date, over 50 separate suits have been filed throughout the country, each seeking the right to equal educational opportunity.

Right to Treatment A similiar series of suits have been filed, primarily on behalf of institutionalized citizens, which focus on the right to receive adequate treatment. In *Wyatt* v. *Aderhold* (1971), the emphasis was on the delivery of services in the least restrictive environment. This was necessary in order that each individual committed to Bryce Hospital would have "... a realistic opportunity to be cured or to improve his or her mental condition." (Wyatt case, 1971). This decision, requiring the immediate hiring of 300 additional employees at the institution, established that the right to treatment necessitates 1) an individualized treatment program; 2) a humane physical and psychological environment; 3) adequate and qualified staff; and 4) provision of programs in the least restrictive manner possible (President's Committee on Mental Retardation, 1974). Other class action right to treatment suits, such as *Davis* v. *Watkins* (1973), incorporated many facets of the Wyatt case holding. Decisions requiring the awarding of damages when adequate treatment is not provided and development of community alternatives (*Ricci* v. *Greenblatt,* 1972), as well as finding that confinement without treatment is probably "cruel and unusual punishment," a violation of the Eighth Amendment of the United States Constitution (*Welch* v. *Likens,* 1974), have all utilized the Wyatt case precedent.

Improper Classification and Placement Procedures Perhaps more basic to the question of what services are to be delivered is who shall receive these services. Dunn (1968), Mercer (1971), Gilhool (1973), Kirk (1964), and Garrison and Hammil (1971), among others, have all raised serious questions regarding the large number of children who are inappropriately classified as having a handicapping condition. This is most often evidenced in children in rural areas. The studies also have shown that this mislabeling, coupled with a lack of appropriate services, results in inappropriate placement. As with two previously discussed rights, successful litigation has brought about considerable positive change. The first of these suits, *Diana* v. *State Board of Education* (1973) was filed by nine Mexican-American school children on behalf of bilingual children in California who might have been inappropriately labeled "mentally retarded" and then placed in classes for retarded children. The court ordered the retesting of all children already placed in classes for the mentally retarded. More importantly, the court recognized the placement of a disproportionate number of Mexican-Americans in classes for retarded children as requiring an explanation to the court.

Barely 2 years later, in *Larry P*. v. *Riles* (1972), the decision states that "no black student may be placed in an EMR class on the basis of criteria which rely primarily on the results of I.Q. tests as they are currently administered, if the consequences of use of such criteria is racial imbalance in the composition of EMR classes." The rationale for the decisions in these cases was compelling. The California legislature amended the education code in that state to provide a legal framework for pluralistic assessment, among other criteria. The evaluator must investigate such factors as developmental history and cultural background and substantiate any findings of retarded intellectual development by individual test scores. Estimates of adaptive behavior also must be made, and may include observations made at the child's home (California Education Code).

These and other cases (*Lebanks* v. *Spears,* 1973; *Guadalupe Organization* v. *Tempe Elementary School District,* 1972), have had great impact on the rights to education and treatment for all handicapped individuals. The judgments rendered call for an *individualized assessment* upon which must be based an *individualized program* in an appropriate setting. Certainly, the fiscal implications arising from all education oriented litigation are immense. The per pupil cost for special education is greater than for regular education in all categories of exceptionality (see Table 1). Yet, as was shown in the Mills case (1972), scarcity of available monies is no excuse for the denial of appropriate services. Rather, a reallocation of resources must be made. State legislation (Abeson and Ballard, 1976) and the Education for All Handicapped Children Act of 1975 have committed state and federal governments to very substantial fiscal support for educating handicapped children. In concert with recent litigation, legislation has further refined and strengthened the rights given to all citizens by the United States Constitution.

Education for All Handicapped Children Act The Education for All Handicapped Children Act, PL 94-142, was signed into law in November 1975. Most of its provisions took effect October 1, 1977. This act received overwhelming approval by both House and Senate and stands as a legislative landmark for people who have handicapping conditions.

There are numerous statements describing PL 94-142 in detail (see *References*). However, this section is intended to provide a summary of information concerning some of the major features of PL 94-142 for the purpose of describing part of the context of education for persons with handicapping conditions.

The stated purpose of the Education for All Handicapped Children Act (PL 94-142) is:

"... to assure that all handicapped children have available to them ... a free, appropriate public education which emphasizes special education and related services designed to meet their unique needs, to assure that the rights of handicapped children and their parents or guardians are protected, to assist States and localities to provide for the education of all handicapped children, and to assess and assure the effectiveness of efforts to educate handicapped children."

The act specifies that the population of handicapped children includes those who are "mentally retarded, hard of hearing, deaf, speech impaired, visually handicapped, seriously emotionally disturbed, orthopedically impaired or other health impaired children or children with specific learning disabilities who by reason thereof require special education and related services." It is noted that persons of school age with developmental disabilities are included within this larger population of handicapped children.

In order to meet the stated purpose of the law for these children, the following mandates have been stipulated by the act:

1. A free, appropriate public education for handicapped children aged 3 to 18 must be assured by all states by September 1, 1978, and for handicapped persons aged 3 to 21 by September 1, 1980. If however, a state does

not provide a public education for nonhandicapped children between the ages of 3 through 5 and 18 through 21, it is not required to provide an education for handicapped children.

2. Priorities specify that federal monies should first be used for the education of handicapped children who are unserved. The second priority is to serve severely handicapped children, within each disability category, who are inadequately served.

3. In order to target the funds toward the children who meet the requirements of the definition (and not, for instance, to children who have learning problems primarily because of socioeconomic status), the law stipulates that a state cannot count over 12 percent of its total school-aged population as handicapped for the purpose of receiving federal funds. In addition, no more than one-sixth of this 12 percent can be labeled "learning disabled."

4. In order to qualify for assistance from the federal government under this act, a state must meet certain eligibility requirements (including a policy assuring the right to a free, appropriate public education, the deadlines, the priorities, the maintenance of Individual Education Plans (IEP) for every handicapped child, nondiscriminatory testing, and the establishment of procedural safeguards). These requirements are in addition to the usual federal requirement of a State Plan.

5. Each state desiring to receive federal funds under PL 94-142 must submit a State Plan to the Commissioner of Education; each Local Education Agency desiring to receive federal funds under the act must submit an application to the State Education Agency. The State Plan and the application must contain the following guarantees and assurances (which are essentially accountability mechanisms at both levels):
   - assurance of a goal of full educational opportunity for all handicapped children and a detailed timetable for accomplishing this goal
   - assurance that the eligibility conditions will be met
   - assurance of extensive child identification and evaluation procedures
   - a guarantee of policies and procedures to protect the confidentiality of data and information
   - assurance of parent or guardian consultation
   - assurance of complete due process procedures
   - assurance that special education will be provided to all handicapped children in the least restrictive environment
   - maintenance and use of programs and procedures for a system of comprehensive personnel development, including in-service training
   - provision for an annual evaluation (at the state level) of the effectiveness of programs in meeting the educational needs of handicapped children

6. There is a substantial increase in federal aid to the states to help them

reach the goal of a free, appropriate public education for all handicapped children. Authorizations, which are worked out through a formula, are estimated to be around 387 million dollars for fiscal year 1978 and increase to around 3.16 billion dollars by fiscal year 1982. However, it must be remembered that these are authorization figures, not the actual amount which will be appropriated for expenditure.

7. Each state's allotment comes from the federal government to the State Education Agency (SEA): much of the allotment then passes to those Local Education Agencies (LEA) which have submitted an application to the SEA which the SEA has approved. Fifty percent of the allotment was to pass through to LEA in fiscal year 1978; thereafter 75 percent must be passed to the local level.

8. Federal dollars passed through to the local level must be used to pay the extra cost of educating handicapped children. Each local school district applying for aid is still responsible for maintaining current expenditures for special education based on the average annual per pupil expenditure in that school district. Federal aid cannot be used to supplant state or local monies for educational services until the goal of full services is reached.

PL 94-142 requires the SEA to assume responsibility for ensuring that all requirements of the act are met. This provision serves to centralize accountability and to provide for more careful implementation of the comprehensive state plan for educating handicapped children. If parents (or guardians) are dissatisfied by either the LEA's or SEA's provision of a free, appropriate public education for their child, they may use the extensive due process procedures (including a hearing) to remedy the situation to their satisfaction.

Questions and issues about the appropriate handling of special education within public education may have been resolved by careful research. For the present some of these questions have been resolved by the courts. The combined effects of litigation and legislation have resulted in a marked change in how educational services to handicapped children are to be delivered. Historically, segregation was the byword, with emphasis on self-contained classes or schools of homogeneously grouped handicapped children. This emphasis now has changed to mainstreaming, following the principle of least restrictive environment. Thus, the likelihood is greatly increased that many children, identified as needing special education services, will receive all or part of these services in regular classrooms.

NEED FOR PLANNING IN SPECIAL EDUCATION

It is essential that persons associated with special education have a clear understanding of the planning process, because many professionals and parents of children with handicapping conditions are becoming involved in providing full services for these children for the first time. Effective coordination and planning of programs are key to providing quality services.

Implementing a "full services" program means a number of things. First, each person who needs special educational help should have his or her individualized program of full services. The process by which this program is developed is a planning process, engaged in by a team of professionals, the child's parents, and, where appropriate, the child. Second, full services for any agency providing special educational services amounts to more than the aggregate of all special educational programs for each individual. Instead, the agency must have a program plan for itself that integrates these programs into a meaningful whole. A structure must be provided within which to manage all of the individual plans, to identify program or agency needs, and to generate and maintain a flow of resources necessary for providing full services within the agency. Beyond each LEA is the SEA, which in turn must have its own plan. This chapter will concentrate primarily on the planning function at the local level.

The Education for All Handicapped Children Act of 1975 provides the mandate for these two levels of planning. The LEA Special Education Plan is the second level of planning. The Individualized Education Plan and the LEA Special Education Plan are documents required by law, but they most frequently do not reflect all planning activities that must take place if the provision of full services is to be accomplished. However, both levels of planning can be accomplished by the same generic planning process.

The steps in this planning process include:

1. Identification of goals
2. Assessment of needs to accomplish goals
3. Identification and analysis of constraints and resources to accomplish goals
4. Specification of objectives necessary to achieve each goal
5. Specification of activities necessary to achieve each objective
6. Specification of indicators to show whether each objective has been reached
7. Specification of the overall evaluation plan.

An eighth step is also essential to most plans. It takes place after a plan has been carried out. This step consists of taking the results of evaluation and determining how the initial plan should be revised to carry out further what is intended.

Seven steps, sometimes referred to as "The Seven Steps to Heaven," are for the most part basic to any planning effort. Simply stated, one must first determine what one wants to do. Next one must gauge the size of the task. Then one must find out what is in the environment that will either help or hinder the effort to do what is intended. After this, it is usually necessary to break the goal into its component parts or objectives, a matter of simplifying the goal. The next step asks the questions: "What needs to be done to achieve each objective?" And after that, "How will one know when it is done?" The plan will be complete when there are satisfactory answers to all these questions.

Any planner knows that this basic list of steps can be altered in a variety of ways, depending on the planning effort. Planning at an organizational level, for example, should include a consideration of organizational beliefs and environmental climate, as well as the careful specification of mission. There are other ways to further detail the basic planning process, but for the moment this simplified list is sufficient.

The process for generating a child's IEP includes those steps. The first step is more or less inferred with the referral of a child suspected of needing special help. These goals are to determine whether, in fact, the child does need special help and, if so, to provide it. Next comes the assessment of needs to determine the child's strengths and weaknesses: what is his performance level in each of the relevant areas of his education program? Constraints and resources can relate to determining the extent to which the LEA can or cannot provide the type of setting and the type of personnel needed by the child. The next step is specifying instructional objectives necessary to provide the child with the special help he needs. The IEP can include listing the educational activities associated with each instructional objective as well as the means of determining whether or not the objective has been reached.

The LEA Special Education Plan must consider the same steps, or questions, at an organizational level. Goals relate to providing full educational services to all children who need them. Assessment of needs relates, in part, to how many children are involved and how to identify them. Identification and analysis of constraints and resources include at least the following considerations: architectural barriers, number of special education teachers and resource personnel, types of special education programs available, staff development and training needs of various school personnel, financial resources available, potential available, and many others. Objectives, activities, and indicators are generated from the planning effort to complete the plan.

INPUTS FOR PLANNING

A basic approach for planning and the context in which planning occurs has been presented. Effective planning is based on data and information of current and projected needs as well. Although data are never 100 percent accurate and projections are always no more than "guesstimates," it is important to select a method for determining existing and projected needs that is at the same time useful and cost-effective.

Needs Assessment

Too often in a search for accurate needs data "the baby is thrown out with the bath water." Numerous planning projects have floundered because of the excessive costs of needs assessments. These costs are financial, temporal, and psychological. If the needs assessment strategy is either too expensive or not in line with potential planning outcomes, the proverbial "tail may wag the dog." In two states 200,000 and 600,000 dollars were spent during 1- and 2-year periods to establish data bases for human service planning for the developmentally disabled. Both systems surveyed existing and potential clients and services on a state-wide basis. Despite expensive and time-consuming efforts, client needs data were marred by errors which began at the referral and diagnostic levels and were exacerbated by the data transfer and synthesis at the regional and state levels. In addition, the services and resources data portrayed accurately a very predictable result; namely, uneven and uncoordinated service systems that had few if any vacancies. Thus the idealistic planning format of matching clients and services received a severe if not fatal setback because of inaccurate needs data and unavailable services.

It is clear that to have such a data base for documenting the real needs of the system would be useful; however, such a documentation could be gained with far less cost to the system. The needs assessment process resulted in a burned-out staff in both cases. Legislators were also overwhelmed by the high costs as compared to relatively meager products. To avoid such a situation, needs should be determined by use of a method selected to be as cost-effective as the potential results of the planning would warrant. If the planning is going to result in actual choices of high magnitude based on the needs data, then the costs could justifiably be significant; however, as is most often the case, if the planning is going to serve more as a rationale for already determined or inevitable directions, then the costs should be commensurately lower.

There are various methods which can be used for determining the need of those to be served. These methods, listed by increasing order of costs, include:

1. **Those presenting needs**—This is the traditional method of finding those who have a need. Individuals are expected to contact a service provided or referral agent and present their need. When sufficient common needs are presented, a new service is developed. This method is least costly in the short run in that it does not require outreach of any kind and results in a match between need and service. Although this method does identify handicapped children with important educational or human service needs, it neglects the uninformed and those who cannot advocate for themselves. Although this method appears to be inconsistent with law and a humane society, its free enterprise nature is inherent in many human service

programs now in existence, *e.g.*, Supplementary Security Income, Head Start, etc.

2. **Those matching services**—This method is also commonly used, and consists of putting a service in place (*e.g.*, classrooms for the multiply handicapped), then advertising its existence until it is filled. This is a cost-effective strategy for serving those with certain prescribed needs, but neglects those who do not fit. Widespread use of this method accounts for the uneven patterns of educational and human services we have now. In its most pronounced form this is the basis for the service islands of excellence, created by federal and state demonstration programs, with empty seas between.

3. **Population estimates**—This approach is now being used more often as the use of "computer-think" increases. The logic is that if only accurate estimates by catchment areas were available, planning would be simplified—if not simple. Unfortunately, too often it becomes "simpleminded" instead.

A problem with using population estimates is that those that exist reflect political realities more often than needs and population realities. The estimates in common use have, by and large, come from advocacy and consumer organizations that used them to develop legislative and financial support. They are, therefore, often inflated and usually insensitive to state and local differences. Very few of these types of estimates have been confirmed by population studies and well designed sampling surveys. For example, in studies by West Virginia (Lindberg, 1976) and Chicago (Hamilton, 1977), the cited incidence of handicapped persons was substantially different from the projected estimates. In a second example, the 3 percent figure which the National Association for Retarded Citizens uses is taken from the use of the normal curve of intelligence. Below 2 standard deviations from the mean falls approximately 3 percent of the population. This assumes that all such persons also fail to be socially adaptable.

Some of the most often used population estimates are those for the larger handicapping conditions: 3 percent for mental retardation, 0.2 percent for cerebral palsy, and 2 percent for epilepsy (Hammer and Richman, 1975). For educational purposes, PL 94-142 limits the total population to be identified to no more than 12 percent. Given the coexistence of many handicapping conditions, *e.g.*, mental retardation and epilepsy, this is a very high figure and results in finding false-positives.

A set of well developed population statistics is still needed. It must be sensitive to the fact that handicapping conditions are both biological and sociological in nature and, therefore, the estimates would most likely vary with ages of client (*e.g.*, preschool versus high school); geography (*e.g.*, inner city versus rural); income of families (*e.g.*, low income versus high income); and other factors such as educational levels of community. Perhaps the best estimates to use to date are those by Stedman (1970) and Baroff (1974). These present hypothetical estimates based on accepted incidence figures and vary them with other population statistics, *e.g.*, differences in size of population in various age ranges. Planners would do well to modify those estimates to fit the socioeconomic conditions of their communities. If more accurate estimates were needed, a sampling strategy commensurate with needs and potential results could be used to make statistics more sensitive to the community population.

4. **Head counts**—This method is often seen as the most accurate and the ideal assessment of need; "the end all and the be all of needs assessment." Unfortunately, this is not the case. As stated earlier, the best and most feasible method would be the one which matches purpose, costs, and potential benefit. This head count method is practical only for specialized purposes. First, a method that depends on actually contacting people and counting individuals is very expensive. Second, it may have serious repercussions from those contacted in terms of increasing expectations and invasion of privacy. Finally, and perhaps most importantly, it is an inaccurate process. It depends on human specifications and understandings that currently do not exist. If one were trying to locate all mentally retarded persons in a specified area, how much common understanding of the condition could one expect from surveyors, parents, professionals, politicians, self-interested persons, fearful people, etc.? If professionals do not agree about the definition and means for determining who has mental retardation, how much understanding could one expect among members of the community? This technique should be abandoned for all but research and population estimate purposes, where methods could be well defined and costs could be acceptable because of potential widespread use of the results (*i.e.*, more accurate population estimates).

5. **Child find**—This is the program established by PL 94–142 and the Bureau of Education for the Handicapped as the method to determine the population in need within a state. The program varies from state to state and combines many of the before-mentioned methods. In addition, individual states have used enrollment figures, client lists from other human service agencies (*e.g.*, developmental day care services, mail-out surveys, and use of local and regional contact teams).

The program has met with varied success from state to state. Most have had difficulties in getting the program started but some, such as Idaho and Connecticut, have had notable success. When one considers the expense of the national program, estimated at somewhere between 10 and 20 million dollars, and the fact that only small numbers of additional handicapped children have been located, one could question its cost-efficiency. On the other hand, the data have been useful at both the state and federal levels in giving hard numbers to special education advocates and silencing some critics who question the needs and benefits of expanded programs for handicapped persons. An alternative to these methods is the single port of entry.

6. **Single port of entry**—This is a concept that is relatively new to human services and education and is receiving increasing attention. Single ports of entry are designed to provide a single location and administrative framework for integrating human services. Although implementation strategies vary from one region to another, in most, this implementation involves a single location for coordination outreach, referral, and follow-along services. By combining these services across agencies, significant amounts of resources and wear and tear on the consumer can be saved. If consumers have multiple needs for economic, social education, and health services, they need go only to one central location to gain their legitimate piece of the service pie, rather than from agency to agency. Although education agencies have not often been a part of this baker's dozen, educators could profit from this interagency cooperation in numerous ways.

Most handicapped children in the schools do have need for other human services, and a well constructed set of support services can make for a personal and home climate more conducive to education. As Hobbs suggested in *The Futures of Children* (1974), the school might be the best location for the single port of entry for school-age children.

The single port of entry is in part a needs assessment strategy. This is because individuals in need of any of a range of services go directly to the point of referral and present their needs. The number of incoming people and their presentation of needs can be used for planning of service expansions, gap filling, reduction of duplications, the development of new services, and service integrations. With aggressive outreach this method reduces the time and communication gaps between presentation of need and location of services. With an expandable, retractable, and flexible service network, services can be shaped to fit the clientele rather than the other way around.

Needs assessment data are critical to the planning process, but even more important may be the process for gathering the data. Each method has its advantages and disadvantages and none can be said to be best in all cases. Instead, just as services need integration and pluralism, so do needs assessment strategies. For effective planning to take place, planners must first plan effectively for cost-effective needs assessment strategies in line with their goals and resources.

Manpower

In the past decade the area of education for the handicapped has undergone rapid and significant change. From these changes have emerged a number of varying trends that promise to enact profound changes within the field, particularly regarding personnel. Currently, there appears to be a great deal of flux and lack of cohesiveness within these trends. Some are viewed as being possibly detrimental to the progress already made. This controversy is illustrated by such diverse examples as those calling for a loosening of the requirements for educators of the handicapped at the same time that others are demanding a greater number of qualified specialists to deal with more and/or expanding special education programs. The expansion of special education and increased personnel allotments has been largely due to the more active involvement of federal and state government with particular emphasis on funding. By 1970, there were over 400 colleges and universities (an increase from the 70 which existed less that 20 years ago) with special education programs; over 300 of these institutions were receiving federal support for teacher training. In fiscal year 1975, the Bureau of Education for the Handicapped (BEH) awarded nearly 200 million dollars to states and special programs. Of this, 37.7 million dollars were allocated for training of teachers, supervisors, and paraprofessionals (*Education Daily,* 1976). The two federal programs directed toward increasing special education personnel are: 1) The Education for the Handicapped Act, Part D, which provides for graduate-level training through fellowships to those students pursuing careers in special education, and 2) programs under the Education Professions Development Act which are designed primarily for the provision of special education training for regular classroom personnel. However, even these steps do not change the fact that there still remains an urgent need for trained special educators. In fact, special education is one of the few areas in education with a major personnel shortage. This lack of personnel extends in all areas and also to the provision of ancillary and trained paraprofessionals to work with and provide assistance to the special educator. There is also a need for inservice training in special education to better enable regular educators to identify and meet the special needs of handicapped children. Although this demand is readily acknowledged, there are many complicating factors. Throughout the United States there is a wide variation in demand versus supply of special educators. Although in some states 60 to 70 percent of handicapped children receive special instruction, in others fewer than 15 percent are served. Wide variation also exists as to the types of education services available. A viable relationship does not always exist between the *need* for special educator personnel and *funding* available to pay them. Recent increases in state level expenditures may alleviate this problem.

Perhaps the area of special education in which there is the most urgent need is that of the need for increased numbers of skilled professionals for the early education of the handicapped child. Educator's experience and experimental data tentatively suggest that a great deal more would be accomplished if special programs were initiated at an early age. Although complete data is nonexistent, current estimates approximate that there are about 1 million handicapped children (birth to 4 years) in the United States.

A continuing shortage of minority and bilingual special educators exists. This need for bilingual personnel is particularly apparent in the Spanish-origin population of the United States which continues to grow rapidly because of high birth rate and the substantial immigration of young adults.

Clearly, there is a need for additional personnel to deliver services to children with special needs at all levels and across all categories. Accurate projections of supply and demand would provide much enlightenment in this area of great concern. The general lack of data, the disagreement among professionals as to the needs of handicapped children, and the multiplicity of systems all complicate efforts for a concise national trend which would clearly indicate manpower needs.

It is reasonable to state that in the area of personnel there have been giant strides toward attaining a greater balance between need and available resources. However, greater numbers of more highly qualified personnel are needed. To accomplish this, funding in federal, state, and local budgets for personnel training and development is needed. There is a need for school districts to become aware of and implement the upgrading of qualification requirements for existing and incoming personnel. As the recent court decisions and legislation have determined, children with special needs must receive an appropriate education. This presumes staffing our schools and other service delivery systems with qualified personnel.

Continuum of Services

As the focus for education of handicapped children has been placed on the public schools, new approaches for the delivery of appropriate services have been developed. Upon entering the school, handicapped children and their parents are finding that many activities are now being oriented toward normalization, or mainstreaming. The normalization principle, as applied to handicapped children, provides conditions for them which are as close as possible to the norms accepted by society. Translated into educational programming, the term "mainstream" refers to providing education for handicapped children in the regular classroom in addition to providing needful students the supportive services of teacher consultation with specialists, tutoring by an itinerant teacher, resource room attendance, or a combination of these services (Kirk, 1975). Traditional self-contained classrooms continue to exist, delivering services to the more severely handicapped children who best function in such an environment. The burden of proof lies with the school to provide the least restrictive and most educational environment.

Self-contained classrooms are of two basic types, categorical and non-categorical. In each instance, the children receive their education in a single classroom. The children are, in this manner, segregated from any interaction with nonhandicapped children. In a self-contained classroom, instruction is the responsibility of a single teacher and, occasionally, a teacher's aide. Children are assigned to the class on the basis of categorization, *e.g.*, educable mentally retarded or learning disabled, oftentimes resulting in the ages of students spanning several years. In the noncategorical, self-contained room, the difference is that the children of approximately the same age are grouped together, regardless of the label affixed to their disability. There are some schools which utilize a team-teaching approach. There, teachers and their classes are placed together in pods. Teachers are given responsibility for particular students and/or the instruction of certain subject areas.

Many schools, in a more overt attempt to eventually place handicapped children in regular classes, have moved to the "resource room concept." Under this system, the child leaves his class at certain specified times for a resource room where he receives assistance in a particular subject or skill area. Resource programs may have either an ability or skill orientation or a combination of both (Jenkins and Mayball, 1975.) In the former, the focus is on basic school tasks such as arithmetic or reading. The latter concentrates on central processing mechanisms related to perceptual, motor, and psycholinguistic abilities.

For various reasons some schools do not have resource rooms, opting instead for a consulting teacher program. As developed by Hugh S. McKenzie (1970), a consulting teacher program brings the specialist into the child's regular classroom. There, the child is both observed and formally evaluated. The consulting teacher then develops an individualized program of instruction for the child and works with his teacher in implementing it. If necessary, the consulting teacher will visit the child's parents, explaining the program and enlisting their assistance.

Another model being utilized is the Child Development Consultant. The National Institute of Mental Health funded five university programs to prepare specialists in child development to work with handicapped children. The professionals are broadly trained during a 2-year Master's degree program to provide consultation to teachers and in service training. Where the model is effective, school personnel establish a supportive, individualized program of instruction for every child in the school and a carefully monitored, positive mental health atmosphere.

One area that has received increasing attention from Congress and BEH is early education. Under the Handicapped Children's Early Education Assistance Program, over 250 model First Chance Centers have been developed and funded. These centers provide services for preschool children from birth to 8 years and their parents. Service delivery methods vary from center to center, but all include individualized programs and parent training.

Table 1. Service delivery costs per child at the elementary school level (estimated costs)[a]

Model[b]	Number[c] served	Direct[d] costs	Indirect[e] costs	Total costs	Training[f] costs	Training[g] costs	Per child training costs	Total cost (training and services)
Institutional	5	20,000[h]		20,000	10,000	1,000	200	20,200+
Special class (self-contained)	6	4,200[i]	800[e]	5,000	24,000[j]	2,400	300	5,300
Resource class	20	1,000[k]	1,200[l]	2,200	30,000[m]	3,000	150	2,350
Consulting teacher specialist	20	750	1,200	1,950	36,000[n]	3,600	180	2,130
Child development consultant[o]	40	500	1,200	1,700	36,000	3,600	90	1,790
Early education[p]	8	2,400	1,200[q]	3,600	30,000	3,200	400	4,000
Regular education	25	1,400		1,400	22,000	2,200	40	3,600

[a]These costs are estimates from data from several sources and do not reflect any actual situation; they should, however, accurately reflect proportional costs and different base rates (Blum and Pauly, 1975; Weber, Foster, and Weikart, 1978).

[b]We cannot assume that there would be equal benefits or equal access for all handicapped children. However, handicapped children could be expected to move from more restrictive environments to more normal environments with some increased benefit.

[c]Estimated number served per full-time staff.

[d]Estimated cost of the service per child.

[e]Estimated cost of additional services.

[f]Estimated cost of training (preservices and inservice).

[g]Cost divided by an estimated 10 years of service.

[h]Cost divided by number of children served.

[i]Estimated costs: MA teacher, one aide, room, materials (per child).

[j]Training: 4 years at 5,000 dollars plus 4,000 dollars (inservice).

[k]Additional overhead costs: administrative.

[l]Estimated average cost for regular classroom instruction per child.

[m]Training: 5 years at 5,000 plus 3,000 dollars.

[n]Master's degree plus inservice training.

[o]Inservice training provides for a school focusing on special education.

[p]Preschool, 2+ years, divided by 6 years of benefit.

[q]Regular class placement following early education.

61

Although not proven to be highly successful, performance contracting has been utilized as a method for attaining success in the classroom. One of the most extensive experiments in this area was undertaken during the 1970–1971 school year. The United States Office of Economic Opportunity (now the Community Service Administration) sponsored a project in which private firms operating under incentive contracts (the more children learned, the more the firms were paid) developed educational performance contracts for several school systems and delivered programmed instruction. Their results were compared with those of public schools operating under a traditional instructional method (Gramlich and Koshel, 1975). Because these programs enjoyed only minimal success in most instances, schools have continued to place the responsibility for delivery of educational services on teachers.

Mainstreaming of handicapped children into regular classrooms has become the watchword of the late Seventies. Ultimately, it is hoped that almost all children will be served within the regular classroom. The success of this effort will depend on the success of in-service training and re-education for today's teachers, and new training goals, methods, and procedures for tomorrow's teachers.

Table 1 presents cost comparison of the various models briefly described in this paper. The costs are estimated from a variety of sources and reflect approximate current average costs nationwide. Costs, of course, vary widely from state to state and district to district, but the relative costs of the compared models do not. All things being equal, it is clear that the mainstreaming approaches are less costly than the specialized approaches. Of course, all things are not equal. Current models cannot accommodate all types of handicapped children. Instead, the multiply handicapped are restricted to the more costly service methods. However, it is possible that given the willingness and the start-up costs, in the long run even the multiply handicapped would be much better off in mainstreamed classes for social, cultural, legal, as well as economic reasons. What remains to be acquired is the determination and resources to complete the mainstreaming effort.

PROCESS FOR PLANNING

Two levels of planning must be carried out to ensure that a full service program exists for handicapped children within an LEA. Level I planning is used to construct an IEP for each child who has special needs. Level II planning is used to develop a management system for generating and maintaining the flow of resources necessary for the full service program.

Level I Planning

This planning effort is conducted by an interdisciplinary team. Within an LEA, the key team members are the principal, who heads all such teams, the child's regular classroom teacher, the special education teacher who most likely will be providing special services to the child, and the child's parents. Other personnel may complement this core group, depending on the child's needs. The school psychologist who contributes to the assessment of the child's performance level may be a member. A child who is reading substantially below grade level will need the help of a remedial reading teacher, who will assess the child's needs and work out this part of the child's special program; therefore, the reading teacher should be included on the team. Other specialists or resource personnel could be included, depending on the child's need for their services. The critical question about team membership is whether or not a particular person or type of personnel is knowledgeable about the child and his needs or some type of special educational service needed by the child.

The work of the placement team breaks down into two main tasks. The first is to determine what type of special programming the child needs. The second is to determine the type or types of educational setting in which the child's total program should be carried out.

The process for developing an IEP and the description of who develops it have been well stated by others. The National Association of State Directors of Special Education has published a manual entitled *Functions of the Placement Committee in Special Education* (1976) and, Turnbull, Strickland, and Brantley have produced a handbook entitled *Developing and Implementing Individualized Education Programs* (1978). Both of these handbooks serve as helpful resources to those interested in learning a detailed, step-by-step approach to IEP construction.

A most important outcome of IEP development is that of determining the placement match for a child. The placement match is decided by team consideration of the child's special and nonspecial needs and the placement options available in which these special needs may be served. Figure 1 is a pictorial display of variables constituting a Least-Restrictive Environment Decision-Making Model. The left-hand side of this figure briefly summarizes information about the child and is used to determine the child's special and nonspecial needs. Once special and nonspecial needs are delineated from assessing the child's performance level in all educationally relevant areas, the team assesses each need with respect to the child's adaptability to different least-restrictive environment options. Can the child better achieve a particular goal in a regular class setting or a special class setting? Given a particular setting, what special resources should be in place to make it most favorable for his learning? These questions and others should be asked with consideration of the child's characteristics—what is best for him or her, not what is available in the educational agency.

Least-restrictive environmental options available in the agency, itself, constitute the right-hand side of Figure 1. Now the question can be asked:

64

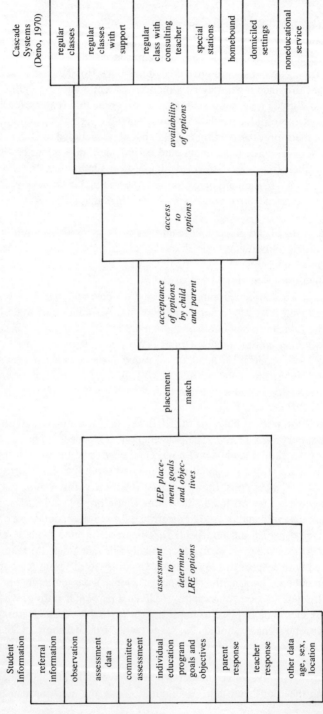

Figure 1. Least-Restrictive Environment (LRE) Decision-Making Model.

Given the kind of placement settings the child needs, what are the available options in the educational agency? If all settings needed are available, then a placement match is easily accomplished. If not, then reconsideration of placement settings for the child needs to be made.

There are certain desirable outcomes from this method of determining the placement match for each child needing special help. It is very likely that many educational agencies do not presently have all available placement options. The information flowing out of this decision-making model can be used in Level II planning. It provides the principal with an indication of how many times a child needs a particular placement setting which is not currently available, therefore indicating a need for additional resources. It might also suggest the need for resources within settings.

It might be that a regular classroom is thought to be the suitable placement for achieving certain IEP goals. However, certain conditions in that setting are not favorable. Architectural barriers, insufficiency of regular classroom teacher skills, lack of suitable equipment or materials, or inadequate resource/consultant teacher time are some of these conditions. Systematic collection of this type of information by the principal becomes a form of needs assessment about constraints on developing a full services program within the school. If the process is conducted systematically a match should result between a child's needs and the best place and resource fit available.

LEVEL II PLANNING

Current requirements for the delivery of educational services to handicapped children markedly increase the amount of time needed to plan and deliver these services. Meanwhile, there has been no reduction in the amount of time needed to operate the regular education program. Principals, chairing the placement team for each child suspected of needing special education, may have literally hundreds of hours of meeting time he or she never had before. Meeting time increases for any regular classroom teacher who refers a child, although certainly not as much as for the principal. Teachers may also find themselves working with the child in the classroom in new ways, since they are not likely to have much experience with special education.

Providing a full services program for handicapped children and maintaining the regular education program requires much more time and additional skills. Level II planning can help in the understanding of how to accomplish a satisfactory balance in the overall program.

Level II planning is recommended at the district level as well as within each school building. The planning group at the district level should include the coordinator (or director) of special education, the coordinator of staff development, and representatives from each category of school personnel. One or two principals, regular classroom teachers, special education teachers, and other resource personnel can be selected for the planning group. They will provide input based on their special professional perspective. They may also serve as communication links back to their professional group. Personnel who should be involved in Level II planning at the school building can follow a similar pattern. Here, the principal is the likely chairperson of the group, rather than the director of special education.

It may be very useful to acquire the services of an outside planning consultant to lead the group through the planning process. Good planning consultants can save the group much time through their knowledge of planning process, group dynamics, and otherwise helping the group to develop a plan they literally "own." In no case is it recommended to contract with a planning consultant to draw up a plan for the educational agency. Plans obtained in this manner are the kind that collect dust on shelves. Plans must be action oriented and owned by the group if they are to be carried out.

Suggestions for Level II Planning

The general task of the planning group is to design a plan to provide full services for handicapped children, while maintaining the desired thrust of the regular education program. The following steps should be considered in order to accomplish this task.

1. **Consideration of organizational beliefs**—Given the general task mentioned above, each member of the planning group should be asked to contribute his or her beliefs about the organization with regard to the task. Beliefs are statements of principle or philosophy relatively well accepted by the group. They also guide the group's behavior (Goode, 1973). This step helps to demonstrate any differences in values among group members. It also helps to strengthen certain beliefs that are commonly accepted. The generation of a list of belief statements serves as the foundation for the entire planning activity and serves as a continuing reference point for the group.

2. **Consideration of problems**—The planning group next begins to list the kinds of problems the educational agency faces in accomplishing the task. They consider the question: "What are the barriers to providing a program of full services?" This discussion should be relatively short and informal. It is to record a list of problems, but the main function of this step is to help the group begin to get its collective "mind" around the task.

3. **Development of mission statement**—A mission statement is a brief statement of the purpose of the plan. "It is the mission of Galactica Public Schools to provide full educational services for handicapped children within the overall program of regular education," is an example of a mission statement. The mission statement defines the scope of appropriate activity with respect to the agency. It helps the planning group to

focus their activities. It will also communicate to all organizational personnel what the organization is committed to do. Therefore, a good mission statement can serve to motivate personnel in achieving the objectives of the organization.

4. **Stating the goals**—A goal is a statement of a result desired on a continuing basis for the forseeable future. "To ensure that all students develop functional competency in reading, writing, speaking, listening, and reasoning," is an example of a goal. The main purpose of goals is to make the intent of the mission statement more explicit. Goals partition the mission statement into definable parts that can be more easily managed. They will subsequently serve as anchors for specific objectives and corresponding strategies. They also link these objectives to the mission statement. In this way, they also help to ensure that focus of evaluation remains on results rather than on a program or process. It is not necessary that goals are stated in measurable terms, but they should indicate what is to be measured.

5. **Specific objectives**—A specific objective is a statement of desired achievement which is specific in terms of when it should be completed, what results are expected, and how it is to be evaluated (Goode, 1973). Objectives provide an exact description of desired outcomes. "An objective of Galactica Public Schools is to have all students with an I.Q. of between 90 and 110, who terminate their participation in the elementary-secondary program in the 1979–1980 school year, demonstrate a reading ability at least on the ninth grade level as measured by the XYZ Reading Inventory; others shall demonstrate a reading ability commensurate with their I.Q. scores."

   A set of specific objectives linked with a goal provides an operational definition of that goal. The set of objectives describes what is to be achieved by what time. Objectives, therefore, serve as a key to the evaluation system that should be developed as part of the plan. The criteria and techniques for evaluation are an integral part of each objective.

6. **Strategies**—A strategy is a method used to accomplish an organizational objective or group of objectives. Typically, more than one strategy may be available to accomplish an objective. The task is to select one that most effectively and efficiently gets the job done. One strategy for achieving the specific objective mentioned above is to hire enough reading specialists so that there is one available for every student who is presently within an I.Q. range of 90 to 110, but who is reading below the ninth grade level. This strategy would increase the likelihood of achieving the objective, but the costs may well be somewhat excessive. Selecting strategies requires creativity and careful thought. It is frequently useful to generate a list of alternative strategies. These can be weighed

against each other in the effort to select strategies which have the greatest likelihood of being most effective and practical.

7. **Action Plans**—An action plan is an explicit statement of work to be accomplished (Goode, 1973). Action plans are written for each specific objective. The plan breaks down the objective into all of the tasks needed to be carried out to accomplish the objective. Each task can then be assigned to persons or groups of persons within the organization who then will carry out the task. Tasks should be scheduled in appropriate sequence. They should also have assigned deadlines. Costs can also be associated with tasks by calculating the amount of time required to complete a task and multiplying it by the salary rate of personnel required to do it. Costs of other resources needed to complete the task, such as equipment, space, supplies, etc., can be calculated for the task to give a total cost figure for each task. Costs for all tasks in an action plan can be aggregated to arrive at a budget figure for achieving the objective. Aggregation of costs for all objectives for all goals provides the budget for the overall plan.

Action plans of this type provide individual staff members with very specific information about their work load. Each staff member can determine which and how many tasks they are to be involved in by simply noting where their name is located in the plan. Staff also can understand how their assignments relate to the total organizational program, thereby enabling them to associate their efforts with the mission of the agency.

These steps are basic to engaging in Level II planning. Many educational agencies are in a transition period. They are moving from one kind of delivery system to another which is more complex and time consuming. Any transitional period is characterized by confusion, miscommunication, and increased constraints on accomplishments. Level II planning can help to reduce the negative aspects of change.

PRODUCTS OF PLANNING

The products of planning should be based on an effective evaluation of system outputs. Perhaps the most important need in evaluation is to determine the impact of educational planning on those children receiving services and their families. A monitoring system should be developed by which to collect information bearing on a series of questions relating to impact of the services implemented under the IEP.

The questions which might be asked concerning outcomes are:

a. **Personal Outcomes**
  1. Family
     a) Is there an increase in the use of support services?
     b) Is there an increase or decrease in stress?

      c) Is there increased parental acceptance of the child's handicap?

      d) Are there changes in parenting practices?

  2. Child

      a) Does the child exhibit changes in behavior?

      b) Is that changed behavior an improvement?

      c) Does the child have an increased self-acceptance?

b. **Social Outcomes**

  1. Family

      a) Is there an increase in social activities outside the family?

      b) Is there an increase in social interaction inside the family?

      c) Is there an increase in interaction with the school?

  2. Child

      a) Does the child exhibit improved social skills?

      b) Does the child have increased interaction with peers?

      c) Is the nature of that interaction more positive?

c. **Economic Outcomes**

  1. Family

      a) Are costs to the family increased or decreased? (Costs might include costs of obtaining records, evaluation, transportation, time lost for job to attend meetings, and so forth.)

      b) What is the impact of the handicapped child on economic decision-making within the family?

  2. Children on the job market

      a) Are the individual's job skills increased?

      b) Is there an increase in employment?

d. **Educational Outcomes**

  1. Family

      a) Did the parents change the child's school setting?

      b) Do the parents have an increased knowledge about their child's handicapping condition? About child development? About the child's progress in school?

      c) Do the parents have an increase in their parenting skills, such as mastery of special education techniques?

  2. Child

      a) Does the child's tested I.Q. score increase?

      b) Does the child's achievement score increase?

      c) Is the child able to master and independently perform more complex tasks?

      d) Are there changes in the program, setting, or curriculum for the child?

Although these questions, as a group, may be beyond the scope of individual school systems to answer, in order for a school system to measure the relative impact of its program planning, some of them should be addressed. Those that relate to the child and family could be addressed in part by the teacher with the use of periodic observational log. Support service personnel (psychologists and social workers) could address those questions most directly related to the educational performance of the child. Should a school system wish to address the issues more broadly and systematically, a sampling procedure for selecting a number of individual children and families to review and interview in depth could be cost-effective. In order to warrant significant amounts of money for planning purposes and activities, school systems should be able to document commensurate changes in the child, the family, and the school program. A periodic monitoring of these expected changes should be built into the planning effort itself.

ISSUES IN EDUCATIONAL PLANNING

The new expectation of education to provide all handicapped children with a public education commensurate with their needs and as close to the mainstream as possible has called for new roles and training for professionals. In fact, these new roles are an about-face from those that have been established over the past 20 years. Regular education must once again learn to provide ready access for the students who make the necessary progress. School psychologists and other ancillary personnel must learn to focus on providing inclusion rather than grounds and support for exclusion. Administrations must assume responsibility for providing a climate and the resources to support mainstreaming rather than the development of separate services. After years of moving downstream with the support and sanction of most authorities, consumers, and university personnel, the boat must be reversed and all must paddle together to make progress against the current of tightening resources, negative attitudes, and lack of know-how. Running parallel to these changes is the expanding role of the schools in services to the handicapped in general. If Nicholas Hobbs' recommendation in *The Futures of Children* (1974) that schools should become the service advocates, centers, and coordinators for all human services, we can expect both a changing and greatly enlarged role for the schools.

The crystal ball of the future is clouded by a confusion of trends and purposes, goals and objectives, needs and rights, and movements and countermovements. Projected population statistics for 1984 indicate there will be 42.8 million school-aged children, down 7 million from 1974. This includes 29.5 million kindergarten-age to 8-year-old children, down 5 million from 1974; and 13.3 million 9- to 12-year-old children, down 2 million from 1974 (Simon and Frankel, 1976). Using an incidence estimate of 12 percent handicapped, a total of 5.1 million handicapped children would need and have a right to publicly supported educational services in 1980. This would be more than the estimated 4.7 million school-age handicapped children in 1974 needing special services, and a quantum leap over the 2.9 million who were receiving them in 1974. If these estimates are accurate, our country will still need a two-fold expansion in services and service resources during the 1974–1984 decade. From 1970 to 1976, special education experienced approximately a 300 percent growth in federal monies for the handicapped. Federal legislation already passed may add another 400 percent by 1978. This boost should put education for all the handicapped within grasp of each state.

A substantial area of need is in trained manpower. A recent study of one state's needs indicates that less than 60 percent of the current teachers of the handicapped have special training and that most need continuing education and updating. The study identified two other important needs. Forty percent more teachers were needed for school-aged handicapped who are unserved. Special educators were also needed for the nonschool-aged handicapped under 5 years and between 16 and 21. The need for accelerated manpower development becomes blatantly obvious in the face of such studies. Fortunately, new manpower roles and training strategies are being developed and utilized. The use of cross-categorically trained personnel, transdisciplinary personnel (generalists trained by specialists in a variety of fields), paraprofessionals, parents and volunteers, resource personnel, case managers, and consulting teacher specialists, plus the retraining of regular classroom teachers and broadening of roles of specialists such as school psychologists to be school mental health advocates are a few of these changes. Each new development is, of course, slowed down by the demands on resources and ideas of the past.

Research has had the effect of both increasing and decreasing the load on the educational system with respect to services for the handicapped. On the one hand, the load has been increased by findings demonstrating the educability of handicapped children previously considered of minimal educable potential. For example, not too long ago, it was thought that Down's syndrome children had very limited intellectual and language potential. A host of studies from Kennedy Center at Peabody College, The Early Childhood Center for the Handicapped at the University of Washington, and the Mailman Center in Miami has demonstrated the healthy potential of such children to profit from education. Other studies have shown similar potentials for autistic, deaf-blind, cerebral palsied children, as well as others thought previously uneducable.

Of course, these demonstrations reveal the need for new and more resources in instructional design, timing, and trained manpower. Research has also shown the faulty efficacy of special class placement for many mild and moderately handicapped youngsters. The outgrowth of such research, mainstreaming, may eventually result in a better education for all at less cost, but during the transition, the costs of attitude changes, retraining, and legal battles present mountains to climb. Research has also been effective in uncovering and demonstrating the efficacy and the utility of early intervention for the handicapped. Increased attention is also being paid to vocational education. A recent report from BEH indicates that only 25 percent will be without employment and under the care of social services. Again, implementation of these findings in practice does not come without high social and economic costs.

Fortunately, changes being made in the service delivery system for handicapped individuals harken a brighter future. These systems began with islands of excellence, but they are now engulfing larger amounts of unchartered seas. The most important single trend is the development of more generic services to help handicapped citizens. This trend is represented by the development of the Early Periodic Screening Diagnosis and Treatment Program (EPSDT) and the many state screening programs in use or under development. Early childhood programs, such as Head Start with its mandatory 10 percent inclusion and the many state kindergartens and nursery school programs, are also under development. The public schools mainstreaming and zero/reject programs and the expansion of educational opportunities directed toward the handicapped and their families (which include a variety of telecommunication programs) are well under way. The expansion of vocational education and vocational rehabilitation to include handicapped individuals previously forsaken as low risks is beginning to take place.

These new developments do not come without economic consequences and concerns. Since 1929–1930 (except for a low point during the World War II years of 1943–1944), there has been a steady increase in the proportion of the gross national product (GNP) spent for education; during this period the GNP was also rising. Beginning with the last economic quarter of 1973 and continuing on into all four quarters of 1974, the GNP did not rise. During 1974, real and disposable income fell 2.5 percent for the first time since 1947. At that time, unemployment hit a record high, and the nation suffered the worse crisis of lack of crude oil and refined products in its entire history. The outlook brightened somewhat after 1975, when the GNP rose dramatically. Since that time the GNP has increased slightly, but inflation is taking its toll. It now appears that the economic situation of the nation is becoming one to be dealt with prudently. It is reasonable to hypothesize that if the economy does not soon begin to improve or at least stabilize, all manner of havoc could be wrought upon the existing and proposed budgets for education, especially those for the handicapped at the federal, state, and local levels. Another factor certain to play an important role is that the nation is now in the midst of a taxpayers' revolt. Indications are the nation is in a more conservative trend than earlier in the 1970's. Traditionally, a conservative administration is apt to cut corners in all areas of federal spending. This viewpoint is also spreading to the state levels, as recently expressed by Governor Edward G. Brown, Jr.

of California when he stated "... we are entering an era of limits... It's now a question of reordering priorities and choosing one program over another, based on a rigorous standard of equity and common sense."

Although these predictions and statements may appear droll, they cannot be discounted and measures must be taken to work with, or in some cases counteract, them. Reflecting upon Governor Brown's statement, one realizes how applicable it is to the area of special education. The focal point of concern is that special education not be pushed aside and scrambled in the "priority" battle. This has already occurred too many times in the past during a more secure economic climate. Ultimately, the issue of increased special educational services may be settled by attitudes of the general population. It is hoped that the increased formation and awareness of advocate and consumer groups will have a direct bearing on the policy of budgetary spending for the handicapped. The economic crunch can be viewed in a more positive style if one considers that dollar value will receive a primary emphasis. That is, there will be more concern with the overall value to the consumer in the total areas of eduation. The method which is most beneficial and economically feasible will be given priority, whether it be mainstreaming a child inservice education, or the cost-benefit of vocational education. Other steps should be taken in order to effectively utilize the budget and to satisfy the two important objectives of 1) assuring equal access to programs and 2) achieving maximum efficiency in the use of resources. If this is to become a reality, more information than is now available is needed.

Certainly, government policy over the next few years will play a major role in determining the future of special education. Increasingly, the federal government is sharpening its new federalism. More federal funds with fewer strings are available, creating a situation which likens the federal government to a bank giving no repayment loans to states, increasingly focusing its attention on service rights, standards, financial accountability, human services, and education. State and local governments increasingly resist the few strings attached and are growing stronger in their assertion of states' rights. If the trend continues, the federal government's role of balancing and elevating services from one region of the country to another will be lost. In some cases, as in the more progessive states, this will not be a problem, for attention to local and state needs is well demonstrated, and federal strings have only got the puppet hopelessly tangled in its efforts to free itself. In other states and localities, the needs of the disenfranchised poor and handicapped now making themselves clear on the horizon may sink with the sunset of federal influence. If this occurs, the progress of federal and state laws and court decisions in assisting the rights, needs, and services for handicapped citizens may be in for darker days. Whether this will or will not occur may ultimately depend on the positive or negative realization of another trend—that of consumerism.

One of the most important trends in human services for the handicapped is the increase in consumerism. This movement is visible at all points of the service continuum from federal legislation to direct services. Recognition at the federal level is led by the Developmental Disabilities Act of 1975 which calls for the establishment of state planning advisory councils with handicapped individuals and parents as participants. At this level, consumers and their representatives have legal, monitoring, advocacy, and planning functions.

Consumers are also gaining increasing recognition at the service delivery level. In reality, they are becoming more involved in the due process functions of educational planning for themselves and their children. The Education for All Handicapped Children Act and most state statutes require the involvement of parents and handicapped children at all important decision-making points: evaluation, placement, follow-up, etc. Finally, there is growing recognition of the consumers' role in providing education for themselves and their children. The Handicapped Children's Early Education Program (First Chance) and the Head Start Program both emphasize the importance of parents helping themselves, their children, and fellow parents with support from professionals and paraprofessionals. If this trend continues at its current pace, 1975–1985 may be known as the age of the consumer and may substantially challenge the roles and functions of professionals. In fact, in the hands of consumers lies the balance between continued movement toward quality, coordinated, comprehensive services for the handicapped, and the islands of excellence of the Sixties. Professional planners who wish for progress to be made must listen for and perhaps follow the sound of a different drummer, or much of what they seek to accomplish for those they wish to serve will never be included in the parade. Consumer influence or lack of it will be the primary independent variable in the allocation and reallocation of funds and resources in the future. The future success of public education in quality and quantity may be dependent on their success.

REFERENCES

Abeson, A., and Ballard, J. 1976. State and Federal policy for exceptional children. In F. J. Weintraub, A. Abeson, J. Ballard, and M. LaVor (eds.), Public Policy and the Education of Exceptional Children. Council for Exceptional Children, Reston, VA.

Baroff, G. S. 1974. Mental Retardation: Nature, Cause, Management. Hemisphere Publishing Corp., Washington, DC.

Berman, P., and Pauly, F. W. April 1975. Federal Programs Supporting Educational Change, Vol. II: Factors Affecting Change Agent Projects. (HEW R-158912) The Rand Corp., Santa Monica, CA.

Blum, P., and Pauly, E. W. April 1975. Federal Programs Supporting Educational Change, Vol. II: Factors Affecting Change Agent Projects. (HEW R-158912) The Rand Corp., Santa Monica, CA.

Bruininks, R. H., and Rynders, J. E. 1971. Alternatives to special class placement for educable mentally retarded children. *Focus Except. Children* 3:1–12.

California Education Code, Section 6102.08.

Christoplos, F., and Renz, P. 1969. Critical examination of special education programs. *J. Spec. Ed.* 3:371–379.

David v. Watkins, Civil No. 73-205 (N.D. Ohio, 1973).

Deno, E. 1970. Special education as developmental capital. *Except. Children* 37:229–237.

Developmentally Disabled Assistance and Bill of Rights Act (PL 94-103), 1975.

Diana v. State Board of Education, Civil No. C-70, 37 RFP (N.D. California, January 7, 1970 and June 18, 1973).

Dunn, L. M. 1968. Special education for the mildly retarded—Is much of it justifiable? *Except. Children* 35:5–22.

Education Daily. 1976. 8:181.

Education for All Handicapped Children Act (PL 94-142).

Gallagher, J. 1972. The special education contract for mildly handicapped children. *Except. Children* 38:527–536.

Garrison, M., and Hammil, D. D. 1971. Who are the retarded? *Except. Children* 37:13–20.

Gilhool, T. 1973. Education: An inalienable right. *Except. Children* 39:597–610.

Goode, J. M. 1973. Leader's Guide for Comprehensive Educational Planning. American Management Association, Hamilton, NY.

Gramlich, E. M., and Koshel, P. 1975. Educational Performance Contraction: An Evaluation of an Experiment. The Brookings Institute, Washington, DC.

Guadelupe Organization v. Tempe Elementary School District, No. 3, Civil No. 71-435 PHX (D. Arizona, 1972).

Hamilton, B. B., Betts, H. B., Gustave, J., Gillette, H. E., Greene, G. M., Garrity, S. D., and Libman, A. S. March 1977. A Study of the Medical and Allied Health Services Delivery System for Substantially Handicapped Developmentally Disabled Adults: Chicago (Research Report Summary R-26). Rehabilitation Institute of Chicago, Northwestern University.

Hammer, P., and Richman, G. (eds.) 1975. The Orientation Notebook. Developmental Disabilities Technical Assistance systems, Chapel Hill, NC.

Harvey, J. 1969. To fix or cope: A dilemma for special education. *J. Spec. Ed.* 3:389–392.

Hobbs, N. September 1974. The Futures of Children: Categories, Labels, and Their Consequences. Vanderbilt University, Nashville, TN.

Jenkins, J. R., and Mayball, W. F. 1975. Describing resource teacher programs. *Except. Children* 40:35–36.

Kirk, S. A. July 1975. Labeling, categorizing, and mainstreaming. (Paper presented at the meeting of the International conference of special Education, University of Kent, Canterbury, England.)

Kirk, S. A. 1964. Research in Education. In H. A. Stevens and R. Heber (eds.), Mental Retardation: A Review of Research. University of Chicago Press, Chicago.

Larry, P. v. Riles, 343 Supp. 1306 (M.D. California, 1972).

Lebanks v. Spears, Civil No. 71-2899 (E.D. Louisiana, 1973).

Lilly, S. 1970. Special education: A tempest in a teapot. *Except. Children* 37:597–586.

Lindberg, D. July 1976. Prevalence of Developmental Disabilities in West Virginia. Department of Sociology and Anthropology, Davis and Elkins College.

MacMillan, D. H. 1971. Special education for the mildly retarded: Servant or savant? *Focus Except. Children* 2(9):1–11.

McKenzie, H. S. (ed.) 1970. The 1968–1969 Yearly Report of the Consulting Teacher Program, Vols. I and II. Consulting Teacher Program, College of Education, University of Vermont, Burlington.

Mercer, J. R. 1971. The meaning of mental retardation. In R. Koch and J. Dobson (eds.), The Mentally Retarded Child Living in the Community. Special Child Publishing Co., Seattle, WA.

Miller, J. G., and Schoenfelder, D. S. 1969. A rational look at special class placement. *J. Spec. Ed.* 3:397–403.

Mills v. *Board of Education of District of Columbia,* 348 F. Supp. 866 (D. District of Columbia, 1972).

National Association of State Directors of Special Education, DC. 1976. Function of the Placement Committee in Special Education: A Resource Manual. National Association of State Directors of Special Education, Washington, DC. 1976

Pennsylvania Association for Retarded citizens v. *Commonwealth of Pennsylvania,* 334 F. Supp. 1257 (E.D. Pennsylvania, 1971).

Ricci v. *Greenblatt,* Civil No. 72–469–T (D. Massachusetts, 1972).

Simon, K. A., and Frankel, M. M. 1976. Projections of Education Statistics to 1984–85. U.S. Government Printing Office, Washington, DC.

Smith, J. Q., and Arkans, J. R. 1974. Now more than ever: A case for the special class. *Except. Children* 40:497–502.

Stedman, D. J. 1970. The hypothetical community, a template for planning mental retardation programs. *N.C. J. Mental Health* IV:26–29.

Turnbull, A., Strickland, B., and Brantley, J. 1978. Developing and Implementing Individualized Education Programs (1978). Charles E. Merrill, Columbus, OH.

Valetutti, P. 1969. Integration versus segregation: A useless dialect. *J. Spec. Ed.* 3:405–408.

Welch v. *Likens,* 373 F. Supp. 487 (D. Minnesota, 1974).

Weber, C. U., Foster, P. W., and Weikart, D. D. 1978. An Economic Analysis of the Ypsalinti Perry Preschool Project. High/Scope Education Foundation, Ypsilanti, MI.

Wiegerink, R., and Simeonsson, R. 1975. Public Schools. In J. Wortis (ed.), Mental Retardation and Developmental Disabilities, Vol. VII. Brunner/Mazel, New York.

Wilbur, C. V., Foster, P. W., and Weikart, D. D. 1978. An Economic Analysis of the Ypsilanti Perry Preschool Project, 1978 (Number 5). High/Scope Educational Research Foundation, Ypsilanti, MI.

Wyatt v. *Aderhold,* 334 F. Supp. 1341 (M.D. Alabama, 1971).

Chapter 3

Perspectives on Planning for Prevention of Mental Retardation

Andrew E. Lorincz

The best way to deal with mental retardation is to prevent it from occurring. Where technology and methodology are available, the prevention of mental retardation and its associated handicapping conditions is a goal that seemingly is realistic and attainable. Planning programs for reducing the prevalence of these conditions involve concerted action and interaction with professionals, the public, and the political governance of these populations. Such planning, of necessity, involves input from numerous practitioners in the health, education, and social-behavioral disciplines.

The sequence of the material that follows is designed to provide an overall perspective of prevention planning as it relates to environmentally and genetically determined mental retardation as it exists and is understood predominantly in the United States of America. Excellent detailed publications on the prevention of genetic disease as well as overviews of mental retardation and other developmental disabilities are available as published textbooks (Baroff, 1974; Carter, 1978; Johnston and Magrab, 1976; Milunsky, 1975; National Research Council, 1975).

Prevention of mental retardation or its complications can traditionally be considered on three levels: primary, secondary, and tertiary. *Primary prevention* encompasses any activity that attempts to eliminate the directly known causes of mental disorder or disability. *Secondary prevention* encompasses activities involving the early detection and prompt treatment of disorders so that they do not become more serious. For example, hypothyroidism, galactosemia, or phenylketonuria (PKU), which if early diagnosed and appropriately treated, prevents mental retardation. *Tertiary prevention* encompasses activities, treatments, or interventions provided a developmentally disabled individual so that, in the course of habilitation, that person is enabled to live independently and with minimal permanent functional disability.

RECOGNIZING CAUSES OF MENTAL RETARDATION

The first step in planning for prevention of mental retardation is recognizing the causes or etiology. A brief glance of most tables of etiological classification of mental retardation quickly reveals two major categories: *acquired* and *genetic*. Acquired causes are nosologically related to prenatal, perinatal, or postnatal origins. These, in turn, are broken into subgroups as due to infection, trauma, toxins, hormonal deficiencies, new growths (benign and cancerous), sociocultural deprivation, other noxious environmental hazards such as radiation, and a large category designated as acquired mental retardation of unknown origin.

The genetic causes, in turn, are categorized as those due to chromosomal abnormalities; metabolic disorders of either amino acid metabolism, carbohydrate metabolism, lipid metabolism, purine metabolism, etc.; as well as presently unknown genetic causes of mental retardation.

Although it is recognized that frequently no etiological cause is discerned, considerations of apparent mechanisms of causation of mental retardation nevertheless can be helpful. Crocker (1978) has listed such mechanisms as follows:

1. **Hereditary issues**—*single-gene abnormalities* with known biochemical markers ["inborn errors of metabolism," *e.g.*, PKU, Hurler's disease, galactosemia, maple sugar urine disease (MSUD)]: *other genetic syndromes* with variable retardation aspects (*e.g.*, neurofibromatosis); *special chromosomal abnormalities (e.g.*, translocation in Down's syndrome); *familial retardation* of probable polygenic origin
2. **Early influences of embryonic development**—*Sporadic germ cell changes* or *mutations* [*e.g.*, trisomy 21 or Down's syndrome); aberrations occurring during embryogenesis (*e.g.*, "prenatal influence" syndromes with structural changes from infection such as cytomegalic inclusion disease or rubella); from drug ingestion (*e.g.*, thalidomide, phenylhydantoin, fetal alcohol syndrome); from early uterine bleeding]
3. **Other pregnancy problems and perinatal morbidity**—Placental anomalies, multiple births, postmaturity, "fetal malnutrition"; prematurity, birth trauma, and newborn adjustments including asphyxia, hypoglycemia, and hyperbilirubinemia
4. **Acquired childhood diseases**—Infection (*e.g.*, encephalitis or meningitis); endocrine disorders (*e.g.*, hypothyroidism); intoxications (*e.g.*, lead or mercury poisoning); head trauma; intracranial tumors; special

sensory handicaps (e.g., deafness or blindness); asphyxia from near drowning or as a complication of anesthesia or cardiac arrest

5. **Environmental and social problems**—Deprivation; parental psychosis, neurosis, or character disorder; childhood psychosis, autism

6. **Unknown causes.**

Prevention activities, therefore, can and do span a broad spectrum of activities that range through improved nutrition of pregnant mothers, the control of disease by immunization, the improved treatment of disease, genetic counseling, identification and/or treatment of inborn errors of metabolism, the early identification of learning problems, childhood accident prevention, harmful drug identification, improved recognition and care for pregnancies at "high risk," improved maternal health, and improved birth alternatives.

Unfortunately, there is an inability to collect data on cases of mental retardation which "might have been." In the realm of prevention, victories are not easy to document or demonstrate. One can never show exactly how many cases of an illness have been prevented, only comparisons to a lessening number of what used to be.

POLYGENIC SOCIOCULTURAL RETARDATION

Psychosocial or polygenic sociocultural retardation is estimated to be the cause of over 75 percent of all mental retardation, whereas the remainder can usually be attributed to specific clinical causes (Garrard and Richmond, 1978). Public education regarding risks during pregnancy and the education of parents on better child-rearing practices are general goals for all communities interested in planning for the prevention of so-called psychosocial mental retardation. Effects of prenatal undernutrition as well as severe postnatal undernutrition, especially during the first year of life, have been documented as an etiological cause (Culley, 1978). Obviously, programs that address the prevention of such undernutrition represent primary prevention efforts in the field of mental retardation.

Techniques to provide to high risk infants appropriate stimuli, which may be missing from the environment, need to be better identified and transmitted to families that are at risk. These frequently include low income families, families where the parents are of lower intelligence, and, commonly, very young, single parent families (Garrard and Richmond, 1978). Such nonmedical or nonorganic mild mental retardation, in part, can be considered an artifact of society, of inequities in the distribution of environments, and of the diagnostic labeling process itself.

Many feel that psychosocial mental retardation may be secondarily prevented or at least mitigated through early intervention programs (Meier, 1975). Evidence has also indicated that the effects of deprivation (i.e., severe restriction of the experiences necessary for developmental growth) can be reversed either in the home or in institutions, provided that the quality of care, the crucial ingredient, is adequately improved (Garrard and Richmond, 1978).

SOCIETAL AND INDIVIDUAL ORIENTATIONS TOWARD PREVENTION

Although certain organic types of mental retardation are spread rather evenly throughout the population, the persons at the bottom of the socioeconomic status ladder are the most likely victims of mental retardation. Ashmore (1975) concludes that, in part, this victimization springs from certain behavior patterns which are not conducive to maintaining health for self and family.

Most of the victimization of the poor, however, is simply due to being poor. That is, the poor have less access to good hospitals at the time of birth, less access to proper diet for mother and child, less access to an environment free of poison and accident, and less access to home, neighborhood, and school environments that are intellectually stimulating. All of these conditions have been implicated in the development of mental retardation, and any overall attack on this problem must seek to reorganize society so that the poor have more equal access to services and environments which foster health, rather than disease and deficit.

Ashmore (1975), in discussing self-perception and the probability of success of preventive action, appropriately commented as follows: "Although the perception that a particular preventive action will be successful is dependent on a number of factors, one minimum requirement is that the individual see himself as able to exert some control over his fate through personal action. The individual must see himself as having some personal control over his future. There is some evidence that the poor—those who engage in preventive behavior least often—are also those who see themselves as incapable of influencing their future through their own behavior." In truth, this may be the major limiting factor for the effective use of education and improved technology in the prevention of mental retardation.

BIOMEDICALLY DIAGNOSED RETARDATION

Although clinically known causes of mental retardation account for only about one-quarter of all mental retardation, the degree of retardation involved is, in general, more severe than mental retardation that is attributed to psychosocial reasons.

Approximately 3 percent of the United States' population is estimated to be mentally retarded. Of this group, approximately 95 percent are estimated to have mild to moderate retardation, whereas the remaining 5 percent have severe to profound retardation. Of the latter 5 percent, anywhere from one-fifth to one-third presumably have diagnosable etiologies which are genetically determined. Although the occurrence of specific heritable disorders is infrequent, the aggregate occurrence of all such disorders is such that early diagnosis through appropriate screening programs can be highly cost-effective. In specific terms, of the greater than 3 million babies born in the United States each year, 15,000 are estimated to have diagnosable chromosomal defects, and another 30,000 to have diagnosable heritable disorders which frequently result in profound or severe mental retardation.

In spite of the awareness that early detection of many such disorders is cost-effective, and in spite of the availability of published methods for such early diagnosis through clinical laboratory analyses, a large gap exists in translating the basic science information to clinical service and practice. The reasons for this gap are many. The knowledge to perform and interpret the complex array of highly specialized laboratory studies requisite for definitive laboratory and clinical diagnosis has generally not been acquired by health practitioners in the field. Moreover, when metabolic defects are suspected, practitioners generally lack the information as to which laboratory tests should be ordered and where quality controlled laboratory testing can be obtained. Many of these complex laboratory procedures are available only in highly specialized laboratory research programs. Most basic research is funded by grants which are not geared or approved to provide broad service delivery. Thus, many potentially useful specialized analyses are just not generally available for public prevention programs.

Historically, the profoundly and severely retarded have been institutionalized for lifelong custodial care simply on the basis of potentially evident profound or severe functional retardation. Frequently such institutionalization occurs without the benefit of definitive etiological diagnosis. Appropriate early and definitive detection might well serve to reduce unnecessary institutionalization by making remediation available at an early age before irreversible damage has occurred. Moreover, appropriate genetic counseling, based upon such definitive diagnosis, could reduce the future occurrence of such disorders in the same families.

There is a need for even more cost-effective utilization of genetic counseling centers. What is still required is a national awareness and understanding of the existence of heritable disorders, as well as an awareness that all profoundly and severely retarded persons, regardless of etiology, deserve and require:

1. Lifelong comprehensive supportive services
2. Adequate evaluation to rule out or identify specific genetically determined conditions, *e.g.* PKU, galactosemia, mucopolysaccharidoses, hypothyroidism, amino acidopathies, gangliosidoses, etc., that could be prevented from recurring in the same family (primary prevention), provided that the diagnosis was known

3. Appropriate referral to genetic counseling services for their families
4. Appropriate remediation for the affected individual where available

The resources available for prevention of clinically caused mental retardation are numerous, frequently highly technical, and, unfortunately, not equally available to all sectors of the public at large. Brief overviews of resources available and resources required to plan for prevention of other clinically caused retardation follow.

Total Elimination Via Immunization of Diseases That Result in Mental Retardation

These generally are major public health problems that require, first of all, basic knowledge and technology in the development of effective vaccines. In recent years, smallpox has been effectively eliminated. In the near future, measles (rubeola) can be similarly eradicated as a cause of mental retardation. To accomplish these results, planning for related goals is needed.

A major goal is to achieve and maintain high levels of immunity for the particular disease, *e.g.*, the measles vaccine that was developed in 1963. Local and state health departments may provide vaccines to susceptible populations, provided these are routine programs for childhood immunization and steps are taken to establish and enforce immunization requirements. That is, this goal can be achieved when immunization is required for school entrance and when health care professionals, as well as the public, understand, support, and participate in the planned immunization program.

In planning, there must be an on-going program to identify and know where susceptible persons are located. Similarly, it is necessary to know where the disease is located. This can be aided by physician reporting; however, an actively planned public health surveillance is frequently more effective and desirable. The health care system must be able to respond promptly when the disease occurs, *i.e.*, outbreak control methods must be developed.

Although total elimination of a particular disease may not be achieved, plans to significantly reduce the incidence and sequelae of other diseases (*e.g.*, syphilis and tuberculosis) are equally important, particularly when technology exists for early detection and treatment.

Maternal-Fetal Blood Incompatibilities

In those instances when the mother acquires an "allergic reaction" to her unborn baby's blood cells (*e.g.*, Rh incompatibility and ABO blood group incompatibility), there is a major potential for fetal central nervous system damage. These blood group factors are hereditary traits. Problems arise only if there has been significant previous mixing of incompatible fetal and maternal blood. With such prior mixing, the mother may respond by producing antibodies that have the capability of destroying red blood cells. Such antibody effects in subsequent pregnancies, where there is incompatibility between fetal and maternal red blood cells, may result in massive hemolysis of fetal blood with resultant hyperbilirubinemia and central nervous system damage (kernicterus).

By proper monitoring of maternal blood group types as well as maternal levels of Rh antibody activity, those pregnancies where appropriate preconditions exist (*e.g.*, Rh-negative mother and Rh-positive fetus) can be managed to partially limit anticipated hemolytic effects. With appropriate clinical treatment of early diagnosed erythroblastosis, as through exchange transfusions, central nervous system damage caused by neonatal jaundice may be secondarily prevented.

Primary prevention of blood group incompatibility is now also possible through the proper use of immunoglobulin administered to Rh-negative women at risk for initial Rh maternal sensitization. When they bear Rh-positive children or have abortions such incompatibility can be avoided.

Although knowledge of such primary prevention techniques has been extant for over a decade, public and professional utilization of such primary prevention techniques still remains to be broadly effected in this country. In a 1976 report, the Center for Disease Control estimated that, based on the number of immunoglobulin doses sold by United States manufacturers, in 1974 about 80 percent of tbe 449,100 women estimated to need the serum were receiving it, leaving about 91,300 women a year at risk. Various reports show that the utilization rate is uneven among the states and that particular problems exist in rural areas and for the management of abortions nationwide (Comptroller General of the United States, 1977).

Mental retardation and other complications caused by Rh hemolytic disease can be prevented through aggressive actions to identify Rh-negative women and provide them with immunoglobulin when they bear Rh-positive children or have abortions. Although the extent of the problem is not known, many women apparently are not receiving immunoglobulin. The scope of the problem could be more accurately determined if more states had comprehensive systems for testing pregnant women for Rh incompatibility, reporting disease incidence, and reporting immunoglobulin utilization. In lieu of state laws requiring such tests, the family planning programs could assist by including Rh blood typing as a routine part of family planning services.

Inborn Errors of Metabolism

Lipidoses Incidence data for lipidoses, as for other serious disabling inborn errors of metabolism, are limited. Published estimates of incidence of the lipidoses are based mainly on two population groups: Ashkenazic Jews and Swedes. Frequencies for Tay-Sachs disease, adult Gaucher's disease, and type A Niemann-Pick disease in Ashkenazic Jews are, respectively, 1 per 3,600, 1 per 2,500, and 1 per 40,000. Hagberg *et al.* (1969), reporting

Swedish population studies, placed the birth incidence of metachromatic leukodystrophy at 1 per 40,000 and Krabbe's disease at 1 per 53,000. Estimated incidence for all lipidoses in the six New England states is roughly 1 to 2 per 18,000 live births (Kolodny, 1975).

Neither cure nor effective treatment is available for these sphingolipidoses. Prevention is presently the method of choice for their control. Ascertainment of high risk pregnancies is almost always through the prior birth of an affected child. The great majority of carriers for these traits are unaware of their genotype.

The problems of large scale heterozygote detection in the lipidoses have been reviewed by Kolodny (1975). To date, Tay-Sachs disease is the only lipidosis in which large scale heterozygote screening has been attempted. The factors favoring this development were:

1. The existence of a defined high risk ethnic subgroup in the population
2. The existence of a reliable laboratory enzyme test for heterozygote detection
3. The availability of prenatal diagnosis (through amniocentesis) which allows the possibility for a carrier-carrier couple to have normal children

Despite the above, no large scale heterozygote screening program conducted in the United States has ever succeeded in reaching over 15 percent of the population at risk, even when the screening program has been publicly funded.

Disorders of Carbohydrate Metabolism   Alterations in the function of other body systems may result in dysfunction within the nervous system. For example, the child with hypoglycemia may present clinically as a seizure disorder. Prompt recognition and therapy of the underlying disorder may prevent permanent nervous system damage and resultant retardation. A constant supply of bloodborne glucose, together with oxygen for its oxidation, is required to maintain normal nervous system function. Proper management of hypoglycemia, regardless of the cause, requires prompt recognition and correction by glucose administration followed by delineation and correction of the specific underlying cause where possible.

Some disorders of metabolism, which may result in hypoglycemia, include pancreatic islet cell hyperplasia (overproduction of insulin), Beckwith-Wiedemann syndrome, adrenal insufficiency, severe hepatic insufficiency, maple syrup urine disease (leucinosis), methylmalonic acidemia, and the spectrum of glycogen storage diseases, galactosemia, congenital hypothyroidism, pituitary insufficiency, hereditary fructose intolerance, sugar malabsorption syndromes, leucine-sensitive hypoglycemia, and mannosidosis. Groover (1978) adequately catalogs and summarizes these disorders as well as other endocrinological disorders that may be manifest by mental retardation, such as disorders of calcium metabolism (hypocalcemia and hypercalcemia), disorders of magnesium metabolism (hypomagnesemia and hypermagnesemia), and others. Among the carbohydrate metabolic defects, probably one should include the complex array of disorders with basic defects in the metabolism of the connective tissue mucopolysaccharides (glycosaminoglycans) that are frequently associated with progressive mental retardation. The literature regarding these disorders was recently reviewed by Lorincz (1978).

Disorders of Amino Acid Metabolism Disorders of amino acid metabolism have been estimated to occur 1 in 5,000 to 10,000 births, and to represent 10 percent of the profoundly mentally retarded. The detection of these abnormalities early in life is important because prevention of mental retardation is possible in many cases either by dietary restriction or by the use of large doses of vitamin cofactors in vitamin-responsive disorders, *e.g.,* B6-responsive homocystinuria (Guthrie, 1972; Shih, 1975).

Screening for PKU alone has proved itself not merely medically, but also economically sound. Given the further development and perfection of multiple (multiphasic) screening tests, mass screening can become not merely a way of rapidly detecting PKU and other treatable genetic diseases, but also a source of invaluable information on biochemical differences in large populations (Guthrie, 1972). When a woman with PKU becomes pregnant, the chances that her children will be retarded is extremely high (MacCready, 1972). With hundreds of PKU cases being detected and treated annually, the population at risk of prenatal phenylalanemia can be expected to rise rapidly as the "first generation" of screened and treated girls reaches childbearing age. The prevention of such cases of retardation requires a solution to a problem of medical information transmission. How does the physician, years from now, ensure that the patient and/or her then physician have the information needed to avert risk?

Nonetheless, the economics of mass screening rest on the demonstrated fact that prevention is less expensive than nonprevention. Multiphasic screening for multiple aminoacidopathies (*e.g.,* MSUD and homocystinuria) is superior to mass screening for PKU alone (Comptroller General of the United States, 1977; Guthrie, 1972; Buist *et al.,* 1975). Similarly, use of regionalized public health and/or private metabolic laboratories makes such mass screening even more effective at a small cost and may increase quality control of laboratory procedures as well (Guthrie, 1972; Brandon, 1976).

Problems in Prevention of Metabolic Disorders

The aggregate occurrence of the diagnosable specific heritable metabolic disorders that result in profound and severe mental retardation·is great enough to warrant major national strategies to screen for and definitively diagnose these disorders, whether they are presently "treatable" or "untreatable."

The need for designating a specific group within the Department of

Health, Education and Welfare with responsibility for implementing and monitoring a national prevention strategy, clarifying government agency roles, and determining which of and how the Department's programs can best assist in this effort is outlined in the Comptroller General's Report to Congress (1977).

Multiphasic lab screening methods targeted to better screen and diagnose genetically determined metabolic causes of severe mental retardation remain to be developed along the patterns suggested by Watts (1978), that is, to screen for aminoacidopathies, carbohydrate disorders, macromolecular storage, lipid metabolism defects, organic acidemias, and other disorders. The application of such studies to highly visible clinical populations of severely and profoundly retarded should result in more effective utilization of genetic counseling resources, provided, of course, that appropriate follow-up to definitively diagnose persons screened as positive is available and provided.

The scientific and technical knowledge to diagnose many of these conditions is extant, although frequently expensive and complex. The advent of analytical methodologies (e.g., bacterial inhibition bioassays, atomic absorption spectrophotometry, and radioimmunoassay utilizing specific immunologic antibodies) makes large scale studies possible. Newer techniques of mechanization, automation, data processing, and data retrieval have the potential of providing cost-effective, efficient, and accurate multiphasic analyses on micro and ultramicro quantities of blood, serum, urine, saliva, tears, amniotic fluid, or other biological tissue sources. Such automation has already been effected in a few exemplary regional programs for screening the total newborn population for PKU, a number of other aminoacidurias, hypothyroidism, and galactosemia, as well as heterozygote detection for certain abnormalities of hemoglobin synthesis.

Unfortunately, such mass screening programs have had limited public and professional acceptance. Other logistical as well as legal problems are byproducts of such large scale disease detection programs. Multiphasic laboratory screening of general populations as yet has not been widely accepted by frontline medical practice physicians. Although automated, centralized, efficient, multiphasic laboratory programs exist that are capable of providing data in terms of specificity, reliability, sensitivity, and yield, the use of such techniques may still be blocked by the attitudes of practicing physicians. The physician's traditional clinically oriented philosophy, added to a fear of losing professional control over one's own practice, precludes wide acceptance of such screening programs (Bates and Mulinare, 1970).

ROLE OF LAW IN THE PREVENTION OF GENETIC DISEASE

Only recently has society challenged the notion that technological developments that offer benefit to humanity must be incorporated into society. Some major principles that a genetic screening law should embrace are well presented by Reilly (1975). Included are scientific rationality, paramount concern for the physical and psychic health of the individual screened, assurance of high quality genetic counseling for all persons with significant test results, recognition that a program of public education is integral to the dual goals of reducing genetic disease and eradicating genetic discrimination, and special attention to the problem of maintaining strict confidentiality of any screening records that are stored.

The willing participation of an individual in a public screening program requires that he or she know why the test is offered, what test results could mean for personal health or procreative decisions, significant risks associated with the test itself, and availability of counseling services and treatment, where they are indicated.

Clearly, screening designed to prevent retardation from PKU, hypothyroidism, galactosemia, or MSUD demands that the neonate be tested, despite the inability of the newborn to voice consent to the procedure or to understand its results. At that state of a person's life, parental consent is operative.

However, the state that decides to do this screening should develop a mechanism to ensure that the infant receives the test result and adequate counseling at an age when he or she will be able to understand the implications of the test. Informing the parents is not enough. This is evident from the previously noted problem involving babies born to mothers affected with PKU.

The law best serves a program designed to reduce genetic disease by guiding technological implementation. Successful PKU screening, accomplished without legal mandate in many countries, proves that compulsion is an unnecessary feature. For now, perhaps the best course would be to continue neonatal screening programs for those disorders that are amenable to treatment and to develop laws that inform couples seeking a marriage license that free genetic testing is available if they wish to utilize it. The benefits of premarital screening should also be recognized. However, elimination of genetic disease must proceed with paramount concern for the procreative rights of the individual.

PREVENTION OF ACQUIRED MENTAL RETARDATION

A detailed discussion of individual and societal responsibilities to prevent acquired mental retardation due to environmental toxins, trauma, and other etiologies of acquired mental retardation, is beyond the scope of this presentation. The principles to be followed in the prevention of lead poisoning summarized by Graef (1975) are applicable to other environmental toxins. The problems and significance of preventing trauma due to inappropriate automobile safety are summarized by Reichelderfer (1976). Lieberman *et al.* (1976) has reviewed problems of professional responsibility in teaching auto safety.

NEED FOR CONCERTED ACTION

Dr. Allen C. Crocker (1979), noted pediatric educator and leader in the field of mental retardation prevention, has appropriately commented that, "The prevention territory as it relates to mental retardation consists of a vast collection of hopes and assertions, heterogeneous in nature and viewed disparately by different workers. Certain concrete models exist in the biomedical field where gratifying effects have been achieved, often relating to relatively low-incidence syndromes. Rather amorphous aspirations characterize the areas of social planning and behavioral influences, many times accompanied by a paucity of accountable data."

Despite these reservations, Dr. Crocker and others have initiated formation of communication linkages with several national organizations, which already have significant prevention programs. Included in these organizations are the American Association on Mental Deficiency (AAMD), the National Association for Retarded Citizens (NARC), United Cerebral Palsy (UCP), National Foundation-March of Dimes, American Association of University Affiliated Programs for Developmentally Disabled (AAUAP), National Tay-Sachs and Allied Diseases Association, National Genetics Foundation, American Society of Human Genetics, and the Genetic Services Program of the Health Services Administration.

Such a national consortium for the concerted action for genetic diseases and developmental disabilities still remains to be established on a firm basis. Similarly, coordination of the new prevention resolves of the Department of Health, Education and Welfare and activities of the President's Committee on Mental Retardation (PCMR), as well as the aforelisted organizations, remains to be planned for and implemented.

ROLE OF EDUCATION FOR PREVENTION

All facets of mental retardation prevention need to be better understood by the public as well as professional service providers. Although earlier public education has been recommended, clearly Junior and Senior high school presents a last "universal" opportunity for systematically reaching "potential parents-to-be." A useful curriculum guide for Junior and Senior high school students has been published by Litch (1978).

Nearly all people with handicapped family members want and need to work together to solve common problems. They have a need to learn more about specific handicapping conditions, and they need to work cooperatively

in advocating for better health care, education, and legislation for their handicapped members. Numerous self-help or mutual aid groups have come into
being. They frequently provide a nidus in the community for prevention
activities related to specific problems, as, for example, the National Tay-
Sachs and Allied Diseases Association, Inc. has done. The excellent guide
compiled by Haffner (1979) suggests activities for such groups, lists extant
groups, and is written for broad public information dissemination.

Although only limited "islands of success" exist in the overall education
for prevention of mental retardation, and despite the lack of significant planning and acceptance of large scale prevention programs, one must still recognize that the very best way to deal with mental retardation is to *prevent it from
occurring*.

In *all* planning for services to developmentally disabled persons, considerations for prevention impact at all levels (that is, primary, secondary and
tertiary prevention) should be assessed and, in truth, should be mandated for
incorporation into all proposed plans.

REFERENCES

Ashmore, R. D. 1975. Societal and individual orientations toward prevention. In A.
Milunsky (ed.), The Prevention of Genetic Disease and Mental Retardation, Chapter
2, pp. 51-63. W. B. Saunders Co., Philadelphia.

Baroff, G. S. (ed.) 1974. Mental Retardation: Nature, Cause and Management. John
Wiley & Sons, New York.

Bates, B., and Mulinare, J. 1970. Physicians' use and opinions of screening tests in
ambulatory practice. *JAMA* 214:2173-2180.

Brandon, G. R. 1976. Regionalization of public health metabolic laboratories. *Public
Health Lab.* 34:56-60.

Buist, N. R. M., Murphey, W., Brandon, G. R., Foley, T. P., Jr., and Penn, R. L.
1975. Neonatal screening for hypothyroidism. *Lancet* 2:872-873.

Carter, C. H. (ed.) 1978. Medical Aspects of Mental Retardation, 2nd Ed. Charles C
Thomas, Publishers, Springfield, IL.

Comptroller General of the United States. October 3, 1977. Preventing Mental
Retardation—More Can be Done. (Report to Congress, HRD-77-37.)

Crocker, A. C. 1978. Personal communication.

Crocker, A. C. 1979. Personal communication.

Culley, W. J. 1978. Nutrition and mental retardation. In C. H. Carter (ed.), Medical
Aspects of Mental Retardation, Chapter 6, pp. 73-82, 2nd Ed. Charles C Thomas,
Publishers, Springfield, IL.

Garrard, S. D., and Richmond, J. B. 1978. Mental retardation without biomedical
manifestations. In C. H. Carter (ed.), Medical Aspects of Mental Retardation,
Chapter 2, pp. 24-36, 2nd Ed. Charles C Thomas, Publishers, Springfield, IL.

Graef, J. W. 1975. The prevention of lead poisoning. In A. Milunsky (ed.), The
Prevention of Genetic Disease and Mental Retardation, Chapter 15, pp. 354-368.
W. B. Saunders Co., Philadelphia.

Groover, R. V. 1978. Neurologic manifestations of endocrinologic disease. In C. H.
Carter (ed.), Medical Aspects of Mental Retardation, Chapter 24, pp. 605-646, 2nd
Ed. Charles C Thomas, Publishers, Springfield, IL.

Guthrie, R. 1972. Mass screening for genetic disease. *Hosp. Pract.* 7:93–100.
Haffner, D. 1979. Learning Together: A Guide for Families with Genetic Disorders. DHEW, BCHS publication (in press).
Hagberg, B., Kollberg, H., Sourander, P., and Akesson, H. O. 1969. Infantile globoid cell leukodystrophy (Krabbe's disease). *Neuropaediatrie* 1:74.
Johnston, R. B., and Magrab, P. R. (eds.) 1976. Developmental Disorders—Assessment, Treatment, Education. University Park Press, Baltimore.
Kolodny, E. H. 1975. Heterozygote detection in the lipidoses. In A. Milunsky (ed.), The Prevention of Genetic Disease and Mental Retardation, Chapter 7, pp. 182–203. W. B. Saunders Co., Philadelphia.
Lieberman, H. M., Emmet, W. L., II, and Coulson, A. H. 1976. Pediatric automotive restraints, pediatricians, and the academy. *Pediatrics* 58:316–319.
Litch, S. (ed.) 1978. Towards the Prevention of Mental Retardation in the Next Generation. A Health Education Curriculum: Course of Study-Resource Manual for Junior and Senior High School Students. Fort Wayne Printing Co., Fort Wayne, IN.
Lorincz, A. E. 1978. The mucopolysaccharidoses: Advances in understanding and treatment. *Pediat. Ann.* 7:64–98.
MacCready, R. A., and Levy, H. K. 1972. The problem of maternal phenylketonuria. *Amer. J. Obstet. Gynecol.* 113:121.
Meier, J. H. 1975. Early intervention in the prevention of mental retardation. In A. Milunsky (ed.), The Prevention of Genetic Disease and Mental Retardation, Chapter 17, pp. 385–409. W. B. Saunders Co., Philadelphia.
Milunsky, A. (ed.) 1975. The Prevention of Genetic Disease and Mental Retardation. W. B. Saunders Co., Philadelphia.
National Research Council, Committee for the Study of Inborn Errors of Metabolism. 1975. Genetic Screening: Programs, Principles, and Research. National Academy of Sciences, Washington, DC.
Reichelderfer, T. E. 1976. A first priority—Childhood automotive safety. *Pediatrics* 58:307–308.
Reilly, P. 1975. The role of law in the prevention of genetic disease. In A. Milunsky (ed.), The Prevention of Genetic Disease and Mental Retardation, Chapter 19, pp. 422–441. W. B. Saunders Co., Philadelphia.
Shih, V. E. 1975. Homozygote screening in the disorders of amino acid metabolism. In A. Milunsky (ed.), The Prevention of Genetic Disease and Mental Retardation, Chapter 10, pp. 264–276. W. B. Saunders Co., Philadelphia.
Watts, R. W. E. 1978. Progress in screening for inborn errors of metabolism. *Experientia* 34:143–152.

ACKNOWLEDGMENT

This project was supported in part by Maternal and Child Health Training Project 910, Department of Health, Education and Welfare, Public Health Service, Bureau of Community Health Services, and Grant 59-P-2034914, OHD, Region IV-Developmental Disabilities Office, as awarded to the Center for Developmental and Learning Disorders, University of Alabama in Birmingham.

Chapter 4

Community Health Planning

Herbert J. Cohen

In 1970, the White House Conference on Children issued a series of recommendations relating to the handicapped. Among these was a declaration "that a comprehensive health care system be developed that will insure not only basic health needs for all children, but also diagnostic, treatment and educational services for all handicapped children without restrictive means tests, residence requirements or other arbitrary barriers." (White House Conference, 1970).

A comprehensive system of health care is only one of several critical services required to provide for the overall needs of the handicapped. Other requirements include community residential programs; educational, vocational, social, recreational, and transportation services; and mechanisms for assurance of the protection of client's and patient's legal rights. However, it is surprising that, despite the fact that handicapped individuals have greater medical needs than the general population, satisfactory health care is frequently a low priority, or even an omitted component, in service planning for them.

A comprehensive health service system must include prevention, early detection, diagnostic evaluation, and access to a broad range of community-based treatment facilities. It also must reflect a clear recognition of the overwhelming trend in delivery of services to the handicapped towards community care and the deinstitutionalization of the currently institutionalized population. A variety of outpatient and inpatient services must be included in a plan for comprehensive health care. There is growing recognition of the need for prevention, and for early identification and treatment of the developmentally disabled.

CHARACTERISTICS OF AVAILABLE SERVICES

In most communities there is no coherent system of medical care for the population at large; instead, there is a complex conglomeration of services offered by publicly supported facilities, medical care providers, private physicians, clinics, and medical groups. In an urban environment, the local public (city or county) or voluntary hospitals provide much of the rather episodic health care available to the urban poor. Hospital emergency rooms are the usual source of such care, frequently for nonemergencies. This is often supplemented by hospital-based clinics. Outpatient care is separated from inpatient care and the two types of services are likely to be provided by different physicians or staff. The more affluent are more likely to be cared for by the private physicians who also supervise the patients' care while they are hospitalized.

For the handicapped child or adult, medical care is similarly fragmented. If these individuals reside in the community and are poor, they will be subjected to the same social class, racial, or ethnic barriers to systematic care that their neighbors experience. The families who can afford to purchase private health care or who have adequate insurance can seek private health care for their handicapped relatives. However, money is no guarantee of good service. Because of prejudice, the lack of public interest and proper training of professionals, or even ignorance, the handicapped, and particularly severely retarded people, may be turned away from medical services or given limited attention. Unfortunately, the same negative attitudes and exclusionary policies may apply in private offices, hospital clinics, or emergency rooms.

Stories which exemplify the problem abound. A retarded adult arrives at the local municipal hospital emergency room with a high fever, but is immediately referred to a psychiatric emergency room because of "behavior problems." His temperature is never taken. Another family with two retarded daughters is asked to leave a doctor's office because the doctor's staff believe that the girls might soil the carpets in the office waiting room. A retarded woman is refused admission to a voluntary hospital for acute medical care because it is feared the staff cannot handle her "behavior."

Residential settings for the developmentally disabled present other problems. Institutions have an internal system for providing health care to all residents, but a major problem is the quality of health care provided in these institutions (Nelson and Crocker, 1978). In many cases, the physicians hired to work in state institutions are poorly trained or unlicensed, and have no access to postgraduate study or adequate supervision. These physicians, as well as the nurses in the institutions, are usually isolated from other health care providers in the community.

There are, therefore, two separate mechanisms for provision of general health care for the handicapped: 1) isolated, segregated, usually inadequate health care in state institutions or 2) inconsistent care provided for people living in the community. It is obvious that the dual system of health care in the community and the separation of institutional health care from community health care is a far cry from the goals of normalizing services for the handicapped and of providing satisfactory health care for all of these individuals. The ideal solution would be the development of a comprehensive, integrated, single class system of care for all, including the handicapped and the developmentally disabled.

The phase-down of state institutions, which is accelerating because of the deinstitutionalization movement, plus the effective legal advocacy that has resulted in court judgments such as the Willowbrook Consent Decree (*New York State Association for Retarded Children* v. *Carey*, 1975), are producing a declining institutional population (see Chapter 5). This, plus the growing advocacy for the rights of the handicapped, reinforced by the federal legislation such as Section 504 of the Federal Rehabilitation Act and PL 94-142 (Education for All Handicapped Children Act), should improve access to all services in the community, including health care.

The dilemma faced by service planners is whether or not to create a separate system of health care for the handicapped which enables providers to deal with the special needs of these patients or to rely on gaining more complete access to the existing, but still problematic, health care available within the community. The latter approach is more normalizing, but may not be entirely satisfactory. Meanwhile, in the institutions, the pressure to meet accreditation standards and to comply with federal regulations for Intermediate Care Facilities for the Mentally Retarded (ICF-MRS) in order to qualify for federal reimbursement has exerted pressure to reform and improve the quality of institutional health care. Such pressures may have the salutory effect of upgrading the health care provided within institutions. One approach has been to establish systematic linkages with quality health care providers in local communities. This results in better access to local hospitals for institutional residents and also brings community health care providers into the institutions and institutional clients outside to receive other needed services.

However, achieving these changes requires commitments to break down existing patterns of care, to eliminate prejudices against the handicapped, and to provide extensive training to health care providers in the community, to medical students, to nursing students, and to other health professions who will be serving these patients in the future.

DEFINING HEALTH NEEDS OF HANDICAPPED PERSONS

Because it is difficult to identify the true frequency of specific types of developmental disabilities within communities, defining the health needs of handicapped persons is a complicated task. Studies of the severely and profoundly retarded (less than 50 IQ) suggest that the rate of occurrence is between 3 to 4 per 1000 in most communities (Abramowicz and Richardson, 1973). Yet, data on other disabilities usually are estimated, because there are serious problems defining disorders and deciding who should be included in categories such as "cerebral palsy," "epilepsy," and "autism." Despite this problem, comprehensive surveys have been attempted. One of the most useful reports is the Isle of Wight study by Rutter, Graham, and Yule (1970). This study reports the incidence of cerebral palsy to be 2.9 per 1000 (other studies have reported 1.0 to 5.9 per 1000 with the majority of the more accurate studies reporting 2 to 3 per 1000). The Rutter study includes the incidence of a number of other disorders: severe developmental language disorders, 0.8 per 1000; blindness, 1.3 per 1000; deafness, 1.2 per 1000; epilepsy, 5 to 9 per 1000 in the general population and 40 percent in children with a diagnosis of cerebral palsy (other reports have ranges from 30 to 40 percent). Figures for autism have been very difficult to ascertain because diagnostic criteria have not been adequately standardized, although a figure of 0.33 per 1000 has been utilized recently in the Five Year Comprehensive Plan for Services to Mentally Retarded and Developmentally Disabled Persons in New York State (1978).

It is important to note that the frequency of some disabilities may be changing because of factors such as the increased abortion rate, the widespread application of birth control procedures, the impact of intrauterine diagnostic procedures, and the aggressive interventions utilized in intensive care units for high risk premature and newborn infants. As a result of the overall declining birth rate, coupled with the application of better medical practices which prolong the lives of retarded and multiply handicapped children and adults, there are indications of a decline in the absolute number of handicapped children in most communities and an increase in the percentage of adults with handicaps among the total population of disabled people seeking services.

Given this problem of accurately defining the handicapped population, there are serious difficulties in pinpointing the quantitative need for specific medical services. However, we can, based on clinical reports and experience, define qualitative needs. For example, we know that the frequency of seizures is relatively high among the severely retarded. In the institutionalized mentally retarded population, an incidence of 34 percent was reported in a study by Wright, Valente, and Tarjan (1962). Among people living in the community, the rates are, again, highest in individuals with cerebral palsy and severe and profound mental retardation. However, there is no adequate data on the frequency of seizures accompanying mild retardation or learning disabilities, although it is suspected to be higher than in the normal population. The same frequency distribution for seizures in the severely retarded or physically handicapped also may apply to chronic respiratory disease as it relates to neurological and physical defects. However, this is unlikely to be a significant problem among the more mildly developmentally disabled.

In planning services, one must, therefore, have an understanding that there are specific medical problems that require special attention because of their increased occurrence in the handicapped population. This includes not only managing seizure disorders and frequent respiratory illnesses, but also attending to psychological problems, handling physical or sensory (hearing and vision) deficits, treating associated congenital anomalies, and providing genetic services.

To understand the qualitative need for medical services, there must be a realization that such services reflect the developmental needs and developmental patterns of the individuals served. For example, young children with handicapping conditions require considerable early medical attention because of some of the associated medical problems. They also need routine prevention care. As they mature and enter school, their need for education, training, and habilitation increases and their medical needs, except in unusual circumstances, have a corresponding decrease. This relatively low frequency of medical problems persists into young adulthood, with the exception of adolescence, when psychological problems increase and some physical disorders such as seizures are also more problematic. Finally, as handicapped individuals age, the pattern is similar to normal adults, since they require increasing health services in their later years.

Concerning the quantity of health care that will be needed, the eventual requirements will depend on the demand generated for such services and the degree to which personnel allocated to provide these services are capable of meeting the demand. We must also bear in mind that we have no available method of predicting how much of the required services can or will be provided by generic workers, as opposed to service providers who specialize in serving handicapped individuals.

To obtain accurate data defining the quantitative need for specific types of community health services, longitudinal data on a cohort of community-based clients should be collected. Unfortunately, most data generated thus far have been on institutional populations, since the latter are captive groups. However, the institutional population does not reflect the problems of handicapped individuals living in the community.

The only recent attempt at a comprehensive assessment of health needs for a specific handicapped population in a community was the Hamilton *et al.* (1978) Chicago study of medical and allied health services delivery for substantially handicapped disabled adults. The objective of this study was to determine the type and extent of services available, the sources of funds, the character of unmet needs, and the problems which existed. The study population was a cohort of 3800 adults served by existing local agencies. Records were reviewed and questionnaires were sent to consumers and providers. The three largest consumer disability subgroups in the study were the mentally retarded (79 percent), the cerebral palsied (61 percent), and epileptics (18 percent), with considerable overlap of respective subgroups. An analysis of categorical problems identified indicated that neurological abnormalities were most frequent, communication disorders second, and behavior problems third. Associated medical problems were quite common, but the types of problems were numerous with no particular associated medical conditions standing out in excess of the others. Sixty-two percent of the existing medical problems identified in these adults were considered treatable and 87 percent would have been treatable in childhood by current standards of care. Of the existing associated medical problems in the adult population, it was felt that 42 percent could have been prevented or improved to a point at which the current treatment should not have been necessary. The most common unmet needs in the Chicago study, according to consumers, were for dental, ophthalmological, and general medical care.

Most striking among the findings of the Chicago study was that medical services were generally available, but that they were poorly coordinated, inaccessible, or difficult to reach with available transportation. Health services were funded by a large variety of mechanisms. In some cases, funds were directly provided to the consumer, and in others to the provider. No single governmental agency appeared responsible for health planning. Essentially, a nonsystem existed with no systematic efforts to develop services based on identified needs.

COMPREHENSIVE HEALTH CARE

Outpatient Services

There are three major components of comprehensive outpatient health care for the handicapped: *specialized diagnostic services, general health management,* and *provision of mental health services.*

Specialized Diagnostic Services The identification and correct diagnosis of developmental problems is of particular importance in the handicapped population. It is a process which involves screening, referral, and a diagnostic evaluation by a number of specialists.

The most important screeners for developmental disability are parents who monitor their childrens' development. Public and community education, including efforts directed at educating prospective parents, are useful in this regard, particularly in high risk pregnancies (young adolescents, elderly primagravidas, and women with a history of high fetal wastage or high multiparity). One concern, however, in these high risk situations is that, unless the educational process is carefully conducted, parental anxiety may be raised to a point at which child-rearing practices become distorted and the child's behavior adversely affected. Abnormal behavior could be a self-fulfilling prophecy.

Other important screeners for developmental problems include physicians who provide care for infants and toddlers, as well as nurses and paraprofessional staff at public clinics who provide preventive or continuing health care for less affluent families. Formal screening programs are also available in some communities. The concerns and problems related to screening programs and recommendations for improving these activities are discussed elsewhere in this chapter.

The process of referral for comprehensive evaluation is dependent upon a number of factors. These include the degree of certainty of the screener about the child's potential for developmental disability, the screener's knowledge of or linkages to more comprehensive diagnostic services, and the availability of more sophisticated diagnostic evaluations within the community.

In some instances, there are knowledgeable consultants, particularly pediatricians who specialize in the care of the developmentally disabled or pediatric neurologists and child psychologists whose knowledge and experience with handicapped children prepares them to confirm (or rule out) the presence of the developmental abnormality suspected by the screener. However, most experts in the field agree that the optimal method of evaluation is through the efforts of an interdisciplinary diagnostic unit which includes, at a minimum, medical, psychological, and social services plus special educational input. The most effective clinics function in an interdisciplinary manner with considerable interaction, exchange, and sharing of views among the involved professionals.

A comprehensive diagnostic clinic must be able to consider all of the possible problems manifested by a handicapped child (or adult), including the various associated medical problems or congenital defects. The medical role is important in determining the role of physical or neurological dysfunction in causing the disability and to assess the roles of specific organ system abnormalities in producing the individual's symptoms so that needed treatments or procedures can be recommended or implemented. Among the required medical specialists who are called upon for their expertise are pediatricians, internists, neurologists, ophthalmologists, otolaryngologists, physiatrists, orthopedic surgeons, and psychiatrists. Genetic specialists are also important, particularly for establishing the presence of genetic disorders and offering primary preventive services through both counseling and intrauterine prenatal diagnostic techniques. These and the related types of preventive services that constitute important components of comprehensive health care are discussed in detail elsewhere in this book (see Chapter 5).

The other important components of the diagnostic process include comprehensive *psychological testing* to establish intellectual level, areas of strength and weakness, the presence of perceptual problems, and signs of behavioral disturbance and to recommend intervention; *social service evaluation* to assess the impact of the home and social environment on the affected individual's behavior; *special educational* or *psychoeducational evaluation* to determine the individual's current academic skills, areas of proficiency and weakness in learning, and to pinpoint useful remediation techniques; *speech and audiological services* to evaluate the understanding and comprehension of language, the ability to hear normally, the quality and quantity of expressive language and oral mechanics, and to recommend or initiate interventions or therapies; *occupational and physical therapy services* to measure functional capabilities, motor coordination, and muscle strength and to provide needed exercises and rehabilitative techniques for improving motor performance and the capability for acquiring new skills used in activities of daily living; and *nursing services* to provide health assessment and to assist families in planning and providing home care and management, including consultation about hygienic, dietary, and equipment needs. Other professionals, including nutritionists, vocational counselors, recreational therapists, and orthotic specialists, all may have useful consultative roles in helping handicapped individuals with their respective nutritional, vocational, recreational, and orthotic needs.

Another important adjunct to the diagnostic process is the availability of laboratory services. In addition to routine blood and urine analyses, specialized laboratory procedures may be needed to screen for metabolic disorders and to provide specialized x-ray procedures, when needed, for differential diagnosis of brain disorders. These include electroencephalograms, arteriograms, and computerized axial tomography (CAT scan). A cytogenetic laboratory is needed to study chromosomal and related genetic disorders.

Many diagnostic clinics are equipped to provide an appropriate variety of medically related treatment programs and interventions, as well as to offer follow-up diagnostic and consultative services and periodic reevaluation of client's/patient's progress. This approach is useful in providing continuity of services for affected individuals.

The opportunity for a child or an adult to receive an independent outside evaluation, separate from the school, day, or residential treatment programs that he or she attends, is useful to assess his or her progress objectively. However, such evaluations are most useful when there is feedback not only to the family and affected individual, but also to the outside program provider.

General Health Management   In addition to specialized diagnostic services, there is a need for continuing comprehensive health, medical, and dental management of the handicapped. Preventive health care (see Chapter 3) and ongoing medical and dental treatment are even more necessary for the developmentally disabled than they are for the general population because of the additional medical and special treatment needs and higher frequency of associated handicaps.

Mental Health Services   One frequently neglected area of care for handicapped individuals is management of their psychological problems. The mentally retarded and physically handicapped are not typical psychiatric patients. Psychiatric clinics serve few retarded people, preferring to refer them to mental retardation facilities. The latter may have psychiatric consultants, but limited outpatient psychiatric treatment. It must be realized that handicapped people may have mental health needs just as anyone else may. However, disabled people may feel more vulnerable and more stigmatized than others. This insecurity, complicated, in some cases, by a more labile nervous system, makes handicapped persons quite susceptible to emotional disorders. The image of the happy, friendly child or adult with Down's syndrome is contradicted by the experience of clinicians who have seen numerous psychotic adolescents and adults with that syndrome.

Inpatient Services

With the exception of the need for inpatient physical rehabilitation services, there are no specialized inpatient services that developmentally disabled people require that should not be provided routinely by hospitals in most communities. These services include acute medical, surgical, and psychiatric treatment.

The major problem is access to inpatient care. This presents few problems for handicapped children, particularly young children, who are usually treated the same as others. However, older handicapped children or adolescents with aggressive bebavior, autism, or severe physical handicaps are felt by hospital staff to be difficult to manage; therefore, it is sometimes difficult for such patients to gain admission to hospitals. The same is true for retarded adults. Although part of the problem may be discrimination, it is understandable that hospital personnel in some situations feel that they are not adequately staffed to deal with these more difficult patients. Under such circumstances, supplementary staffing arrangements provided by a mental retardation agency have helped to make the hospital stay less traumatic for both patient and hospital staff. It is helpful when such staffing flexibility exists, or when special contractual agreements with agencies that provide home aides or private duty nurses can be worked out and supported by state or local governmental funding agencies. When these kinds of arrangements are available, access for the severely handicapped to public facilities is improved and need for special institutional "hospital units" or other separate isolated arrangements for the severely handicapped is negated.

Inpatient rebabilitation treatment is an option that should be available to provide time-limited intensive rehabilitation programs for children and adults at times of specific need, particularly after surgical procedures for patients with neuromuscular impairment, or when intensive outpatient treatment is not feasible because of family or transportation problems.

SPECIALIZED SERVICES FOR SPECIAL POPULATIONS

Although the traditional view of the developmentally disabled is that they have a single disability, most experienced practitioners recognize that their clients or patients frequently have multiple problems. These "problem cases" are distinguished by their histories of having been served by more than one public agency and more than one health care provider or clinic. Their associated handicaps, problems, or complications are as chronic and as permanent as their primary handicapping conditions.

The most important associated handicaps include behavior problems, seizure disorders, motor or physical disabilities, and deafness and/or blindness. Those individuals with more than one disability are often labeled multiply handicapped, a term certain to mean different things to different people. Among many professionals, the term signals a combination of mental retardation with a physical disability. To others, it means a combination of cognitive deficits and significant emotional or behavioral problems. To still others, it means individuals who are deaf, blind, and retarded. Whatever the combination of disabilities, special emphasis must be placed on efforts to provide comprehensive services, effective case management, plus special attention to the problems related to the associated handicap.

Behavior Problems

One of the most exasperating clinical problems is dealing with the handicapped individual with emotional problems. In many communities, it has been extremely difficult to obtain psychiatric help for retarded or physically handicapped individuals. This problem in obtaining such services is ironic, in view of the long history of psychiatric domination of the mental retardation field which was and, in many instances, still is subsumed under mental hygiene systems which operate state institutions. Yet, most psychiatric training programs do not provide any extensive or systematic exposure to handicapped people. As a result, there are few psychiatrists who feel qualified or have an interest in severely disabled people. It is fascinating that of over 1000 members (90 percent physicians) of the interdisciplinary organization, the American Academy of Cerebral Palsy, only 5 of the current membership roster are psychiatrists. As a result of the apparent disinterest of psychiatrists in these problems, the literature on the psychiatric management of the cerebral palsied or physically disabled child is practically barren. Therefore, obtaining diagnostic psychiatric services and traditional psychotherapy for severely disabled people is a difficult task, except in a few specialized clinics. On the other hand, there are a sizeable number of psychiatrists interested in working with learning disabled children and these services are available in many communities, if the family has the means to pay for them.

A key approach to the treatment of behavior problems in the handicapped includes use of *medications and behavioral therapy*. Medications for behaviorally abnormal children and adults usually are divided into two major categories: 1) use of tranquilizers for treatment of anxiety or aggression and 2) use of a variety of medications, particularly drugs such as ritalin and dexedrine, for children with hyperactivity. The use of tranquilizers for behavior problems in the handicapped is very widespread. Surveys of institutions for the mentally retarded have generally indicated overuse and misuse of medications. Use of multiple drugs is commonplace, and drugs at times are used to pacify residents, or serve as a substitute for inadequate programming or a staff's inability to manage a resident's behavior. Efforts to determine the impact or evaluate the effectiveness of the medications prescribed are usually absent. Unfortunately, the same is true for drugs prescribed for clients in the community, where compliance is known to be generally poor for all types of medications. There is little information available on the frequency with which tranquilizers are prescribed for mentally retarded and developmentally disabled persons living in the community, since these drugs may be prescribed by a wide variety of practitioners in different settings.

Even clinics for developmentally disabled individuals have problems keeping track of their patients for whom medications have been prescribed. Clinic doctors are often unavailable when families try to contact them and families themselves do not follow up on reporting positive effects or side effects of medications. What has been devised in such clinics is a variety of systematic attempts at improved medication follow-up. These include:

1. Establishing a regularly scheduled medication clinic supervised by an experienced psychiatrist or other physician
2. Providing patients with a single point of contact with the clinic and a phone number of a nurse or nurse practitioner whose schedule makes her more readily available to patients or their families (the nurse can maintain regular contacts with patients)
3. Utilizing a variety of reporting forms devised to measure the medication's impact on behavior, side effects, compliance, and performance in school
4. Testing blood specimens to monitor serum drug levels
5. Where this luxury is available, sending staff to observe behavioral changes in other settings (school, home, or treatment programs).

The controversial issue of use of medications for hyperactive children deserves some discussion. Although there has been a tendency in some communities to overuse medication to control hyperactivity, as summarized by a recent discussion of the issue in the *Medical Letter* (1977), a publication devoted to analyzing the value of medications, most experts feel that judicious use of a drug such as ritalin in selected hyperactive children may be beneficial and is likely to result in demonstrable improvement. To complicate matters further, there is evidence that most medications, and even placebos, have produced positive effects on children by diminishing their hyperactivity, as summarized by Millichap (1973). Solomons (1973) has pointed out that the reporting of medication's effects and medication follow-up are generally inconsistent. This makes careful analysis of the impact of drugs rather difficult in most clinical settings.

However, despite the shortcomings in the use of drugs in behavioral management, the preponderent evidence is that they are of value. Certainly, the available evidence supports their careful use, although there is little data to support the use of alternatives such as restrictive diets, including the Feingold diet (excludes dyes and salicyclates), use of megavitamins (large doses of B vitamins), and sugar-free or high carbohydrate diets. Certainly, drugs should never be relied on as an alternative to, or substitute for, appropriate educational programming.

The second major approach to the management of behavior problems is through use of *behavior modification techniques*. Although most program providers are impressed by the gains that can be accomplished both in institutional and community settings by using positive reinforcement techniques, it is evident that carryover is greatest in the community when parents are participating in the programs. Much more controversial are the use of aversive techniques in order to diminish undesired behavior. It is generally agreed that such techniques should be measures of last resort and used very infrequently; *i.e.*, only when the behavior to be modified is a severe threat to the client's health or welfare, or to his environment.

Behavior modification techniques appear most effective in modifying behavior in moderate to severely retarded people, but the techniques have, with some adjustments, been melded into treatment approaches for other types or degrees of disability with some reported success. It is always preferable that these techniques be designed and supervised by a professional experienced in their use.

Seizure Disorders

The frequency of seizures in developmentally disabled persons is considerably higher than in the general population. As noted earlier, the rate in institutionalized retarded and the severely and profoundly retarded individuals appears to be over 30 percent. The frequency in individuals with cerebral palsy is even higher, the highest percentage being found in patients with postnatally acquired hemiplegias.

Appropriate management of seizures requires a number of key elements:

1. Good historical and observational information about the types and frequency of seizures experienced by the patient
2. Competent neurological consultative services
3. Satisfactory supportive laboratory services, including an EEG laboratory, experienced technicians, and EEG interpreters; neuroradiological services and anticonvulsant serum (blood) level measurements
4. A mechanism for regular follow-up
5. Back-up inpatient hospital services
6. Available emergency medical services to treat cardiorespiratory emergencies or status epilepticus

7. A system for administering medications (including assigning responsibility to properly instructed individuals to assure that medication is given correctly; this must be the case whether the person lives in an institution or in the community
8. A mechanism to report adverse effects quickly and to receive appropriate consultation when problems arise.

Although most developmentally disabled people have their seizures reasonably well controlled using the current repertoire of medications, there are a number of refractory cases for whom all available drugs have a limited impact. These patients remain a continuing management problem. Some of these patients eventually are diagnosed as having a degenerative disease, some deteriorate as a result of frequent poorly controlled seizures, and some improve with maturation for unknown reasons. However, one must bear in mind that times of psychological stress and physiological change (such as adolescence and pregnancy) are known to exacerbate seizures. We have observed this when individuals changed residential settings or experienced a family crisis. Proper management of seizure-prone clients in the community includes provision of careful medical follow-up during times of anticipated stress or physiological change.

Motor or Physical Disability

The most common major physical disability involving motor functioning is cerebral palsy. Cerebral palsy is a nonprogressive motor disability resulting from brain damage. Almost 60 percent of people with cerebral palsy are mentally retarded. The combination of these two disabilities is common in former premature infants and infants with brain damage as a result of neonatal anoxia.

The ultimate level of motor and functional achievement in people with cerebral palsy depends on their degree of motor impairment, as well as their level of cognitive ability. Severely retarded people with cerebral palsy generally have greater problems learning to ambulate than do the more mildly retarded.

The management of the physically handicapped, cognitively impaired individual requires the traditional multidisciplinary staff, plus specialists in management of the physical disability. The latter includes a physiatrist (medical rehabilitation specialist), orthopedic surgeon, occupational and physical therapists, as well as speech pathologists. Treatment techniques include a variety of exercise programs, reflex inhibition techniques, facilitation of certain motor activities, bracing, and surgery. Similiar techniques may be used for both retarded and nonretarded individuals, but retarded persons usually require the additional understanding of their cognitive deficits when receiving treatment.

Two other key issues must be highlighted regarding these patients. First, the prediction of future intelligence is most difficult in the young physically disabled child. Performance on tests of adaptive functioning and language requires motor competence. Personal-social skills require social exposure. All of these areas may appear to be deficient in the young physically handicapped child and result in misleading test scores. Clinicians are wise to be modest in considering the predictability of their test results under such circumstances. Young children with physical handicaps should be given the benefit of the doubt about their intellectual potential for as long as possible.

A second related issue is the importance of early intervention regardless of the degree of disability. Experience indicates that more aggressive early management and rehabilitation is not only useful in achieving the maximum potential for many children, but also can avoid the development of the very severe deformities observed among institutional residents with severe retardation and cerebral palsy. In addition, it facilitates nursing care. Therefore, early intervention has long term rewards, whereas early neglect is, in the long run, more costly to everyone.

Deafness

A significant hearing deficit is a common finding in certain mental retardation syndromes such as congenital rubella or abnormalities associated with developmental defects of the first branchial arch (Treacher-Collins syndrome). Deafness is found associated with athetosis due to kernicterus (brain damage due to hyperbilirubinemia in the neonatal period, usually as a result of a blood incompatibility) or as a complication of an infection (as in measles or meningitis). Deafness may be found in mentally retarded people who had neonatal disorders requiring treatment with ototoxic drugs. Another cause is related to chronic middle ear disease in infection-prone children with associated immunological problems.

Retarded and cerebral palsied individuals must be tested to make sure their hearing is normal. Such testing should take place as early as possible, preferably in infancy, if there is the slightest suspicion of a hearing deficit. Routine screening tests are useful; however, more sophisticated audiological testing, including the use of auditory evoked response testing, is necessary when hearing abnormalities are suspected. Early diagnosis is essential for the multiply handicapped child who has a hearing impairment, inasmuch as positive treatment results are greatest when intervention is earliest. Competent audiological and otolaryngological staff must be available to carry out the necessary procedures to identify the degree of hearing deficit, the cause of any remediable conditions (particularly chronic infection and some correctible structural defects), and to provide appropriately selected and fitted hearing aids. After the diagnosis is made, speech clinicians must be available to provide the necessary therapy or remediation. This must be an important component of the overall treatment plan which takes into account the client's associated disability or disabilities.

Blindness

Although severe visual deficits are usually more easily identifiable than hearing deficits, problems with vision can also be missed. Early diagnosis and remediation are essential. Conditions such as congenital cataracts or congenital glaucoma, if identified early, can be treated promptly with resultant improved vision and/or prevention of further visual loss. It is essential that an ophthalmologist who is experienced in dealing with children's problems be available. However, even the most competent ophthalmologist may have some difficulties in pinpointing the exact degree of visual deficit in very young, uncooperative, or profoundly impaired subjects, except when there are retinal changes which indicate the very severe pathology known to be associated with very limited vision.

Programming for blind children requires the talents of specialists trained to help children use other sensory modalities to compensate for their visual deficit. Obviously, if there is a major associated deficit in cognitive functioning or associated deafness, the problem of instructing the client and effecting progress is considerably greater, but as verified by dedicated practitioners, not impossible.

COORDINATION OF SERVICES

Funding Mechanisms and Their Impact on Planning and Coordination

Most health planners and providers recognize a need for mechanisms to coordinate service provision. However, plans to integrate and coordinate health services are complicated by the diverse methods of payment for services. Although fewer health care services are now paid for directly by the handicapped consumer, most consumers prefer to preserve this option. The relationship of a patient to a private physician is still valued in this country, and still exists even in a primarily socialized system such as Great Britain.

Direct governmental support and insurance plans are the other major funding mechanisms. Unfortunately, these are quite numerous and their diversity leads to some of the current confusion and problems. Payments from various components of the Social Security Act such as Medicare (Title XVIII), Medicaid (Title XIX), and from private insurance plans (Blue Shield, Blue Cross, GHI, etc.) are the major means of reimbursing doctors and hospitals. Medicare pays for nursing home care. Medicaid pays for hospital clinic visits. Title XIX reimburses residential services for the mentally retarded in Intermediate Care Facilities for the Mentally Retarded (ICF-MR). This latter funding mechanism was originally applied solely to large congregate care facilities, primarily large institutions that could meet the required standards. However, smaller Intermediate Care Facilities (ICF's) in the community now are being funded as well. With this advance comes the concern that medically oriented standards are being applied to residential living environments in the community, an approach that is not normalizing. Nevertheless, the trend in that direction is fostered by the lure of federal reimbursement which, by applying what were originally hospital-related standards to community facilities, may subvert normalization criteria. On the other hand, this process does increase funds available for community residential care. In New York State, through a mechanism called Subchapter C funding, Title XIX monies are being utilized to reimburse day programs for severely and profoundly retarded or multiply handicapped adults, if programs meet required ICF service standards.

To complicate matters further, there are additional federal programs that support health care activities which affect handicapped children. For example, Early Periodic Screening Diagnosis and Treatment (EPSDT) provides for health screening of poor children whose families receive public assistance. The Child Health and Planning (CHAP) mechanism is another effort to provide comprehensive evaluation and treatment for indigent children, although its application to handicapped children has been limited. PL 88-156, otherwise known as the Maternal and Child Health and Mental Retardation Planning Amendments, amended the Social Security Act to provide program support for Crippled Children's Services in States. This pays for assessment and follow-up of handicapped children, plus orthopedic, rehabilitative, or prosthetic devices to help them. In some states, funds from another section of the same law are provided to University Affiliated Facilities and related programs to assist them in operating clinics for handicapped children and to offer professional training in this field. Federal funds are also available through the Federal Rehabilitation Acts. The most recent, PL 95-602, provides funds for vocational evaluation and diagnostic services for handicapped adults, and also funds for research in rehabilitation and for independent living programs. PL 95-602 extends provisions of earlier developmental disability and mental retardation legislation by also providing funds for state Developmental Disability Councils to support some new programs, including health-related projects. In addition, federal Title XX (Social Security Act) funding, aimed at coordinating state social welfare programs, provides financial assistance to a variety of health-related programs for the handicapped, as well as a range of community services, including counseling for expectant mothers.

Other sources of health service funding include 1) the CHAMPUS program (PL 89-10) which reimburses health care for armed services personnel and 2) other components of the Social Security Act providing general funds from which health care can be purchased (Title XVI of PL 92-603 which provides supplemental security income and Title IVA which provides child welfare payments).

On top of this wide array of federal programs, individual states operate mental health and mental retardation institutional and community facilities which serve the mentally retarded. These are, at least in part, supported by state tax levy funds. In some cases, local counties or cities provide additional funds, often as a required percentage of tax revenues to "match" state allocations that support local programs. In such cases, the local contribution enhances counties' or localities' control over the planning and operation of the programs in their communities.

In addition to the mental health and mental retardation programs supported by state and local governmental funding, there are also voluntary agencies providing some services, usually with the assistance of both public funds and their own monies raised from charitable contributions.

States, counties, and cities may support health care directly in their mental health and mental retardation facilities, but some local governmental agencies also operate general hospitals and public clinics to serve their own communities. These facilities usually provide care primarily for the poorer populations in their localities and, in doing so, serve developmentally disabled people as well.

Hamilton *et al.*'s (1978) Chicago study of medical and allied health services for retarded adults cited 35 different funding mechanisms which supported health-related programs/facilities for the adults surveyed in the community. These did not even include some of the other sources described in the above discussion. Obviously, this data demonstrates the diversity of fiscal supports, but also highlights the complexity of the problem of coordinating these services.

Impact of Service Delivery on the Consumer

In the face of this melange of service providers and funding mechanisms, there is obvious overlap in operations and in jurisdictions. Although local communities want to continue to control the planning and implementation process within their own communities, the trend is unequivocally towards increasing federal reimbursement for publicly supported services. The federal support brings with it a plethora of regulations and evaluation mechanisms.

To the individual consumer or family requiring health services, there are enough problems negotiating the patchwork system of educational and social services, and other programs for the handicapped. However, unless individuals are economically able or have sufficient resources to purchase their own health and medical care (which may require some shopping), their alternative is to seek out, then choose among the publicly supported services that they require. If they are lucky, they may have an advocate or effective "case manager" to help them. However, even if they can afford to purchase or are adequately insured to provide for their own routine health care, these individuals almost always have to rely on publicly supported programs to furnish the range of needed multidisciplinary and interdisciplinary services described elsewhere in this chapter.

The individual consumer has little power to influence the system through which services are provided. Yet, by joining with others and practicing group advocacy efforts, consumers can influence policies, particularly those on a local level. When services are disjointed, inadequate, or disregard the needs of handicapped persons, lobbying and seeking representation on local health planning boards, hospital boards, and advisory groups, etc., gives consumers the opportunity to speak up for what they need. When the advocates are outspoken and use legal mechanisms when their rights are violated, they can have some impact in gaining access to available services or creating new ones, although their affect on changing the discontinuity of care in the health system is likely to be minimal.

Given the complex funding mechanisms, it would require a radical reorganization in the support of health care in this country to effect major changes. For handicapped persons, some of the overlap in funding mechanisms has the advantage of offering possible options. In some communities, consumers may have the choice of selecting a voluntary agency or public program and a private physician or a clinic. Although it sounds convenient and simplistic to create a single overall plan for services and a unified funding mechanism, it could be disadvantageous in one way, since it could foreclose consumers from having options as to where and from whom they can obtain services.

EVALUATION OF SERVICES

As most consumer surveys indicate, consumers are unhappy with available services. Hamilton *et al.* 's (1978) Chicago study of medical and allied health services did not cite absence of medical care as a major problem for most consumers. The major problems described by both consumers and providers included inaccessibility of services: inaccessibility related to both transportation problems and physical barriers in some facilities. The most consistent problem identified in the study was inadequate coordination of services and/or unsatisfactory follow-up. The study suggested that a lack of awareness of service availability, lack of accessibility, and lack of effectiveness may all contribute to inadequate coordination of services.

The issue of service effectiveness and its evaluation is a most difficult one. The Chicago survey observed that 42 percent of the existing problems in the handicapped adults studied could have been prevented or minimized by available care. However, no specific consistent elements could be cited as causing the failure in prevention. Improved follow-up procedures and better data collection and record keeping were noted to be common problems of a general nature. One issue which surfaced in the study, and which has been a subject of much discussion among professionals, is the importance of consumer participation. Consumers should have a direct role and direct responsibility in the follow-up process and in the problem solving necessary to improve these services.

Formal evaluation procedures to determine the effectiveness of health services for handicapped individuals in the community are difficult to develop and implement. The technology is limited, the population sample very heterogeneous, and, as described earlier, the methods of service delivery quite variable. As Conley (1973) has stated in his book, *The Economics of Mental Retardation,* there is "an amazing absence of relevant data" about cost-benefit information and an acute lack of reliable field information about service delivery and clients served.

Problematic Areas of Service Delivery

However, there are several areas of service delivery that are known to be problematic. These include: *follow-up of high risk neonates; early screening programs; early intervention programs;* procedures used in multidisciplinary *diagnostic clinics;* and the absence of effective *service linkages* of the diagnostic process to treatment programs.

Follow-up of High Risk Neonates   With the advent of the neonatal intensive care unit (ICU) and the growth of regional neonatal centers for high risk full term and premature infants, there is now a clearly identifiable population of infants with great risk of developmental disability. These regional centers and ICU's are applying very sophisticated monitoring techniques and life-support systems to assist infants with respiratory distress or other serious difficulties.

The successful application of the sophisticated therapeutic interventions in the ICU's is apparently salvaging many high risk infants and also (although the scientific evidence for this is not yet convincing) improving the outlook for some infants who would otherwise be at greater risk of abnormality. Yet, despite these heroic neonatal interventions, the follow-up of such infants tends to be poor. In fact, this may be an important reason why the data on the impact of ICU's are unclear. Many of the infants cared for in ICU's are lost to follow-up. The apparent reasons include: 1) the mobility of the population, which results in people moving to different addresses, particularly in inner cities; 2) the distance that many of the families served by regional centers live from these centers and the resultant transportation problems which complicate follow-up; 3) lack of outreach by ICU staff; 4) absence of formal ties or even communications by those providing follow-up (private physicians and clinics) with neonatal ICU staff; 5) apathy on the part of some families; 6) and the failure of governmental agencies to provide funding for preventive health care and early identification efforts.

There are, however, useful models of infant follow-up available. It is of interest that in many European countries, including England, Germany, Switzerland, and the Scandinavian countries, almost all infants are involved in some system of health care. High risk registries exist and public health nurses are involved in follow-up of such infants. As a result, children with handicaps are usually identified early and referred for treatment. This appears to maximize the potential for ameliorating the disability, as well as to involve the family early in a system of follow-up and support services.

If a similar structure for follow-up care were present in this country, we would have fewer problems in determining the impact of our ICU's. Follow-up could assist in assessing and augmenting the value of our currently applied early intervention efforts. An approach now being attempted at the Rose F. Kennedy Center in the Bronx, as part of an ICU follow-up study, involves the use of grant funds that were obtained to provide comprehensive health care for a cohort of infants who are being followed after they leave the ICU. By offering free comprehensive health services on a regular basis, with an emphasis on continuity of primary medical care plus sophisticated developmental diagnostic services, the rate of follow-up, even with an indigent mobile inner city population, has improved significantly. Although different approaches may be more desirable or feasible in other communities, the development of some rational system of follow-up should be an immediate priority.

Screening Programs The problem of devising and utilizing valid testing instruments to screen for developmental disability is a serious one. Types of screening examinations for infants and toddlers are numerous, but their value in predicting future problems is usually limited, except in the presence of severe disability. Generally, the more severe the disability, the earlier the diagnosis can be made. Meier (1973), in his comprehensive monograph, has described and analyzed the most important screening tests in use. Although some have been reasonably well validated, many have not, and there is a well founded concern about the reliability and training of those administering all such tests. Too often, screening is in the hands of poorly trained individuals who take shortcuts in giving tests. This produces results of limited validity and the kind of misdiagnoses and inappropriate labeling so appropriately criticized by Hobbs (1975) in his excellent critique on the classification of children. Furthermore, children currently being screened and who are suspected of being abnormal are not necessarily being referred for the comprehensive evaluations they deserve. Nor are they being provided with supportive services. The failure to provide such services, after the proper diagnosis is made, usually results in frustration and anger for the family and is of no benefit to the affected child.

An even more serious situation is now developing with regard to screening school age children for developmental disabilities. Some school systems are conducting wholesale screening programs for 5- to 7-year-old children who are either entering school or in the early grades. The kinds of abuses that exist are illustrated by a recent New York State survey (1975) which indicated that 177 of 736 (24 percent) of the operating school districts had early educational screening programs. These 177 districts used 151 different tests, with 61 specific tests mentioned by published titles and 90 locally devised test instruments adapted from standardized tests. Thus, many of the screening tests used by the schools were unstandardized and administered by untrained personnel. Linkages to more sophisticated diagnostic services, including knowledgeable medical and neurological consultation, were often unavailable.

Screening of children for developmental disability should, therefore, be considered only as a device to identify children who may have special needs. These children must subsequently be offered more sophisticated diagnostic services, as well as intervention. Furthermore, there should be well established ties of screening programs to other generic service providers, including health care facilities or physicians. Testing instruments should be standardized, validated, and administered by trained personnel. Ideally, the screening should be part of an overall health screening program which includes visual, hearing, and general medical evaluation, plus specialized consultative services when needed. The time that children enter school is an ideal one to screen for health-related problems because school children, due to mandatory education laws, are a captive population. However, if screening is to take place, it must be done properly.

Early Intervention Programs   It is difficult to evaluate the impact of early intervention programs. There is general agreement that families heartily welcome assistance, support, and guidance in the care of their handicapped child. The United Cerebral Palsy (UCP) Association's National Collaborative Project recently published an interesting report of their national network of early intervention services. Although it appeared that many infants made considerable progress while in the programs, it was difficult to ascertain whether this progress exceeded what might have happened without intervention and was merely related to maturational changes (Meisel, 1977). Conducting controlled studies in situations such as this is complicated, since the subject population is quite heterogeneous. In the case of the UCP program, the most positive measurable impact was on the families who gave overwhelming support to the program, primarily because it helped them with their own problems (Schilling, 1977).

There are numerous studies showing developmental progress in children as a result of a variety of programs. Despite the methodological problems, there is evidence in these reports that certain intervention approaches have been effective. The following approaches have led to increased success in intervention:

1. Working with families or foster families is more effective than working with children alone (Schaeffer, 1975; Kass *et al.*, 1976)
2. Structured, goal-oriented programs using specific teaching materials appear to be more successful than unstructured programs (Bricker and Bricker, 1976; Shearer and Shearer, 1976; Schaeffer and Aaronson, 1972)
3. Improving the home environment and providing instructional materials

appear to help children's development (Levenstein, 1970; Kass *et al.*, 1976; Hayden and Haring, 1976)

4. It is quite useful to have reliable diagnostic data around which to design individual programs (Kass *et al.*, 1976; Scurletis, 1976)

5. It is best to intervene as soon as the disability is diagnosed than to wait very long to provide a program (Bronfenbrenner, 1974; Kirk, 1958, 1967).

There are, of course, pitfalls to early intervention. Sometimes it is unnecessarily used on infants who are prematurely diagnosed as being abnormal and who are then provided with a vigorous intervention program which may not have been necessary in the first place. There are some infants who are reported to have some abnormal findings, but who appear to spontaneously improve with maturation. Another concern is that some programs which utilize parents as therapists in treatment roles with their own handicapped child may produce increased tensions within families. These situations can stimulate guilt in some parents and can provoke increased anxiety and ambivalent feelings. There is also the concern that stimulation programs for children with brain dysfunction may produce adverse effects on their abnormal nervous system instead of helping to facilitate development.

The problem of evaluating early intervention programs continues to be a perplexing one. Although it is difficult to claim that intellectual level is raised and developmental progress is accelerated, it is more reasonable to accept that some of these programs help children to achieve their intellectual potential, while providing the important opportunity (and training) for acquisition or improvement of the social skills and behaviors which are so important for a normal life in our society.

Diagnostic Clinics   One area that is usually assumed to be relatively free of problems is that of clinics for children (or adults) which have been established in many communities to provide comprehensive diagnostic services for developmentally disabled children in a multidisciplinary or interdisciplinary setting. These clinics, as described earlier, are traditionally staffed with physicians (usually a pediatrician or pediatric neurologist), psychologists, social workers, special educators, and speech clinicians. Other consultants and specialists representing other disciplines are usually available.

There is growing evidence, however, that despite the comprehensive evaluations provided to clients/patients and their families, the net results may not be as positive as would be expected. There are indications that families are frequently confused by the multidisciplinary diagnostic process and by the information transmitted to them as the result of the evaluation. They report negative reactions concerning the manner in which they are informed about their child's problems by physicians in these clinics. Clinicians have learned to often discount parent's statements that ''the doctor never told me anything about my child.'' Statements such as this are usually attributed to denial or inattention on the parents' part. However, the studies of Lipton and Svarsted (1974) confirmed that parents seen in a large multidisciplinary diagnostic clinic had a very limited understanding of the respective roles of clinicians in the clinic, had inappropriate expectations about what was to be learned from the evaluation, and absorbed limited and only selected information that was conveyed to them. There must be some concern, therefore, that the clinics are giving children "the million dollar workup,'' but not helping families to fully understand the child's problem. Nor are they necessarily helping the child to understand his or her own problems. The usual practice is to ignore the child. This results in the kind of feelings reported by cerebral palsied adults at a workshop conducted by the American Academy of Cerebral Palsy, and reported by Richardson (1972). These adults report how they were ignored by doctors at clinics whose communications were primarily with parents. Communications with the handicapped individuals themselves, when they were children, were often inappropriate, depersonalizing, overprotective, or completely dehumanizing.

Service Linkages The problem of communication is not the only area of difficulty related to the diagnostic process. The other major failure is that diagnostic units are not sufficiently well integrated into other aspects of service delivery and treatment. Children diagnosed at clinics, which are usually hospital-based, are usually referred to public or private (voluntary) agency programs in other locations. The treatment program is rarely planned or initiated by the staff who diagnose the child, despite the fact that the latter staff usually formulate treatment recommendations as a result of their evaluation. The resultant interagency communication problems, geographical separation of services, and delays in implementation of recommendations all contribute to inadequate services for children and their families. The solution to this type of problem and to the inadequate linkages with service providers requires a breakdown of both the geographical barriers and the problems in communication. For example, hospital-based programs have little relevance to the public schools unless they provide consultations to school staff in the place where the children are being served in the schools. School staff must be invited to participate in the diagnostic process and exchange their views with other professionals. Finally, all involved professionals must improve their communications with each other, as well as with the families of the children they serve and with the children themselves.

New Approaches to Coordinating Services

One interesting method of serving specific groups of developmentally disabled individuals has been through contractual arrangements. Contracts for institutional services have been used as described by Nelson and Crocker (1978) and by Ziring in Chapter 5. Contracts for services to people living in the community, such as in group homes, are not uncommon. Generally, an arrangement is made with a local facility and health provider. One approach, which attempts to be more normalizing for clients/patients, is to arrange for them to receive comprehensive services from facilities or providers already available in the community. For example, we recently made arrangements for clients served by our state-supported university affiliated program, Bronx Developmental Services, to have our clients served in the Comprehensive Family Care Center operated by the Albert Einstein College of Medicine. Rather than hiring a separate group of physicians to provide the required health care (which had to be compatible with the standards mandated by the Willowbrook Consent Decree and include 24-hour medical coverage), we arranged a contract to provide access for our clients to the already existing Comprehensive Family Care Center's system of care. Funds from the contract enabled the Center to expand and enhance its own program, while providing the services our clients needed.

Unfortunately, one has to resort to special contracts for health services because of the limited availability or poor quality of general health care available to handicapped individuals in some communities. It may be normalizing to encourage the use of community facilities without making any special arrangements, but it is more pragmatic and more directly helpful to clients to arrange better services for them through specialized contractual arrangements with qualified, existing health care providers.

Relevant Recent Legislation and Court Actions Affecting Health Services

To achieve coordinated planning of health services in communities for everyone, including the developmentally disabled, one hope for the future is the National Health Planning and Resources Development Act of 1974 (PL 77-157). This law requires that Health Systems Agencies (HSA's) plan for new services and coordinate existing ones with both consumer and professional participation.

HSA's have already taken official positions calling for expanded prevention and early intervention services in the mental retardation field. However, the impact of HSA's has generally been quite limited. A federal General Accounting Office study (1978) of the status of implementation of PL 77-157 criticized the progress thus far achieved. The problems identified included:

1. HSA's lack adequate data to develop health systems plans.
2. HSA's lack qualified staff.
3. Local community groups, professionals, and governmental agencies and health care providers distrust the HSA's.
4. Federal facilities are not included in the act.
5. There are still jurisdictional disputes between HSA's and state planning agencies.

Another key piece of legislation that is having a significant impact on services for handicapped and retarded children and that has important health implications is the Education for All Handicapped Children Act, PL 94–142 (see Chapter 2). This legislation requires that public education programs or the equivalent be provided for all school-aged children. In some states, where state law permits, similar standards are set for 3- to 5-year-old children. The law requires that children be educated in the least restrictive environment possible, encourages mainstreaming efforts, insists that each child have an Individual Education Plan (IEP), and provides some federal funding as a stimulus for the overall implementation of the law's provisions.

One important problem area in PL 94–142 is the provision of health services. The regulations promulgated as a result of the law do not specify the need for medical input into the evaluation of the child or the implementation of the IEP. This is despite the fact that severely multiply handicapped children are now required to receive educational programs. These children, as well as many other developmentally disabled children, have extensive medical needs that must be met. It is ironic that pediatricians and some rehabilitation medicine specialists who were long devoted to the care of multiply handicapped children (and often with their staff, the only service providers, since schools did not usually accept these children in their programs), are now omitted from planning for these children's needs while they attend school.

Fortunately, some states have required medical participation in providing school services for the handicapped by law or by separate regulation. Furthermore, the medical community, particularly the American Academy of Pediatrics, is seeking greater participation of pediatricians in the implementation of PL 94–142, while at the same time strongly encouraging pediatricians to become more sophisticated in dealing with the problems of the handicapped child.

Another federal law having a major recent impact on health services is the Federal Rehabilitation Act. Section 504 of this act requires equal access for all handicapped individuals to all public facilities. The regulations relating to Section 504 were only recently published, after much debate and delay. In essence, this law will force programs receiving federal funds to make their facilities physically accessible to handicapped people and to ban any type of discrimination against handicapped persons which inhibits access to public services. Although there are problems in implementing this type of sweeping legislation, the long range result should be that physically and mentally handicapped people will find it easier to gain physical access to public facilities, including hospitals and clinics, and should have an equal opportunity to obtain other generic services in their communities.

Although federal legislation is influential on a national scale, it is important to recognize that state and local laws are also essential in achieving better health care and in making other needed services available to handicapped individuals. Many states have attempted to improve coordination of care for developmentally disabled persons. A decade ago, Connecticut established regional centers to coordinate local services. California also moved in this direction, while maintaining its large institutional and state hospital system. Only recently, California revised its laws and is attempting to improve the coordination of the regional centers with the state institutions, concomitantly increasing consumer input. Several states created separate Departments of Mental Retardation and/or Developmental Disabilities with the aim of focusing greater attention on and improving services for these handicapped populations. New York and Massachusetts are moving toward regional systems which attempt to link the state institutions to newly formed state-supported, community-based services and to the existing voluntary agency programs. The latter movement in New York was spurred by a federal court action, namely the Willowbrook Consent Decree.

Pressure from the courts has also been an important contributing factor in improving health services. The Willowbrook, Pennhurst, Alabama (*Wyatt* v. *Stickney*), and Nebraska (*Beatrice*) legal actions all have had a major impact on services in their respective states. These decisions and agreements not only set health standards for the institutions but, by accelerating deinstitutionalization and in attempting to monitor the fates of the former institutional clients, they also are establishing standards for mentally handicapped individuals living in the community. Once these standards are established, even though they may be minimal and applicable only to members of a particular "class" of former institutional clients, it is likely that they will be extended to others. In fact, legal actions have already been initiated to gain equal access to services for *people with similar handicaps who had never been institutionalized*.

Manpower and Training

In most communities, there appears to be an abundance of health-related generic professionals (physicians, nurses, psychologists, social workers, educators, etc.) who could serve the handicapped population. However, the major problem is that most of these professionals have had little or no training in the care of handicapped individuals. Those who received their professional training more than 15 years ago had practically no professional contact with severely handicapped people unless they at some point worked in a state institution for the mentally handicapped.

The goal of achieving comprehensive community care for the developmentally disabled by using existing generic services to the fullest extent possible could best be met by providing adequate training for the professionals providing these services. One approach would be to require that at least one specific time period be set aside for training all health professionals using a didactic approach coupled with a practicum of experience with handicapped people. This should be required during their training. Professionals already in practice could be offered postgraduate courses. Ideally, as much training as possible should occur in interdisciplinary settings with experienced professionals, such as are available in the national network of University Affiliated Facilities or Programs.

Specialized programs for handicapped persons require professionals and paraprofessionals with more extensive training and experience. This training should be interdisciplinary and tailored to the needs of the population of disabled clients/patients whom the professionals are being prepared to serve. For health professionals, this training must include experiences in developmental assessment, neuromuscular disorders, sensory deficits, and management of seizure disorders and other associated handicaps commonly found in handicapped patients.

There are particular areas of expertise that have generally been lacking in many communities. Training programs for nurse practitioners and community mental retardation nurses would be particularly useful in inner cities where it is difficult to obtain primary health care because of a shortage of physicians. In most communities, physical, occupational, or speech therapists with experience in working with the severely and profoundly retarded, multiply handicapped child or adult are also scarce. Training programs to teach these professionals techniques used in specialized feeding programs and the use of new adaptive equipment would be beneficial.

It would be helpful if there were some systematic studies of the need for specific health care personnel in the field of handicapping conditions. This data is currently lacking. However, we need not wait for studies to initiate educational programs to teach or at least sensitize health professionals about the health and social problems of the handicapped; action should be begun now.

CONCLUSION

The provision of health care for handicapped people is one of the many services in communities that are often inadequate. The ability of handicapped people to obtain generic health services may, therefore, be limited by the inadequacies of the general health system and also by exclusionary policies that affect them, plus inadequate training for most health professionals.

There is a clear need for specialized diagnostic and treatment services, including early identification efforts, and for follow-up care for the developmentally disabled. These are best provided in interdisciplinary settings. However, specialized clinics need to improve their methods of communication with families, and with the children themselves, in order to be more effective. In addition, there must be greater efforts to link diagnostic services to specialized and generic treatment programs and to coordinate services.

Clients/patients should not suffer from disjointed services because of poor communications among service providers.

In the face of new legislation requiring education for all handicapped children and improved access to services for all handicapped people, there is still a maze of federal, state, local, and private (insurance and self-pay) mechanisms for purchasing or funding services. The latter has created an array of uncoordinated and occasionally overlapping services which are quite difficult for most consumers to negotiate. Based on studies of the current patterns of service delivery, it is unlikely that there will be a more unified system of care until a national health care system is adopted and personal care services are consolidated within a single system of financial support. Furthermore, even if the patterns of financial support miraculously become more rational, satisfactory local planning and coordination of services with an effective system of advocacy and case management for clients will still be necessary.

Comprehensive health care for the handicapped population requires adequate funding, better coordination, improved education and training of health professionals, some alteration in professional attitudes, and the refinement of services based on a thorough analysis, careful scrutiny, and systematic evaluation of current practices.

REFERENCES

Abramowicz, H. K., and Richardson, S. A. 1973. Epidemiology of severe mental retardation in children: Community studies. *Amer. J. Mental Defic.* 80:18.

Boggs, E. M. 1971. Federal legislation. In J. Wortis (ed.), Mental Retardation, Vol. 3. Grune & Stratton, New York.

Bricker, W. A., and Bricker, D. D. 1976. The infant, toddler and preschool research project. In T. D. Tjossem (ed.), Intervention Strategies for High Risk Infants and Young Children. University Park Press, Baltimore.

Bronfenbrenner, U. 1974. Is Early Intervention Effective? A Report on Longitudinal Evaluation of Preschool Programs, Vol. II. Department of Health, Education and Welfare, Office of Human Development, Office of Child Development, Children's Bureau. (DHEW Publication No. OHD 76-30025), U.S. Government Printing Office, Washington, DC.

Conley, R. W. 1973. The Economics of Mental Retardation. Johns Hopkins University Press, Baltimore, MD.

General Accounting Office. 1978. Status of the Implementation of the National Health Planning and Resources Development Act of 1974. U.S. Government Printing Office, Washington, DC.

Hamilton, B. B., Betts, H. D., Rath, G. J., Gilette, H. E., Greene, G. M., Garrity, S. D., and Libman, A. S. 1978. A Study of the Medical and Allied Health Services Delivery System for Substantially Handicapped Disabled Adults: Chicago. Research Report R-26, Rehabilitation Institute of Chicago, Northwestern University, Chicago.

Hayden, A. H., and Haring, N. G., 1976. Early intervention programs for high risk infants and young children: Programs for Down's syndrome children. In T. D. Tjossem (ed.), Intervention Strategies for High Risk Infants and Young Children. University Park Press, Baltimore.

Hobbs, N. 1975. The Futures of Children. Jossey Bass, Washington, DC.

Kass, E. R., Sigman, M., Bromwich, R. F., and Parmalee, A. H. 1976. Educational intervention strategies with high risk infants. In T. D. Tjossem (ed.), Intervention Strategies for High Risk Infants and Young Children. University Park Press, Baltimore.

Kirk, S. A. 1978. Early Education of the Mentally Retarded. University of Illinois Press, Urbana.

Kirk, S. A. 1967. The effects of early education with disadvantaged children. In M. B. Karnes (ed.), Research and Development Program on Preschool Disadvantaged Children: Final Report U.S. Office of Education, U.S. Government Printing Office, Washington, DC.

Levinstein, P. 1970. Cognitive growth in preschoolers through verbal interactions with mothers. Amer. J. Orthopsychol. 40:426.

Lipton, H. L., and Svarsted, B. L. June 15, 1974. Parents' expectations of a multidisciplinary clinic for children with developmental disabilities. J. Health Soc. Behav., p. 15.

Meier, J. H. 1973. Screening and Assessment of Young Children at Developmental Risk. U.S. Government Printing Office, Washington, DC.

Meisel, J. 1977. A guide to program evaluation. In Programming for Atypical Infants and Their Families. Monograph #5, United Cerebral Palsy Association, National Collaborative Project to Provide Comprehensive Services for Atypical Infants and Their Families, New York.

Mental Retardation: Past and Present. Report of the President's Committee on Mental Retardation. (DHEW Publication No. OHD 77–21016), U.S. Government Printing Office, Washington, DC.

Methylphenidate (Ritalin) and other drugs for treatment of hyperactive children. Med. Lett. 19(13), 1977.

Millichap, J. G. 1973. Drug management of minimal brain dysfunction. In F. de la Cruz, B. H. Fox, and R. H. Roberts (eds.), Minimal Brain Dysfunction, p. 321. New York Academy of Sciences, New York.

Nelson, R. P., and Crocker, A. C. 1978. The medical care of mentally retarded persons in public residential facilities. NEJM 299:1039.

New York State Association for the Retarded v. Carey (Willowbrook), 393 F. Supp. 714 (E. D. New York, 1975). Consent Judgment, March 10, 1979.

New York State Department of Education Survey of School District Screening Programs, 1975.

Office of Mental Retardation and Developmental Disability. 1978. Five Year Comprehensive Plan for Services to Mentally Retarded and Developmentally Disabled Persons in New York State. Office of Mental Retardation and Developmental Disability, New York.

Richardson, S. A. 1972. People with cerebral palsy talk for themselves. Develop. Med. Child Neurol. 14:524.

Rutter, M., Graham, P., and Yule, W. 1970. A neuropsychiatric study in childhood. In Clinics in Developmental Medicine, Nos. 35/36. J. B. Lippincott, Philadelphia.

Schaeffer, E. S. 1975. Factors that impede the process of socialization. In M. Begab and S. A. Richardson (eds.), The Mentally Retarded and Society: A Social Science Perspective. University Park Press, Baltimore.

Schaeffer, E. S., and Aaronson, M. 1972. Infant education research project: Implementation and implications of the home tutoring program. In H. K. Parker (ed.), The Pre-School in Action, p. 410. Allyn and Bacon, Boston.

Schilling, M. 1977. Analysis of findings from the parent interviews. In Programming for Atypical Infants and Their Families, Monograph #3, United Cerebral Palsy Association, National Collaborative Project to Provide Comprehensive Services for Atypical Infants and Their Families, New York.

Scurletis, T. D., Headrick-Haynes, M., Turnbull, C. D., and Fallon, R. 1976. Comprehensive developmental health services: A concept and a plan. In T. D. Tjossem (ed.), Intervention Strategies for High Risk Infants and Young Children. University Park Press, Baltimore.

Shearer, D. E., and Shearer, M. S. 1970. The portage project: A model for early intervention. In T. D. Tjossem (ed.), Intervention Strategies for High Risk Infants and Young Children. University Park Press, Baltimore.

Solomons, G. 1973. Drug therapy: Initiation and follow-up. In F. de la Cruz, B. H. Fox, and R. H. Roberts (eds.), Minimal Brain Dysfunction, p. 335. New York Academy of Sciences, New York.

White House Conference on Children. 1970. Report to the President. U.S. Government Printing Office, Washington, DC.

Wright, S. W., Valente, M., and Tarjan, G. 1962. Medical problems on a ward of a hospital for the mentally retarded. *Amer. J. Diseases Child.* 104:142.

Chapter 5
Health Planning for Handicapped Persons in Residential Settings

Philip Ziring

There appears to be general agreement that the quality of health services available to most of our institutionalized handicapped citizens is substandard when compared to that available in the general community. The residents of institutional facilities, for whom the option to choose their doctors or types of health care given is not available, are generally required to live in an environment containing more hazards to health through infection, trauma or other causes than exist in the average community setting. Paradoxically, such facilities, instead of providing an extra measure of supportive health services, often seem to do the reverse. Residents are forced to endure shortages and maldistribution of health care personnel at all professional levels. The staff is often inadequately trained to deal with the complex problems such residents present and is isolated from gains being made in health care in the community as well.

The dramatic decline in the population of residential facilities for handicapped persons during the past 20 years has, unfortunately, not been matched by an extensive commitment by society at large to build health care programs to serve this population in the community. What is becoming apparent, furthermore, is that just as resources are being withdrawn from the support of the large residential facilities, the population remaining in these facilities contains an increasingly high percentage of severely or profoundly retarded individuals with complex neuromuscular disorders or behavioral disturbances, who have health care requirements far greater than those who have made a relatively easy transition to community living. There will have to be a clear and prompt recognition that this present population will not find community placement with great ease and will continue to need considerable financial and professional support to maintain health and promote their developmental potential.

This chapter is based, to some extent, on a review of the current literature on the subject, and on personal observations at a number of residential facilities for the mentally retarded. Primarily, however, it draws upon my recent experience as the Director of Health Services at an institution that was, until a few years ago, the largest public residential facility for retarded citizens in the United States.

THE SYSTEM: WHAT IT IS AND WHAT IT MIGHT BE

No consistent, organized approach to the delivery of health services in residential facilities for handicapped persons has emerged in this country despite decades of experiences which would appear to cry out for one. Particularly and conspicuously lacking until quite recently has been the involvement of major university medical centers in the delivery of direct health services and on-site training of their students at these facilities, despite many years of involvement with such institutions for purposes of clinical investigation.

The health care providers within the residential facilities are governed by sets of policies and regulations meant to be consistent with general practices advocated by a number of agencies such as the Joint Commission on Accreditation of Hospitals (ICF/MR standards). In actual practice, there appears to be considerable variation from these requirements because of the circumstances peculiar to the particular facility such as the density of the residential population, the characteristics of the physical plant, and the number and kinds of staff available to service the population. There are no published standards, for example, as to how many physicians are required to serve this population (or the backgrounds of such physicians). For example, given a population of 300 nonambulatory, profoundly retarded residents, many with seizures or other handicapping conditions, are two physicians too few or six physicians too many? What would be the potential role of physician extenders, such as nurse practitioners, with such clients? How many nurses would be required? What should be the ratio of trained registered physical therapists to such clients? The same questions may be asked of special education, recreation, psychology, and other disciplines. At present, approximately 40% of the professional staff's time is consumed doing "paperwork," attending conferences, and writing reports mandated by innumerable auditing groups. Such activities generally are not given adequate attention at the time of allocation of scarce resources.

The administration of residential facilities for handicapped persons was left, until quite recently, in the hands of physicians, frequently psychiatrists. It is still common for such facilities to be within the province of a state department of mental health. This is a reflection of the societal concept, now fortunately on the wane, that mentally handicapped citizens should be treated as "mentally sick," with its sad implication that developmental disability may respond to the treatment tools of the physician—drugs, neurological and other physical treatments, plus isolation in "hospitals" removed from the normal population.

The "Medical Model," in which the physician and his therapies were paramount, prevailed from the time of the creation of large public residential facilities, but gave way to a different approach termed the "Developmental Model" after disclosure of the often scandalous conditions of many such institutions in the late Sixties and early Seventies. In the opinion of many, the pendulum of such change seems to have swung too far in the other direction and medical opinion is given inadequate weight. At present, it is difficult to recruit or retain physicians trained in interdisciplinary settings to serve handicapped persons in the residential setting. Such facilities are generally unable to compete successfully in the marketplace for young, well trained, and motivated physicians because of the lure elsewhere of greater income, educational benefits, and opportunities to deal with serious acute medical problems and to have gratifying interpersonal relationships with patients. Furthermore, the lack of exposure to meaningful experiences with clients from such residential settings during medical school and postgraduate training is probably a major factor in the difficulty in recruiting new physicians. Those who may have been challenged professionally by this population are not trained to understand such individuals and what services they require. They often feel professionally at a loss to know what to do when they are confronted by retarded patients with major clinical problems, avoiding these patients if possible, and sometimes reacting with anger, frustration, or apathy. The result is that health professionals now engaged in full-time employment in such institutions are commonly drawn from the ranks of foreign medical graduates and older physicians who may have little predisposition or training to work within the framework of the Developmental Model. Interdisciplinary treatment teams preparing individual habilitation plans frequently encounter great resistance from such staff physicians who continue to struggle to preserve some traces of their former prestige and influence in a system determined to treat physicians "just like everybody else." Such resistance is further aggravated in those systems where physicians are supervised administratively and professionally by nonphysicians. The isolation that physicians ordinarily experience in such institutions from their peers in the community is thus further reinforced, making recruitment and retention of qualified physicians even more difficult.

The institutional health care system extends beyond the individual primary care physician providing health maintenance and the management of acute and chronic illness in the client's living unit. There frequently is a secondary level of care in the form of special wards in a "medical-surgical" building, and tertiary care at hospitals in the community. There appears to be growing disenchantment with such secondary care programs when they require close monitoring of seriously ill patients. Many facilities are increasing relationships with community hospitals that can now serve the needs of patients too sick to care for in institutions no longer equipped with the modern technology necessary to deliver medical care on a par with that available in the community. This, in turn, presents additional problems needing resolution. Institutional physicians run the risk of letting their clinical skills atrophy unless they maintain attending appointments for continuing medical education at teaching hospitals in the community, whereas the community hospitals are generally ill equipped to manage impulsive and/or aggressive mentally retarded adults who may have known only the inside of an institution for the preceding 20 to 30 years. Although the hospital personnel may have excellent medical skills, they may be required to make well-considered new decisions because of the nature of the patient's developmental handicap that they would not have to consider in the average community patient. Repairing a hernia or removing a cataract is usually many times more complex in a mentally retarded client from a residential facility than it is in the patient admitted from the community. Physicians, nurses, attendants, and other personnel of community hospitals and major medical centers need considerable training and preparation to successfully serve clients coming out of developmental centers at the present time. Formerly, such conditions were generally managed in the facility's own medical-surgical building (or not treated at all). Now, these clinical problems are coming to the attention of community health care providers in greater numbers and are not yet being dealt with effectively, either medically or with respect to reimbursement.

Although the present system of health care in residential settings could be characterized as disorganized, unresponsive, and in a state of flux, a better system could be set in motion to provide the necessary services in a cost-effective manner. Primary health care could be provided by fewer physicians than are now employed if these physicians could be provided with the proper training and motivation to participate in interdisciplinary treatment team efforts. Physician efficiency could be enhanced by the addition of physician extenders such as nurse practitioners and physician assistants. Appropriate linkages with teaching hospitals in the community should be encouraged. This would enhance recruitment and retention of qualified physicians and would eliminate the isolation of institution-based physicians from their colleagues in the community (for surely both sides have much to learn from each other). In addition, these team efforts would go far in removing the now prevalent stigma of the institutional physician as a second-class practitioner. Assignment of faculty from university medical centers to assist in service delivery as well as training of professional and direct care staff would further enhance the quality of health care in the facilities.

The secondary care level which should be provided on the campus of the residential facility should be limited to provision of those services which the facility is the best position to provide. These include the management of disorders of a subacute or chronic nature that represent special problems—intractable seizure disorders, special rehabilitation programs after orthopedic surgery, or other similar conditions. The staff of such facilities have a better understanding of the needs of handicapped clients with special problems. Staff is generally more motivated to serve handicapped clients, because they have a personal stake in a successful outcome. The easier management of such clients is its own reward, and a successful outcome provides a measure of job security in a period when the resident census of residential facilities is declining. Of equal importance is its cost effectiveness. Attempting to provide such services in an acute care hospital would be far more costly because of the prolonged length of stay required and the high per diem reimbursement rates obtained from third party payors. On the other hand, maintaining intensive care medical services for seriously ill patients on the grounds of such institutions is probably wasteful and inefficient, because equal or superior medical facilities are conveniently located in the community and are specifically maintained for this purpose. In this era of scarce resources, maintaining such a facility in the institution, with its attendant cost of expensive round-the-clock personnel of physicians, nurses, lab technicians, and others, together with maintenance of expensive equipment, is difficult to justify.

Tertiary care medical services should always be available to clients of residential facilities at sophisticated medical centers in the community. Formal arrangements should be made wherever feasible to insure accessibility to these services by handicapped clients. Benefits accrue to the staffs of institution and medical center alike, with opportunities to visit and learn from experiences at the related facility. Students from a variety of disciplines at the medical center should be encouraged to participate in a full range of learning experiences at the residential setting, both because they benefit in learning of the needs of such clients, and because the staff of the facility is challenged by the probing questions of students in training. A further benefit which is frequently overlooked is the morale boost given to the facility staff who are often informed by visiting faculty and students alike that they are generally much better informed about the management of some of these difficult clients than the visitors from the university. Successful integration of clients from an institutional setting into a unit of a major medical center will be markedly facilitated by interchanges of this type.

A component of health care that is frequently lacking in institutional health care services is provision for outpatient care once transfer of the client to the community has taken place. Given the many impediments to the client's access to quality health care in the community (*e.g.*, local private physician's unfamiliarity with management of mentally retarded persons, reluctance to integrate them with other patients in the physician's private practice, generally low and uncertain reimbursement for outpatient medical services from government insurance plans, requirements to fill out numerous forms to be in compliance with governmental policies), the development of comprehensive health care services which would follow the client from the institution to the community appears to be an important and still unmet need. Until such services are readily available in the community for such clients, general medical, mental health, dental, and related services should be made available by the residential facility, albeit in some site remote from the institution itself. Until such services are made available, clients and the caretakers in the community will have to put up with generally inadequate and fragmented health services with the probable result, in many cases, of return to the institution for reasons related to medical and/or behavioral problems.

ESTABLISHING A DATA BASE IN PLANNING HEALTH SERVICES IN RESIDENTIAL SETTINGS

In 1966, there were 213,000 residents in 108 institutions for mentally retarded persons in the United States. Although this population had declined to 168,000 by 1975 and represented less than 5 percent of all mentally handicapped persons in the United States, it was still supported by approximately two-thirds of all public funds spent on mentally retarded citizens. As deinstitutionalization proceeds, the residents who are last to leave the facilities are those whose needs are most complex. Of the approximately 1,500 clients still living at the Staten Island Developmental Center in New York City (more than 6,200 persons were residents there in 1965), 85 percent have IQ scores in the severely to profoundly retarded range, approximately 20 percent are nonambulatory, and the remainder often have other complex handicapping conditions such as severe vision and hearing impairment and/or behavior disturbances requiring special programmatic support. Such persons will be especially difficult to transfer to the community until there is the ready availability of health systems that can provide care which is at least as good as that available at the institution. Few ventures into community placement of such individuals as yet have taken place. The data derived from their experiences will help to determine the human service and financial needs required to make such programs in the community viable. For the moment, therefore, it appears that the pace of community placement of the developmentally disabled from large institutional settings may be slowing down and probably will not pick up again with the desired goal of reduction in numbers of residents and closing of many institutions. In planning for health services in institutional settings in the 1980's, it would be important to obtain data on the number of such multihandicapped individuals, their age, and character of their impairment and severity. Obtaining such information will be no easy task. Institutions, which were responsible for custodial care and management of acute illness over many years, frequently do not have diagnostic information about subacute and chronic conditions readily available. For clients who have been residents of institutions for 20 years or more, the historical records are quite voluminous, but rarely portray the true strengths, weaknesses, and needs of the client with accuracy. Although the task would be monumental, revision of client records and summaries of important and relevant clinical information would have to be provided and analyzed with modern data-processing techniques before planning for the future health needs of clients in residential settings can take place. It also should be borne in mind that assessment of each client will have to be performed by an interdisciplinary team, including physicians, dentists, audiologists, speech pathologists, physical therapists, optometrists, and others. Simple reliance on the physicians' notes will doubtless provide only limited, if not inaccurate, information, because physicians are charged mainly with health maintenance and management of acute illness, leading to underreporting of the client's impairments in vision, hearing, speech, ambulation, and other functional areas.

Once the population of the residential facilities has been characterized in this fashion, it may be possible to determine what health care resources would be required to service the population. It then would be necessary either to identify programs now providing quality health services in residential settings in a cost-effective manner or to establish pilot programs to provide this service in order to establish what constitutes effective, appropriate, and financially sound service for this population in the 1980's. At the present time there is wide variation from institution to institution in the numbers and types of health care personnel to serve institutionalized handicapped individuals. It would make sound fiscal and programmatic sense to establish minimal standards for servicing this population so that present waste, inefficiency, and bureaucratic wrangling over clinical positions between facilities can be reduced to a minimum. Experiments in health care delivery should be conducted using new kinds of health personnel such as nurse practitioners and mental health technicians in such settings to determine whether better services may be produced at lower costs. Arrangements for special services should be sought with university teaching hospitals for provision of consultant and teaching services at the institution and development of special clinical programs for handicapped persons at the medical center. Such innovations are presently being tried in a few residential facilities, but their scope and number need to be expanded to determine their potential impact on services in residential settings in the next decade.

An important part of this projected data collection should be surveys of economic, educational, and attitudinal factors among health practitioners in residential facilities for handicapped persons as well as among their peers in the community. The results of such surveys would aid in drawing up appropriate plans for recruitment and retention of new kinds of health care personnel. Interdisciplinary training programs on developmental disabilities for health care providers in various disciplines need to be developed and promoted for institutional settings beyond what is now available at the University Affiliated Facilities (UAF's). Some UAF's have taken up this challenge, but thus far their numbers are few. Interdisciplinary training for health professionals and direct care personnel is fundamental to the UAF mission and a major commitment toward an association between regional UAF's and residential facilities for the developmentally disabled should be given high priority in planning for the 1980's.

INTEGRATING ROLES OF PUBLIC AND PRIVATE SECTORS

With the decline in the agrarian economy in the United States and simultaneous expansion of the technologically oriented cities, the state increasingly assumed responsibility for the long term residential management of complex handicapped persons. So long has this gone on that institutions where these individuals lived out their years developed a culture of their own, in an isolation enforced by a society persuaded that these people were deviant and even dangerous if permitted too much egress into the community at large. In this increasingly more enlightened era in which we find ourselves, it becomes more and more important to establish new services of many types in the community which, in many ways, the personnel of the residential facilities are in the best position to organize and staff. Such staff too often are overlooked as a major resource in the development of programs in a community lacking both experience and expertise with this population. The time has come for a marriage to take place between persons intimately knowledgeable about the characteristics of the clients of developmental centers and persons in the community knowledgeable about community resources and hopefully without preconceived and pessimistic notions about the capabilities of long term residents of these institutions. Ideally, this marriage should take place in a stepwise fashion with exposure of each side to the life and culture of the other before transfer of clients into the community. Nowhere is this more important than in the area of health services. Appropriate, in-depth training opportunities must be made available to all students in the health professions at all levels of training on the developmental center campus. At the same time, similar experiences must be made available to institutional personnel. Not surprisingly, such a scheme will probably meet resistance on both sides, despite its obvious desirability. Thorough discussion regarding attitudes, benefits, and disadvantages to be overcome must take place before beginning such relationships and should be an ongoing process to insure some measure of success.

In the field of health care, the private sector is probably the most difficult to involve in institutions for handicapped persons. Private practitioners, especially, have little financial need or incentive to become interested in this population, and the paperwork they must face when they do become involved only serves as a deterrant. The mentally retarded client with a state Medicaid card is simply unable to compete for access to care with his more financially independent fellow citizens in the community. Outpatient clinics in hospitals are more prepared administratively to deal with such patients, but the complex services such clients need from numerous hospital professionals virtually guarantee the hospital a fiscal loss every time such a client comes for an outpatient visit. Ambulatory care programs in most teaching hospitals are already a fiscal drain to the hospital's resources; therefore, it is not surprising to view their great reluctance to serve clients who would only accelerate this financial hemorrhage. There is even little comfort in the prospect that such outpatient visits may help to generate more lucrative inpatient days, since the amount of nursing, medical, social service and other expensive personnel such clients need also does not serve as an incentive to become involved. Little wonder, then, that the private sector has shown such little interest in becoming involved with handicapped clients and prefers them to be cared for, by and large, out of general tax revenues by the State.

Obviously, should this situation be perpetuated, it is bound to seriously cripple the deinstitutionalization movement. Clearly, some form of financial incentive or subsidy must be provided by the State if it is going to attract the attention of the private health sector and make quality health services, on a par with the standards of the community at large, available to its clients. Over the long term, with the inevitability of some form of National Health Insurance and some experience in dealing successfully with this population and the State bureaucracy which administers services for clients in residential settings, such subsidies may be withdrawn. For the moment, however, fiscal reality mandates that some form of state support, most efficiently on a regional basis, should be provided to major teaching hospitals and high quality community health care agencies to insure access to the kind of health care that has been denied these clients for so long.

Overseeing the operation of this partnership will be a major responsibility and difficult challenge. Each side, public and private, has been a stranger, if not an adversary, of the other for so long that it will take some time to build a stable, trusting relationship while maintaining accountability. There will have to be agreement from the beginning on the different missions and perspectives on each side. For example, the institution's primary mission is client services and deinstitutionalization, whereas the university medical center's primary concern is in training health care professionals; service is a necessary by-product. A most difficult question to be answered is which side should pay for the service and training. The answer will have to be forthcoming from the highest levels of government which are responsible for serving the handicapped.

Evaluating the effectiveness of the partnership between public and private sectors must be an ongoing process monitored by consumer and parent groups, legislative bodies, governmental agencies at various levels, such as Medicaid, private agencies such as Joint Commission on Accreditation of Hospitals, and in many instances, the courts. There must be enough flexibility built into the review process of the system to permit change to accommodate client need. Measureable parameters and program goals should be established at the outset to insure accountability. Such tangible parameters should include aspects of the training as well as service programs, with improvement in access to quality health care and improved health of the client remaining the overall program goal.

EFFECT OF LEGISLATION ON PLANNING HEALTH SERVICES IN INSTITUTIONAL SETTINGS

Legislative initiatives at the federal and state level have brought both problems and progress to institutional health services. For example, Title XIX of the Social Security Act brought new sources of federal funds to hard-pressed state institutions in return for agreement to adhere to sets of standards for health services. The Utilization Review and Independent Professional Review programs continually audit such facilities for compliance with federal regulations. At least one force behind the deinstitutionalization movement has been the inability of certain facilities to comply with certain aspects of these regulations because of the age of their physical plants. Renovation and construction costs in some cases are so prohibitive that complete compliance with architectural aspects of the codes would be impractical. Other legislation requiring physicians' participation in development of individual habilitation plans for each client also have frequently been met by resistance. Physician complaints of too much paperwork, insufficient stenographic support, and inequitable treatment by the interdisciplinary team and administration are commonly heard, and although such complaints may have some merit, they often represent resentment of the decline in the medical model, loss of a personal power base, and inadequate training and motivation to deal with the complex new system being imposed.

New legislative efforts dealing with improving access to quality health care for handicapped persons is long overdue. Legislative support for programs training new health professionals for institutional and community settings serving the developmentally disabled and legislation which takes into account the especially high health care costs such individuals generate in inpatient and outpatient hospital settings as well as in the institutions themselves would go far toward improving the climate of health care for developmentally disabled individuals.

ROLE OF THE COURTS

In April 1975, Governor Carey of the State of New York signed a Consent Agreement concluding a landmark class action suit brought in federal court by a number of groups representing the residents of the Willowbrook Developmental Center. Perhaps more than any other single factor, the involvement of the court in the day-to-day operation of the institution has brought about more change at a faster pace in this facility than any other. Among other things, the document specifies in detail the numbers and types of employees the institution must have on site at all times, the types and duration of programs it must make available to the clients, and further specifies that the institution must be reduced to a population of 250 clients or fewer by 1981. Millions of dollars and countless hours of thousands of individuals have been spent in an attempt to comply with the terms of the Court Decree with considerable, albeit incomplete, success. From the health care point of view, the decree has meant reducing the crowded, unhygienic conditions of the institution, a process which had been set in motion several years previously when the institution was closed to any new admissions. There has been a prompt decline and virtual disappearance of serious infectious diseases. More medical, nursing, and direct care staff have been hired, who give more individual attention to the clients. Every client has been mandated to receive 6 hours of programming daily, regardless of level of function or disability, enhancing the sense of well being and improving skills in activities of daily living for many. On the other hand, the consent decree created a new set of problems for the health care providers in the institution. Few physicians knowledgeable about institutional health care provided input to the court for the final version of the decree. The result was that the medically related portions of the document were written from a layman's view of what should be done about medical care; thus, an important opportunity for major health care reform within an institutional setting may have been missed. The present staff of the institution devotes a major amount of time to documenting efforts to comply with the terms of the consent decree while simultaneously, with the remaining time available, working on the development of major new health initiatives and programs which demand urgent attention, and that were not considered in the decree. Examples of the latter are new programs developed with major medical centers in the community to deal with the comprehensive management of clients with severe neuromuscular impairment, comprehensive management of mentally retarded clients with severe maladaptive behaviors, and development of a comprehensive ambulatory care program.

On balance, the consent decree has had an unquestionably positive impact on the lives of the residents of the institution. It, in turn, has led to a succession of similar court actions around the country. In general, the institutional system is ill prepared to deal with the demands of the courts, and significant resources must be devoted in the future to assist the staffs of the state facilities and senior management personnel to bring about the necessary changes required by the courts in expeditious fashion.

IMPACT OF NEWS MEDIA

The revelations of some of the deplorable conditions at Willowbrook in the late 1960's and early 1970's on television ended the public's ability to avoid facing up to its responsibilities to thousands of handicapped citizens. The public outcry that followed the news stories led to various legislative investigations and ultimately to the class action suit resulting in the Willowbrook Consent Judgment. Almost more than any other group, the physicians working at Willowbrook have borne the brunt of the media assault. They were accused of being ineffective senior administrators, of prescribing excessive amounts of psychoactive drugs and conducting unethical research, and it was they who were accused of sitting idly by while residents lived under unspeakably horrid conditions. The physicians were tried and convicted in the media, with the result that many skillful, ethical, and compassionate physicians were irrevocably traumatized by the experience. Remnants of the distrust and suspicion regarding all physicians in the institution persist on the part of other employees, consumer groups, and court representatives. The result has been a continuing stigma attached to serving as a health care professional in the institution, making recruitment and retention of high quality personnel most difficult.

It is readily apparent that dealing effectively with the news media is an important aspect of planning for health services in institutional settings. Having a positive influence on public opinion is especially important as deinstitutionalization programs proceed, requiring a high degree of cooperation of personnel from the institution, consumer groups, legislators, and court representatives. It is most important that representatives of the news media be properly informed of all relevant issues regarding present day management of the handicapped both in institutional settings as well as in the community so that they can help the public make intelligent, informed decisions.

A MAJOR MEDICAL CHALLENGE TO DEINSTITUTIONALIZATION

In the days when Willowbrook was still open to new admissions and clients were crowded together (often several hundred in a single building) under conditions of inadequate supervision and unsanitary hygiene, viral hepatitis was an endemic disease. Within a few short months after admission, the clients contracted the disease in a spectrum ranging from totally subclinical and inapparent, to fulminant with rapidly progressive liver failure and death. So rampant was the problem that an entire ward was set aside for employees who contracted the disease. It has been demonstrated that there were really two forms of viral hepatitis in the institution—infectious (now known as type A) and serum (now known as type B) hepatitis. The efficacy of gamma globulin was also demonstrated to be helpful in attenuating the disease. With improved hygienic measures, reduction in the census, and halting of all new admissions (usually susceptible) to the facility, hepatitis gradually disappeared from the institution as an acute illness. In fact, there has not been a single new case of hepatitis type A or B in a resident at Willowbrook in approximately 4 years. Blood tests now available reveal that the entire client population is virtually immune to both types A and B hepatitis.

Within recent years, the existence of the chronic hepatitis B antigen carrier state has been demonstrated in some patients who appear to have had full clinical recovery from the infection but for some as yet undefined reason have not developed antibody (immunity) to the disease. In these clients, the presence of the hepatitis B surface antigen (HBAg) has been demonstrated in the blood with great regularity. In many individuals, this carrier state can persist for years and perhaps for a lifetime. It has been found to be very prevalent in many countries around the world where there are crowded and relatively unsanitary living conditions. For example, the carrier state in India has been estimated to be as high as 25 percent. At Willowbrook the carrier state affects approximately 15 percent of the population, although in clients with Down's syndrome, the carrier rate is approximately 30 percent. The carrier rate in the general population of blood donors in the community is about 3 per thousand, whereas the carrier rate among drug addicts, male homosexuals, and other high risk groups is much higher.

Because of the concern for eradicating hepatitis at Willowbrook, clients who are immune, susceptible, or carriers had been identified within a short time after the blood tests to establish this condition became available. Their immune status was noted in their records and was forwarded to appropriate agencies at the time of transfer of the resident to a community setting. In 1977, a teacher in a public school on Staten Island, where 3 carriers from Willowbrook attended classes, contracted hepatitis. Soon, Willowbrook found itself again embroiled in controversy, and eventually, in another court case involving the right of retarded children from Willowbrook, who happened to be HBAg carriers, to attend public schools in the community together with their peers. The outcome of this case is still pending. The facts before the court are straightforward, although difficult on which to base a firm, informed decision. It was learned, for example, that the form of hepatitis that the teacher contracted was type A (not characterized by a carrier state) and had nothing whatever to do with the presence of the Willowbrook children in the school. At the present time, and for the past several years, approximately 44 children who are HBAg positive have been attending public schools in "integrated" classes without a single clinical case of hepatitis B reported in their classmates or teachers. In addition, no cases have been reported from any group home, hostel, or other community program where carriers are living. Furthermore, at Willowbrook itself, where more than 200 carriers still reside and come into daily, intimate contact with susceptible employees, not a single case of clinical or subclinical hepatitis B has occurred in more than 1,100 employees followed serologically for the past 2 years. On the other hand, the New York City Board of Education and the New York City Health Department maintain that because there must be *some* risk to susceptibles from the exposure to hepatitis B carriers in the classroom, special precautions be taken to minimize the possibility of transmission to as great an extent as possible. What seems to be clear thus far is that a community classroom for retarded children bears very little similarity to the crowded Willowbrook ward in the period when acute hepatitis was endemic and that acute hepatitis B is far more contagious an infection than the hepatitis B carrier state. At this moment, the court is still undecided as to whether hepatitis B carriers must be segregated in classes unto themselves (making appropriate educational programming exceedingly difficult) or whether the true risk of transmission is so small that the harm done to the carrier through segregation far outweighs the potential risk and hazard of the spread of the infection to a susceptible individual.

A hepatitis B vaccine is now being field tested and appears to be both safe and effective in conferring immunity to recipients in a high percentage of cases. Until it is licensed (perhaps in about 2 years) and made available to groups considered to be at special risk, the management of the hepatitis B antigen carrier coming out of the institutions for the retarded may pose a special problem. Some state facilities for the retarded appear to have deliberately chosen not to get involved in a testing program to identify their carriers in order to insure successful transfer of clients to the community without undue or unnecessary resistance. With hepatitis B carriers all around us in the general population, but never identified because they have never had their blood tested, client advocates argue it would be a violation of the civil rights of mentally retarded persons to single them out for special treatment simply because they are retarded and from an institutional setting.

Coming to grips with the problem of management of the mentally retarded hepatitis B antigen carrier is a difficult problem without an easy solution at the present time. The least one can do is to make informed decisions based on the facts regarding each specific case, and to inform the lay public with the knowledge at hand. Developing a consistent approach to this issue nationwide as it relates to developmentally disabled individuals is an important concern at the present time. Not dealing with it promptly and effectively may result in a serious setback to the deinstitutionalization movement.

SUMMARY

It is important that while planning for health services for the developmentally disabled in institutional settings, that positive opportunities for service and training be realized together with the major problems confronting us daily. It may yet be possible to change the image of the institution for severely developmentally disabled individuals from a place shunned by all but the most devoted personnel to one which can be recognized as providing new and exciting challenges for many health care professionals in the next decade.

SELECTED READINGS

Kanner, L. 1964. A History of the Care and Study of the Mentally Retarded. 1971. Charles C. Thomas, Springfield, IL.

Lengthening Shadows. 1971. Report of the Council on Pediatric Practice. American Academy of Pediatrics, Evanston, IL.

Mental Retardation: Past and Present. 1977. Report of the President's Committee on Mental Retardation, DHEW Publication No. (OHD) 77-21016. Government Printing Office, Washington, DC.

Nelson, R. P., and Crocker, A. C. 1978. The medical care of mentally retarded persons in public residential facilities. NEJM 299:1039-1044.

Scheerenberger, R. C. 1976. Public Residential Services for the Mentally Retarded. National Association of Superintendents of Public Residential Facilities for the Mentally Retarded, Madison, WI.

Standards for Residential Facilities for the Mentally Retarded. 1971. Accreditation Council for Facilities for the Mentally Retarded, Joint Commission on Accreditation of Hospitals, Chicago.

Wolfensberger, W. 1972. The Principle of Normalization in Human Services. National Institute on Mental Retardation, Toronto, Ontario.

Chapter 6

Rehabilitation Planning

William Kiernan

The word rehabilitation is derived from the Latin verb "habeo," meaning to live with; the prefix "re," implying a returning or going back; and the suffix "tion," denoting a process of. In looking at the entire word the concept of *a process of going back or returning to a level of living* is clear. For some handicapped individuals the term rehabilitation clearly means a returning process, one which helps that individual regain a lost capacity, whereas for others a continued learning process toward greater independent functioning is implied. This latter process is more frequently referred to as *habilitation,* the former, *rehabilitation*. The distinction between habilitation and rehabilitation is becoming less significant both legislatively and programmatically.

The present chapter looks at the scope of rehabilitation services for the disabled adult from a legislative, administrative, and clinical perspective. Recent changes in legislation have required major modifications in service delivery systems from the point of view of eligibility determination and the range of mandated services. From the point of view of the service provider, there is a need for new models of service delivery, new technologies for training, and vastly increased manpower resources at both the direct care and professional levels. The professional guidelines which were prevalent in the past are slowly disappearing, leading to the development of interdisciplinary team approaches to both evaluation and training. Finally, the advocacy movement has provided an opportunity for the handicapped individual to play a greater part in his or her rehabilitation process. These changes have had a major impact upon the process of planning for a comprehensive rehabilitation system during the past decade.

HISTORICAL OVERVIEW OF VOCATIONAL REHABILITATION

Although the terms used to describe the concept of rehabilitation may change periodically, the actual practice of rehabilitation can be traced back many years. In the United States this history begins in 1863 with the recognition of the need to provide services to crippled children represented by the charter of the Hospital for the Ruptured and Crippled in New York. Much of the early emphasis in rehabilitation was directed toward the employment components of the life cycle of disabled individuals. There always had been a recognition that disabled persons needed assistance; however, it was not until 1917 and the passage of the Smith Hughes Act that actual national legislation was enacted to assist in the rehabilitation process. This act provided federal financial assistance for vocational education to certain states which met specified requirements, developed a detailed state plan reflecting how this federal money was to be spent, and appointed a state board to monitor developing vocational programs. This act brought to the forefront the concept of specific vocational training for disabled persons.

The Smith Hughes Act was followed 1 year later by the Soldiers Rehabilitation Act which had, as its main thrust, services to disabled veterans. Disabled veterans who were unable to carry on a gainful occupation, to resume former occupations, or to enter upon some other occupation were considered eligible for specific training services. The prescribed services were directed solely at achievement of a gainful occupation for disabled veterans. However, this was soon changed to allow disabled civilians to be eligible as well. As a result of this federal initiative, individual states were encouraged to develop their own rehabilitation programs. Although there was general enthusiasm and a realization that the country had an obligation to its disabled service men, it was 35 years after the passage of the Soldiers Rehabilitation Act that all states and territories had a rehabilitation program.

Little innovative programming beyond the thrust toward employment was seen in rehabilitation during these early years. The Randolph Sheppard Act of 1936, which further emphasized the vocational and employment aspects of rehabilitation, took note of the fact that in some instances there was a need for certain disabled persons to receive preferential treatment, particularly when seeking employment. Federally sponsored individual proprietorships under the vendor stand section of this legislation promoted not only employment but also ownership of enterprises by the blind.

It was not until the Second World War that the role of the disabled worker emerged as a significant force in the industrialized United States. With the manpower shortage and the increased demand for production of both domestic and war materials, industry became acutely aware of the need to employ those who in the past were felt to be either unemployable or at high risk. Before World War II there was little incentive for industry to look at the disabled individual as a potential employee because of the abundant supply of nondisabled workers. With the war effort, industry was not only encouraged but required to employ disabled persons. Again, because of the shortage in the labor force, industry became much more willing to modify the working environment to accommodate disabled persons.

With the passage of the Vocational Rehabilitation Act of 1943 (PL 78–113), mentally handicapped and mentally ill persons were considered eligible for rehabilitation services. This signaled a change in the direction of rehabilitation programs across the country. For the first time there was a recognition of the need for services, not only for those who had been employed but were unable to retain employment because of injury, but also for those who had never been employed and needed assistance in obtaining employment. Although the emphasis on gainful occupation clearly remained the ultimate goal of the rehabilitation process, it began to be recognized that the rehabilitation effort was not solely a relearning or retraining process but, in some instances, a continuous learning process.

The Vocational Rehabiliation Amendments of 1954 (PL 83–565) reflected another major shift in the rehabilitation movement. These amendments had sweeping changes in the financial provisions, professional training, and expansion of service resources. Research and demonstration projects directed at developing better rehabilitation technologies and greater dissemination of findings were central to this law. Training of professionals through the use of long and short term training services, in-service training programs, and fellowships brought the resources of higher education in closer contact with the world of rehabilitation.

The most sweeping change of all in the area of rehabilitation emerged with the passage of PL 89–333, the Vocational Rehabilitation Act Amendments of 1965. These amendments expanded the eligibility criteria to include all types of disabled persons, with specific emphasis upon services to severely handicapped persons. Although, as in past legislation, an emphasis upon gainful employment remained, the definition of gainful employment was now broadened to include not only competitive but sheltered employment as well. In order to determine eligibility for vocational rehabilitation services only a reasonable expectation of gainful employment was required; extended 6- to 18-month evaluation periods were employed to determine eligibility of the severely handicapped applicant. With the recognition that certain environments could limit employment options for disabled persons, this law established the National Commission on Architectual Barriers. This commission looked at building accessibility and for the first time acknowledged that rehabilitation does not necessarily always mean a retraining of the individual but might, in certain instances, mandate an alteration of the environment to meet the individual's needs.

HISTORICAL OVERVIEW OF VOCATIONAL EDUCATION

Rehabilitation services are provided not just through the efforts of the state rehabilitation agency but through local educational associations as well. Vocational education programs have, in some instances, worked in concert with rehabilitation programs, whereas, in other instances, vocational education services have set up a parallel service delivery system.

From a historical perspective, vocational education has had a developmental sequence similar to that of vocational rehabilitation. Although both programs historically shared the goal of getting the individual into the labor market, vocational education accomplished its goals through a mixture of academic education and vocational education, whereas vocational rehabilitation focused in on those individuals whose skills were affected by a disability. Vocational education had long been recognized as a major right through the Tenth Amendment. The Morrill Act of 1882 first recognized that vocational education should be a part of the educational system of each state by granting land to develop vocational education colleges. Societies such as the National Society for the Promotion of Industrial Education, founded in 1906, have encouraged the development of vocational education programs nationwide. It was not until 1958, with the passage of the National Defense Education Act, that vocational education became a major contributor to training in the technological and scientific fields. As a result of the Vocational Education Act of 1963, all persons had to be provided with the opportunity to receive training or retraining in appropriate areas for which there was potential for employment. With the passage of the Vocational Education Amendments of 1968 (PL 90-576), consideration for training in the vocational education system was given to persons with physical and mental handicaps. At least 10% of all state allotments under the Vocational Education Amendments had to be directed towards programs for the handicapped.

The vocational education legislation of the 1970's has made little alteration in the basic vocational education program as stated by PL 90-576. There continues to be an emphasis on the "hard to reach and hard to teach" students, with clear preference for the disabled student. The Education Amendments of 1976 (PL 94-482) require that there be a consolidation of programs with a continued emphasis upon serving the disabled student.

From this brief historical review it is apparent that the major thrust of both the vocational rehabilitation and vocational education legislation has been directed at the needs of the less disabled who could render or return to society what society has invested in their rehabilitation on a financial basis. This cost-conscious approach to human services has more recently given way to an ethical and moral view of society's obligation to all handicapped persons and not just a few. This shift has been typified legislatively by the mandatory education laws at the state level as well as the federal Education for All Handicapped Children Act of 1975 (PL 94-142) (see Chapter 2), the rights of handicapped persons as stated in Section 504 of the Rehabilitation Amendments of 1973, and the new Comprehensive Rehabilitation Services Amendments of 1978. Regulations at all levels are endorsing the rights of all handicapped persons to receive training and services in the least restrictive environment possible with the ultimate goal of assisting handicapped persons to function as close to normal as possible. It is becoming apparent that the services which were granted to handicapped persons during the early years are now being viewed, not as a privilege, but as society's obligation.

DEFINITION OF HANDICAPPED AND REHABILITATION

Through these legislative initiatives a number of major issues have emerged with regard to defining the handicapped population, and determining the magnitude of the population to be served, the scope of the need, and how the services should be organized, coordinated, and administrated. The questions of definition have been a long standing dilemma, as demonstrated by the recent trend to move away from the categorical approach to both program and legislation toward a functional classification system; a system which looks at actual capacity and not solely diagnosis.

The Rehabilitation Amendments of 1973 placed a major emphasis upon the provision of services to the severely handicapped individual. In an attempt to define the term "severely handicapped" more clearly, the law reverted to a modified categorical approach. This approach recognized the extended duration and increased complexity of the needs of a severely handicapped person which necessitated multiple services over an extended period of time. The definition in the act notes that these limitations may result from amputations, blindness, cancer, cerebral palsy, cystic fibrosis, deafness, heart disease, hemiplegia, mental retardation, mental illness, multiple sclerosis, muscular dystrophy, neurological disorders (including stroke and epilepsy), paraplegia, quadriplegia, and other spinal cord conditions, renal failure, respiratory or pulmonary dysfunction, and any other disabilities specified by the secretary through regulations. This attempt is clearly reflective of the so-called "laundry list" approach to defining handicapping conditions with little recognition of the magnitude of the various disabilities from a functional point of view. It does, however, note that a handicapping condition must be of long duration and must require the services of a wide variety of professionals. Thus, the law attempts to define the term by the scope of professional involvement and not by personal needs. This approach runs the risk of losing sight of the individual needs and individual differences of the handicapped person and may, to some degree, measure the handicapping condition by the number of professionals involved rather than the nature of the needs. This approach is more rigid than the purely functional approach and at times may not allow changing and emerging needs to be recognized and dealt with.

The extension and revision of the Developmental Disabilities Service and Facilities Construction Act of 1970 was an attempt to identify, as a group, those disabled individuals who require similar services early in life and who require a multitude of services throughout their life cycle. The original definition of developmental disabilities included mental retardation, cerebral palsy, epilepsy, and other neurological conditions occurring before the age of 18. The intent of the act was to avoid overlapping and inefficient service delivery and to close the gaps between service needs and service availability for those broad groups of persons. This was one of the first attempts at combining major diagnostic classification groups under one umbrella for the purposes of providing similar services in a more efficient fashion.

From 1970 until the passage of the Comprehensive Rehabilitation Services Act, continuous discussion has occurred among advocates, legislators, and professionals as to the actual definition of developmental disabilities and the inclusion of additional diagnostic classifications of disabilities such as autism and learning disabilities. Subsequent revisions of this act did eventually expand the definition to include autism. However, debate as to the need for a more broad-based definition of developmental disabilities continued. A project of national significance (ABT Associates, 1977) attempted to further clarify the term "developmental disabilities." As a result of this project a new definition emerged and has become the cornerstone of the Comprehensive Rehabilitation Services Act of 1978. Although there continues to be debate regarding the ABT report, that project showed a clear trend toward the establishment of a functional definition of developmental disabilities. This trend has persisted and is apparent in the current legislation as well as in the program initiatives at the state and local levels in education, recreation, and independent living.

The present definition in the new Comprehensive Rehabilitation Services Act is probably the most far-reaching effort to look, not at diagnosis, but at the nature of the need of the person requiring services. Within this act the term developmental disabilities means:

"a severe, chronic disability of a person which—
(A) is attributable to a mental or physical impairment or combination of mental and physical impairments;
(B) is manifested before the person attains age twenty-two;
(C) is likely to continue indefinitely;
(D) results in substantial functional limitations in three or more of the following areas of major life activity: self-care, receptive and expressive language, learning, mobility, self-direction, capacity for independent living, and economic self-sufficiency; and
(E) reflects the person's need for a combination and sequence of special, interdisciplinary, or generic care, treatment, or other services which are of lifelong or extended duration and are individually planned and coordinated."

This new definition places the major emphasis not upon the diagnoses or the amount of professional involvement, but on the needs of the individual. Again the recognition of extended duration is noted with the acknowledgment that because of the complexity of needs, numerous professionals may be involved throughout the life of the individual. The "age of onset" component of the definition is more an artifact of other federal legislation than a statement of the developmental process. The critical aspects of this new definition are the listing of functioning activities rather than diagnoses as in the Rehabilitation Amendments. Although this approach is hardly a panacea, it does appear to take a more positive and clear approach by defining a group of individuals by their need and not by their label.

From an educational perspective, the direction is also toward a functional definition as opposed to a categorical one. However, the Education for All Handicapped Children Act (PL 94-142) does use broad diagnostic categories to define handicapped children. Much of the impetus to switch to a more functional approach in defining the handicapped population can be attributed to the phenomena of labeling and its effect upon the individual and how this individual is perceived by others. From a planning perspective the functional approach allows for the development of programs around individual needs and not generalized trends, and avoids the stereotypic perceptions that can occur when diagnostic classifications are used. Although these terms may in some sense continue the practice of labeling, they place emphasis less on tight diagnostic classifications and more on performance capacity.

It must be acknowledged in any discussion of this nature that the phenomena of labeling may not, in fact, be as detrimental as the perceptions which are associated with the label. While the elimination of or reduction in the use of labels may have an impact upon program development, in the long run, it will probably also eliminate many of the historical stereotypic responses that are associated with the person who has been labeled.

Magnitude of the Need

From a planning perspective probably one of the most complex issues to be faced is the two-fold problem of identifying the magnitude of the target group to be served and delineating the scope of the service needs. If one were to look solely at the current incidence figures available it soon becomes apparent that estimates are less than precise because of the lack of clear definitional criteria and poor data-recording procedures at all levels. Estimates of handicapped individuals may range as high as 18.7 percent of the noninstitutionalized population between the ages of 18 and 64 years according to a recent document published by the Urban Institute entitled "Report of the Comprehensive Needs Study." This could be taken as conservative, since the institutionalized community and persons under the age of 18 years and over the age of 65 years are not counted in these figures. The President's Committee on Mental Retardation Report entitled "One in Eleven: Handicapped Adults in America" indicated a 9 percent incidence rate for adults with special needs when looking at employment data based on the figures of the 1970 United States census.

National figures on the incidence of children with special needs may exceed 12.5 percent. The statement of findings and purpose of the Education for All Handicapped Children Act noted that there were in excess of 8 million handicapped children between the ages of 3 and 18 in the United States. Some figures from learning disabilities organizations indicate that it is possible that up to 30 percent of the school-aged population has some learning disabilities. From a planning perspective this equivocal data presents major difficulties in program development and the development of manpower planning and training strategies at all levels.

Scope of the Need

In identifying the needs of handicapped individuals one must consider the social, vocational, and recreational spheres and determine what services will be required to assist that individual in functioning as independently as possible in the least restrictive environment. Employment without associated support services in the recreational and residential areas will lead to an incomplete program for many handicapped individuals.

Not only does the planner have to know the magnitude of the rehabilitation need but there must also be an identification of the scope of the need if a reasonable plan of action is to be evolved. In keeping with the principles of normalization, all persons have the right to learn, work, and play in the most normalized, least restrictive environment possible. This concept has been established through the judiciary by a myriad of class action suits stressing the need for individualized and normalized programming for all handicapped people. Legislative and regulatory actions have further documented the need for individualization by requiring individual service plans, individual written rehabilitation plans, and/or individual educational plans on an annual basis.

This change in the philosophical direction within human services and, specifically, within rehabilitation, has required that planning look not just at one area but at all aspects of the individual's needs—social, residential, and vocational. Probably one of the easiest means of identifying the range of service needs is to look at the nonhandicapped community and identify the range of activities which are available to them. If one were to look at an entire week of a nonhandicapped person it becomes very apparent that a wide variety of activities are engaged in during this time. Of the total 168 hours available each week, traditionally less than 25 percent of this time is engaged in employment by the adult. The remainder of the time is consumed in a variety of activities, including eating, food preparation, sleeping, watching television, shopping, talking with friends, traveling to and from different locations, and engaging in individual and group recreational activities. Depending on one's individual preferences, the amount of time which is consumed in the three areas of activity (work, social, and residential) will vary. However, it is apparent that a balance is needed between these three major clusters of activity if one is to engage in a lifestyle which is as close to normal as possible.

Each of these various activities is interrelated and in some ways dependent upon the other. If an individual is not engaged in gainful employment or receiving some remuneration this will affect the type of recreational and residential options which will be available. Much of our social and residential activities are highly related to our earning capacity. Correspondingly, sufficient research shows that "all work and no play" eventually leads to deterioration of the individual and, subsequently, his or her capacity to function on the job. Successful performance on the job is highly correlated with one's personal sense of stability and satisfaction outside the working environment. It is obvious that any effort which looks solely at one element of the life cycle, be it vocational, social, or residential, to the exclusion of the others only results in short term and short lived gains.

Having recognized that the needs of the handicapped persons are complex, the role of rehabilitation planning becomes the domain of not just a single discipline but an interdisciplinary team. The need for an interdisciplinary team approach is not only necessary for the adult but for the young child as well. A brief look at the evolving needs of the handicapped individual at different life stages shows that at times the role of one professional may be more significant than another but that this changes as the needs and the environment of the handicapped person change.

At the time of birth, medical supports (including diagnostic and therapeutic services to the child and social service supports to the family) are the key components. They reflect the need to gain medical stability for the child and emotional stability for the family. Infancy and early childhood quite often see a reduction in the medical and social support needs and the onset of the developmental education needs. At times during this period, specific residential or home supports may also be needed. The middle or late childhood years require an even more diverse and complex approach to service delivery with continual medical monitoring of the child's progress, social supports to the family, and expanding special education programs for the child. It is also important at this time to begin to develop social and recreational programs which will broaden the interpersonal experiences of both the child and family.

As the child approaches the adolescent or young adult years, many of the medical issues are usually stable; however, a new set of social concerns for the parents surface. These concerns involve a realization that they, the parents, will not be able to provide the residential support for their son or daughter on an indefinite basis, that school and structured educational programs are drawing to a close, and that the physical and emotional needs of their child are changing. It is during this period that the focus of education must change from a traditional or academic curriculum to a vocational or life skills curriculum. Specific social supports begin to shift from the family to the child. The time is approaching for the child to begin to assume responsibilities for some of his or her actions and to move toward a less dependent role within the family. During these years much of the reinforcement comes from peers rather than parents, thus calling for greater social and recreational opportunities. All too often this stage is viewed as the primary transition point to adulthood, and thus one in which a great deal of change must occur, rather than as part of the growth process which is evolutionary and continues throughout the entire life cycle. From birth to adulthood, growth and development must be directed away from the individual's totally dependent status toward a less dependent one, with an end goal of moving as close as possible to entering the mainstream of society as an independent adult.

During the adult years, many of the services and most of the professional interaction is directed toward the handicapped person. Much of the world of the adult is focused on maintaining a job, a place to live, and some level of social interaction. As was noted before, there is a strong interrelationship between the various social, vocational, and recreational components of the adult world. At times there continues to be a need to provide medical services and social support services to maintain the present level of functioning for the individual in the least restrictive environment possible. Often a major new dimension, that of addressing the residential needs of the handicapped person, is added during this period.

Probably the most neglected area of need is that of the elderly disabled person. Frequently the service system is discontinued when it is most needed. Elderly handicapped persons often will have a resurgence of medical problems in light of both their handicapping condition and the aging process. There is also an increased need for residential or domiciliary services, generally of a more supportive nature. Added social/recreational programs are needed because of retirement and, in some instances, because of an inability of these persons to engage in more physically based activities. Active involvement of social supports at all levels, as in other stages of the life cycle, assists the elderly disabled person in the transition to a less physically active and more relaxed place in social, vocational, and recreational activities.

IMPEDIMENTS TO SERVICE DELIVERY

The life cycle of the handicapped as well as the nonhandicapped person is a dynamic process, thus necessitating a flexible approach to service delivery. It cannot be the domain of a single person to address the needs of the handicapped, but is rather the responsibility of an interdisciplinary team which has available a wide range of service options. As was noted earlier, employment is only one phase of the life cycle process. All too often it is looked upon as the sole criteria for independence and success for the adult. In the past rehabilitation looked exclusively at gainful employment as the primary outcome. However, during the past 15 years, there has been an increased awareness of the needs of more severely handicapped persons. The Rehabilitation, Comprehensive Services and Developmental Disabilities Amendments of 1978 demonstrates a significant expansion of the future role of rehabilitation. It is clearly the intent of this act to provide services to those over the age of 22 years who have completed training in the educational sphere under the Education for All Handicapped Children Act. This act also proposes to develop early intervention programs for handicapped children from birth to 3 years, thus reflecting the comprehensive status of the bill. The overall purpose of the act is to develop and implement through research, training, services, and the guarantee of equal opportunity, comprehensive and coordinative programs of vocational rehabilitation and independent living.

The Rehabilitation, Comprehensive Services, and Developmental Disabilities Amendments of 1978 thus intend to coordinate the various vocational, recreational, and residential programs, so as to eliminate duplication of rehabilitation services and fill gaps in the present service delivery system. The fragmented approach of the present service delivery system for handicapped adults is apparent when one looks at the myriad agencies at the local, state, and federal levels. Specific agencies are concerned with training, as in the case of vocational rehabilitation, vocational education, and Comprehensive Employment Training Act programs (CETA). Others address the fiscal needs of the handicapped through Supplemental Security Income (SSI) and Social Security Disability Insurance (SSDI) programs, general relief programs, and food stamps. Health needs are addressed through such programs as Medicare and Medicaid. Some residential programs have been established through Housing and Urban Development Section 8 and Section 202 funds plus Title XIX initiatives. The Urban Mass Transit Authority (UMTA) provides financial assistance to public transportation systems so that they may be more accessible. In other instances, this program makes cash grants to develop supplemental transportation services. Educational services for the adult handicapped individual may be obtained either on a formal basis through institutions of higher education or on a less formal basis through adult education programs. Recreational services, although provided on a fragmented basis by local parks and recreation plans, have recently been brought to the forefront by the Rehabilitation, Comprehensive Services, and Developmental Disabilities Amendments.

At the state and local levels a similar array of agencies and organizations contribute to the provision of services to handicapped individuals. With the service delivery system as it is presently organized, the potential for getting lost in the system is quite high, as is the chance for duplication of services and provision of services that work at cross purposes. The need for coordination is apparent, as is the need for a monitoring system (such as a case manager) to insure that individuals are not lost and the system is not misused by the service recipients.

One of the topics which is often discussed at local, state, and national levels is the need for a coordinated approach to the delivery of services. Many programs require the development of a comprehensive planning process, but until recently these programs did not require that the plan be integrated with other agency or departmental plans. Reports such as the one issued by the White House Conference on Handicapped Individuals clearly articulate the need for a more systematic approach to planning and service provision. The initial and continuing intent of the developmental disabilities legislation is to provide the means of reviewing the various vocational rehabilitation, vocational education, and training programs. However, the actual role of the Developmental Disabilities Councils in requiring compliance to a coordinated planning effort on an interdepartmental level is unclear. The Developmental Disability Bill of Rights Act in 1978 places priority on the provision of comprehensive services to persons with developmental disabilities, with special emphasis on those individuals whose needs cannot be covered or otherwise met under the Education for All Handicapped Children Act, Rehabilitation Act of 1973 as amended, or other Health, Education and Welfare programs. Special emphasis should be placed in the areas of case management services, child development services, alternative living arrangements services, and nonvocational social development services. In recalling the scope of need for handicapped adults there is an obvious need to look at issues of health, employment, recreation, residential, and financial security as integrated aspects of planning community-based programs. There now exists the statutory base for the development of these comprehensive services in a coordinated fashion.

Part of the difficulty in planning is linked to the poor data collection systems which presently exist. Although planning activities are required in the health field by the Health Systems Agencies, in vocational education by the Vocational Education Council, in rehabilitation by the State Rehabilitation Agency, in developmental disabilities by the Developmental Disabilities Council, and by other welfare and community service agencies, there is a great deal of conflicting information regarding incidence and prevalence figures for the handicapped community. Some handicapped individuals will appear on several different fact sheets because of the complexity of their handicap, the diversity of their needs or their skill in gaining access to the human service system. Thus, some incidence figures can be significantly inflated whereas others may be too low. By personal preference, the handicapped individual can choose not to be known as a handicapped person. This is especially common when the handicapping condition is one which could be considered as covert or easily disguised. In other instances the handicapped individual does not appear in incidence figures because of inefficient screening procedures, lack of outreach, or poor information or referral. Although this situation is becoming less and less common, there continue to be individuals who have not been known to any agency or professional but are in need of services.

There are some handicapped individuals who, by the nature of onset of the handicap, have not been previously identified, as in the case of the individual who experiences a traumatic injury or a major illness which results in a substantial limitation of his or her functional capacities. Lastly, there are those individuals who are labeled as handicapped who, as a result of support services, are no longer in need of service and therefore should not be considered handicapped. Incidence figures are thus subject to a number of factors which must be acknowledged. However, with the use of sound data collection procedures and the development of more rigorous epidemiological procedures, more refined approximations of incidence and prevalent figures can be obtained.

In addition to other problems, it would be inappropriate not to recognize that there is an ever increasing need for training of service providers in rendering direct services to an individual. Much of the legislation cited earlier has sections which examine the development of expanded training and research. Institutions of higher education have federally sponsored training programs in a variety of areas of education, rehabilitation, and other service areas, such as the University Affiliated Facilities that provide training in the interdisciplinary team process and the Rehabilitation and Training programs that provide for the development of additional intervention strategies. Although these programs have more far-reaching mandates than have been noted, it is important to recognize that the development of services without the development of service technology or the training of service providers will in the end generate little benefit for the handicapped individual. Without these aspects of training and research there will be little opportunity to expand and refine our methods of assisting handicapped persons to maximize their potential.

COMPREHENSIVE REHABILITATION SERVICE

Having identified the federal statutes, the scope of the need, and the potential magnitude of the service need for handicapped adults, it is appropriate to look more closely at the range of options (residential, vocational, educational, recreational, and emotional) which must be considered in total rehabilitation planning. The term "handicapped" refers to a broad and diverse group of persons; thus, the scope of the programming must reflect this diversity. Just as each and every nonhandicapped individual has a variety of options to choose from, so must handicapped persons have the right to choose what they want. Beyond this right to choose, however, there is also the obligation of all individuals to accept the responsibilities associated with that choice. A comprehensive rehabilitation plan must be a joint plan, one in which the handicapped person plays an active role and correspondingly assumes a major share of the responsibility for implementation.

RESIDENTIAL PLANNING

Certainly one of the most pivotal influences throughout one's life is the home. During the early years this is the environment which fulfills the majority of the nurturance needs of the young child and the social and emotional rapport for the school-age child. For the adult, home or residential environment remains a significant component of one's adjustment. The natural home environment gives support and nurturance in times of need, an opportunity to develop close interpersonal relationships with others, and a haven which is safe and secure. A large institutional environment during the early years seldom provides the nurturance and support necessary and may, in fact, make the move toward independence in later years even more difficult. For those handicapped persons who have remained in a natural home environment the move to an independent living situation can at times be easier, although concern relative to separation on the part of the parent and child may place emotional and social hurdles as adulthood is approached. Movement from a supportive or protective environment into one which is less so or into a totally new environment needs to be accomplished over an extended period of time. Those who are charged with the care and support of both institutionalized and noninstitutionalized handicapped individuals during early years need to plan for an eventual move into an alternative or new residential environment in later years.

Intermediate Care Facilities

Residential options must reflect a wide range of cognitive, physical, and emotional skills of the handicapped person. In certain instances there will be a need for continued social, medical, or emotional supports of a highly structured nature such as those offered in a institutional environment. Large institutions such as those that now exist for mentally retarded and developmentally disabled persons have been viewed not as developmental but as maintenance or "warehousing" facilities with limited opportunity for growth and development. Movement into smaller, better staffed programs, such as an intermediate care facility (ICF), has begun to occur. The development of these ICF's is directed at the provision of services to individuals as a result of a comprehensive interdisciplinary evaluation and the subsequent individual service plan. The ICF is responsive to the needs of people and thus, as opposed to the large institution- or systems-oriented approach of the past, is client and developmentally oriented. The nature of the ICF is dictated by the capacity of residents for self-preservation and non-self-preservation skills whereas the type of developmental program is a result of the individual service plan of each resident.

Skilled Nursing Facilities

For those handicapped persons in need of a more medically oriented support system there are skilled nursing facilities (SNF). Caution, however, must be used in adopting a skilled nursing facility as a placement because in some instances the use of this type of setting will be determined solely by the medical rather than by the developmental needs of the individual. The National Association for Retarded Citizens (NARC), in a book entitled *The Right to Choose,* noted that the choice of a nursing home must be made with extreme care and with assurances that adequate programs both within the home and within the community are available to meet the individual needs. NARC further noted that for most severely handicapped individuals needing nursing care, placement in existing nursing homes is reasonably adequate as long as young adults are not placed singly in homes, and as long as daily programs are provided which reflect developmental needs.

Specialized Home Care and Respite Care

Specialized home care programs may provide a means of serving severely handicapped individuals who are medically stable but in need of a highly structured, highly supportive, and nurturing environment. As a component of the specialized home care programs respite care services may employ this type of a structured and supportive environment on a short term basis as an adjunct to a natural home environment. In both specialized home care and respite care, the goal of the program is to provide those specific structured supports in the most normalized environment possible with the goal of moving the handicapped person into a less restricted environment at some future date. Using a developmental approach, specialized home care is directed toward the goal of skill acquisition in a variety of self-care and social/emotional areas. In contrast, in many instances respite care is directed toward the goal of providing support or relief to the natural family.

Group Homes and Community Residences

By far the most frequently utilized approach to community residential programming is the development of a group home or a community residence which has the capacity of providing residential services for a specified number of persons in a neighborhood setting. Although little research has been done to determine the specific number of persons that should be served in a single community residence, the NARC defines a community-based residential service as some type of housing, other than the individual's natural home, usually designated for not more than 12 persons having similar needs in terms of age, independence, and/or ability. It is clear that large multi-bed programs such as those which were prevalent and still exist in many state schools are counterproductive to developmental programming (*Halderman* v. *Pennhurst State School and Hospital*). Smaller numbers of handicapped persons residing in the community are able to cope with society and become more integrated into the mainstream than those in the larger and more secluded setting.

The community residence provides an environment which gives continuous assistance and supervision to the handicapped individual. There is an on-going emphasis on the development of self-care and self-help skills with the goal of increased social competence. Those persons residing in such a program are involved in a variety of day options ranging from day activities programs to sheltered and competitive employment. The supervisors or house managers do not function as surrogate parents for the residents but more as a sounding board to community perceptions and a means of learning the skills of interrelating with nonhandicapped persons. Social skill development as well as enhanced social adjustment are the goals for each individual in a community residence.

As the move toward greater independence is achieved, the handicapped individual may move into a cooperative apartment program. The level of support and supervision in this type of program will vary depending upon whether there is live-in or non-live-in staff. In larger apartment complexes there is now regulatory incentive to have a portion of the available units for elderly and/or disabled persons who function better in a communal environment and who may need much less structured supervision. In these instances there may be a supportive staff person who is available to help with food preparation or budgeting on a temporary or permanent basis. For the physically handicapped individual, the development of the centers for independent living programs has led to the removal of architectural barriers in the environment and provision for specific attendant services through the use of personal care assistants. Federal initiative through Housing and Urban Development has provided financial incentives to agencies to develop programs specifically for handicapped persons while subsidies in rent have created the opportunity for handicapped individuals on limited income to move into community residence programs and cooperative apartments.

Total Care

This discussion of residential options would not be complete without looking at the need for total care in certain instances. Inpatient services of both a medical and behavioral nature must likewise be available as an alternative and/or supplemental option in residential services. As in the case of the more long term residential services, the use of the inpatient service is designed as another step in the rung of the ladder toward greater independent functioning. As the range of community residential services becomes more developed, the need for inpatient services should diminish with the greater use of local health care facilities for emergency and routine health care and the increased capacity of staff at long term residential programs to address the various emotional and adjustment needs that some handicapped individuals may at times experience.

This range of residential options, although not intended to be an exhaustive listing or a detailed analysis of the various alternatives, does demonstrate the array of choices which should be available to the handicapped individual. Like the nonhandicapped person, handicapped individuals should have the option to choose the environment in which he or she wishes to live. The choices may range from a completely protected environment, such as an intermediate care facility with 24-hour support services in a variety of different areas, to individual ownership with no supports other than those available to the nonhandicapped adult.

VOCATIONAL/DAY PROGRAM OPTIONS

Vocational or day activity options should be as diverse as residential service options. The type of program that the handicapped adult will participate in on a daily basis must be closely matched to the strengths of the individual, taking into consideration the special social, intellectual and/or physical constraints present. In some cases, because of the complexity of the problem, the handicapped individual will need a great deal of supervision, support, or environmental modification in a day program. Using a developmental approach, training programs such as day activities centers may seek to foster greater self-help skills such as feeding, personal care, and hygiene, increased interpersonal skills in dealing with peers using verbal and nonverbal communication procedures, and community survival skills such as independent travel, use of money, and food preparation. The curriculum of the daily activities program should be variable and responsive to the needs of the handicapped individuals in the program. The instructional material utilized is often that which naturally emerges in the community while the techniques of teaching are individualized, stressing multistimulus input and repetition.

Sheltered Workshops

For the individual who has developed self-care and self-help skills, but has yet to develop the capacity to produce at industrial norms or interact in the work milieu, the resources of a sheltered workshop can provide an opportunity to gain a sense of self-worth while experiencing the realities of the world of work. In a sheltered employment environment the handicapped individual may work at his or her own pace with supervisory staff who encourage not only quality but increased productivity as well. Specific skill training, although not shunned, is less stressed in a sheltered employment environment. The primary goal is the development of good work habits and general work adjustments in these types of programs. Often sheltered employment involves production on factory-like tasks in a nonintegrated work environment. This type of approach has its limitations when aiming for development of greater social and interpersonal skills; however, for some handicapped persons, such a protected environment is essential. As in all programs, sheltered employment should not be viewed as a final goal in the rehabilitation process for the handicapped adult but rather as a transitional one.

Extended Evaluation and Training Programs

Evaluation and training programs are at times viewed as long term programs, although they also are a transitional stage in the rehabilitation process. Vocational evaluation is, additionally, the first step in the rehabilitation process for a handicapped individual. Through the use of an extended evaluation period of up to 18 months, a determination of eligibility for vocational services can be made. Evaluation and training services are usually conducted in a rehabilitation center in which vocational aptitude, awareness, and potential are assessed and specific skill-building programs begun. The goal of evaluation and training is to identify areas of strength and weakness, leading to the development of an individual written rehabilitation plan which will direct the rehabilitation efforts of the future for a specific handicapped individual. Not only does the Division of Vocational Rehabilitation engage in evaluation and training but the Department of Education has the responsibility for providing similar services through comprehensive high school programs and vocational technical school programs. Generally, considerable emphasis is placed on the development of specific skills which will lead to semi-skilled and skilled occupations for those programs in the school districts. In the rehabilitation facilities often the ''soft skills of employment'' (that is, punctuality, attendance, ability to accept criticism and supervision, and capacity to do complex tasks) are stressed, with less emphasis upon specific skill development.

Vocational evaluation and training are stages in the rehabilitation process which utilize a variety of standardized evaluation measures, situational evaluations, and aptitude and interest tests to identify future direction. In some instances the plan may call for sheltered employment or day activities whereas in other instances specific skill training and, possibly, competitive employment will be sought.

Transitional Employment and On-the-Job Training

A great deal of interest over the past several years has developed around the concepts of transitional employment in industry, work in industry, and sheltered enclaves. This interest has been stimulated in part by the realization of professionals that for some handicapped people the total emersion into a normalized environment providing auditory, visual, and tactile stimulation enhances the development of appropriate work behaviors and work habits. With some modification of the work environment, those whose limitations are primarily of a physical nature are able to produce in such a setting at an identified rate and in an accurate and consistent fashion.

Public school work/study programs have long acknowledged the benefits of training in the real work environment for the nonhandicapped and, more recently, for the handicapped student. As a result of the Education for All Handicapped Children Act, local educational associations will have the primary responsibility of educating the adolescent and young adult handicapped students until their 22nd birthday. This has led many local educational associations to look closely at their work/study programs to determine whether this approach is appropriate for the handicapped student. Combined with specific classroom training, the work/study approach can provide the handicapped student with an opportunity to test out newly acquired skills under close and supportive supervision. Work/study can be either remunerative or of a voluntary internship nature, inasmuch as the primary goal is not to provide a long term placement but a short term experience in the world of work.

A similar model has emerged in rehabilitation facilities with the use of paid and nonpaid transitional employment programs (TEP). In the TEP it is again important that close supervision be maintained for both the cooperating industry and the handicapped person. The realistic work environment can provide both evaluation data to the rehabilitation professional and experiential information to the handicapped individual. This learning experience thus allows the handicapped person to begin to make decisions about future career activities based on actual and concrete experiences rather than on wish fulfillment. Any TEP or work/study program must have close supervision if it is to be an effective teaching and learning experience and a springboard to future training and employment.

Closely aligned to the above noted programs is the concept of an on-the-job training program (OJT). Once a clearly identifiable vocational interest emerges, the OJT model provides an opportunity for the handicapped individual to receive an extended orientation to that job while receiving full pay. The OJT model provides financial subsidies to industry in the event that there is an extended training period required by the handicapped person on a specific job. Usually the subsidy is designed to cover expenses related to longer learning time and initial reduced productivity on the job rather than social or interpersonal adjustment to the world of work. The OJT model has generally been utilized by the vocational rehabilitation agencies and the Department of Labor as an incentive to industry to employ handicapped persons rather than as a training tool.

Sheltered Enclave

The sheltered enclave or "workshop without walls" concept has been discussed over the years; however, little progress has been made in establishing this model as a viable approach to the delivery of rehabilitation services. Most sheltered workshops have depended upon subcontract work from industry as their primary means of maintaining the program. The traditional approach has been to have the staff of the workshop bid on a job using broad guidelines developed by the Department of Labor and by establishing a unit price for the product with industry. If the contract is awarded it is then sent to the workshop where clients will provide the manpower to complete the contract. More recently some rehabilitation facilities have attempted to send work teams into industry to perform the work on-site. This approach provides benefits to the company from the standpoint of control of materials and production, and offers to the client of the rehabilitation facility an opportunity to experience a real work setting. In a few instances, rehabilitation facilities have negotiated to have a permanent labor force in industry while remaining under the supervision of a trained rehabilitation staff. Although the potential benefits to industry and the handicapped person are apparent in this approach, little experience in sheltered enclave programming has been achieved to date. The trend in vocational training and evaluation, as in residential programming, is clearly in the direction of greater utilization of the community as the training arena.

Gainful Employment

Since its inception vocational rehabilitation has had, as its ultimate goal, gainful employment. Over the years, as this goal has been altered, there has been a recognition of a variety of different types of employment options. However, there still remains a clear interest in providing an opportunity for handicapped people to receive training which will lead to a full time job in industry. The attainment of competitive employment is, at best, difficult and, on some occasions, not possible for the handicapped person. However, more emphasis needs to be placed upon the removal of barriers, architectural and attitudinal, to employment. This move has begun through the Rehabilitation Amendments of 1973 under Section 503 and 504 at the national level and at the state level by a number of specific statutes which prohibit discrimination in employment for the handicapped. In certain states handicapped preference programs have been started to encourage employment of the handicapped. Most states have a Governor's Commission on Employment of the Handicapped which attempts to stress the role of the handicapped person as a productive worker in society.

The Division of Vocational Rehabilitation has provided counseling and job placement assistance to handicapped persons as a means of facilitating re-entry into the labor market. Although there has been a broadening of the definition of gainful employment, counselors spend much of their time in assisting clients in obtaining competitive employment. For the less severely handicapped client, the resources of the Division of Employment Security and the Division of Vocational Rehabilitation can provide direct placement assistance. For the more severely handicapped client, an intermediate training or retraining step may be necessary before entry into the competitive labor market. A variety of related support services around transportation, environmental modifications, and purchase of the "tools of the trade" can also be provided by the vocational rehabilitation counselor. Post employment counseling and support services are directed at assisting the handicapped person into assuming the full responsibilities of competitive employment. For handicapped persons unable to achieve gainful employment, the range of service options through vocational rehabilitation is greatly reduced. Efforts to broaden the mandates of the state Division of Vocational Rehabilitation have resulted in the passage of the new Rehabilitation, Comprehensive Services, and Developmental Disabilities Amendments of 1978.

EDUCATIONAL OPPORTUNITIES

For the handicapped adult there continues to be a need to learn and develop social and self-help skills as well as vocational skills. Often the traditional academic supports have been greatly diminished and in many instances completely eliminated once employment or day activity programming has begun. There is general agreement among most professionals, however, that the learning process is one which does not cease with the completion or termination of formal education but that, in fact, all individuals continue to learn and develop. For the handicapped person this learning process may not proceed at the customary rate under the usual environmental stimulation but may be extended over a greater period of time. The rate of learning and development for some handicapped individuals may be slower and the style of learning may be nontraditional; however, the phenomena of learning and development do occur. The NARC noted in the book *The Right to Choose* (1973) that according to the developmental model every person is capable of learning and change. "Retarded children or adults are first of all people. They can develop physically. They can grow intellectually. They can adjust socially and gain emotional maturity. They may be slower than others but they are always capable of development. We all develop continually."

With the need for extended learning opportunities and alternatives in the learning environment, greater emphasis has been placed upon the development of adult educational resources at the local level. In an effort to stimulate interest in adult education activities for handicapped persons, the federal government in 1975 attempted to clarify this aspect of the Education Amendments of 1974 (PL 93–380) by indicating through its regulatory mechanisms that states could use up to 20 percent of their formula grant funds to establish and carry out adult basic education programs for institutionalized adults. Although the incentive is present there is some confusion as to how the resources of adult education programs can be brought to bear in providing services to the handicapped individual. In some instances, particularly with the developmentally disabled adult, initial attempts have been directed at the development of enhanced self-help skills in a somewhat self-contained environment. This approach has merit; however, as in regular education, the benefits of mainstreaming from a social and interpersonal nature are lost when such a nonintegrated approach is used. Adult education can also be used to create interest in the arts and crafts areas as well as the basic skill areas. Many of the present evening school or adult education programs provide an environment in which specific instruction as well as expanded social interaction can occur.

Often the common denominator in an adult education program for both the handicapped and nonhandicapped person is that of interest and expansion of one's experiences rather than further development of one's career options or expertise. Students tend to be of diverse ages, professions, and socioeconomic origins. They have selected a specific adult education program, be it a continuation of academic subject matter or development of a craft or hobby, because of personal interest in the topic, that is, course selection is a result of interest and not as a part of a required or structured curriculum. This common level of personal interest and diversity of background can often provide a situation which will foster a bonding of the group and the subsequent development of social and personal ties among a wide variety of people. Although not all adult education programs are of the arts and crafts or hobby nature, many can provide an individual with opportunity to develop nonwork-related areas of interest. These areas of interest can assist the handicapped individual in greater integration into the mainstream of society.

There is a substantial difference between adult and higher educational resources and how they are used which should be examined when reviewing educational resources for the handicapped person. All too often no differentiation is made between skill development directed at a vocation and that which can be considered as avocational. Because of the industrialized nature of the United States, educational resources are directed at the development of one's skills as they relate to the marketplace with little recognition that nonwork-related skill acquisition is essential to one's development as well. Avocational skill development can be more accurately described as the development of a skill designed primarily to satisfy one's self, one in which the major gain is psychological rather than financial. Vocational skills, on the other hand, have as their cornerstone the concept of a financial means through which one can maintain his or her existence in an independent fashion. Earlier in this chapter, however, it was noted that the amount of time which is spent on the job is about 25 percent of the available time during a week and that the other components of the life cycle, that is recreational and residential, are closely related to the vocational component and vice versa. There is as great a need to develop skills which enhance self-esteem, expand interpersonal opportunities in the community, and create the capacity to utilize leisure time as there is to develop vocational and marketable skills.

Higher education has been considered the arena of the healthy, nonhandicapped person until the passage of the Rehabilitation Act Amendments of 1973 and Section 504 which affirms equal access to educational opportunities for all. Historically, both architectural and attitudinal barriers have existed for the handicapped in higher education. However, many of these barriers have been removed in the past few years in response to the 504 regulations and a realization that certain handicapped people, although possessing specific limitations, are able to achieve in the higher education environment. Most colleges and universities have developed offices for handicapped students with major emphasis upon providing assistance and guidance to handicapped students as they progress through the formal curricula. In addition, these offices usually work with the administration in expansion of curricula and facility development so that handicapped students will no longer be unfairly excluded architecturally or academically. A report in the March 1974 issue of *The Journal on Community and Junior Colleges* entitled "The Mentally Retarded: A New Challenge," noted that there were approximately 40 programs in community and junior colleges across the country providing services to developmentally disabled adults. Much of the emphasis on these programs has been directed at recreational activity and the development of greater skills of daily living with less emphasis upon vocational training activities. Although higher education has begun to address the needs of the handicapped student, it is necessary to broaden the scope of the curricula available. Participation of handicapped students at all levels of education must be actively encouraged.

RECREATION

Probably the most neglected area of all is that of recreation. All too often recreational services are viewed as a frill when, in fact, they are an essential part of everyone's growth and development. The opportunity to relate to others and to engage in group and individual leisure time pursuits provides the variety and diversity which enables an individual to function more effectively on the job and with others in the place of residence. Because of the many needs in the residential and vocational areas, recreational opportunities for the handicapped are often overlooked or felt to be less important.

Recreation can take a variety of forms, ranging from highly structured activities to completely unstructured ones, and those that are done individually as opposed to those which are done in a group. For the handicapped individual these choices are often severely limited because of architectual or environmental constraints. Many social and recreational clubs are not accessible. Often, when they are, there is a great deal of reluctance on the part of those who conduct the programs to include the handicapped person. The common reasons range from concern over the safety of handicapped persons to feelings that they will not be able to understand the rules of the game. More often the true barrier is the personal apprehension and lack of ability of the nonhandicapped individual to relate to and talk with the handicapped person.

Specific attempts have been made to extend recreational services to handicapped people, most notably through the Special Olympics for the mentally retarded. This highly structured group activity places less emphasis upon winning or losing and more upon the act of participation, with specific recognition for all those who participate. The primary assumption of the

Special Olympics is that the mentally retarded person cannot compete with the nonretarded and therefore they should have their own activities. There are both pros and cons to this assumption. In many instances mentally retarded individuals are not able to compete; however, they are able to interact and share with their agemates in noncompetitive activities. The Special Olympics has been able to bring to the forefront the need for recreational services, though to some degree it has also highlighted the difference between the mentally retarded and the nonretarded individual.

Recently some emphasis has been placed upon integrated recreational services with greater utilization of local parks, and recreation resources by handicapped persons. These types of programs are often structured and usually of a group nature, allowing close peer interaction. Probably one of the more radical approaches to the development of recreational services and resources for handicapped persons has been the proposal that a representative number of handicapped individuals should be involved in all public recreational activities. For example, if the recognized percentage of handicapped individuals were 12 percent, then 12 percent of the participants in all programs would be handicapped. Opponents to this proposal raise the issue of potential for increased levels of scapegoating in some areas, and individual risk to health and safety. Proponents, on the other hand, turn to the argument that those in charge have not developed their skills efficiently to be able to adapt activities, instructions, or rules, and that, in fact, some handicapped persons will be able to achieve at higher levels and therefore the amount of scapegoating will be decreased. The arguments on both sides deserve investigation; however, it would appear that the true limitation is one of lack of ability to modify the environment rather than lack of the individual to participate in the program.

Numerous types of recreational activities of both an individual and group nature are part of the daily activities of most people. Self-play, such as watching television, doing arts and crafts, and reading, in some instances allows an individual to relax and develop a sense of personal accomplishment and in others just provides some variety in the day-to-day routine. Team sports, games which include more than one individual, social groups, card games, discussion groups, and just "hanging out" provide an opportunity to relate to others in both competitive and noncompetitive areas with no established performance criteria other than having a good time. The list of individual or group recreational options for the nonhandicapped is usually limited by the creative mind of the individual whereas for the handicapped there are specific environmental and architectural barriers to choosing these options. Usually this exclusion is not a result of an absence of interest but a lack of understanding of the handicapping conditions with concomitant stereotypic misconception about the handicapped individual. Because an individual is handicapped it is not uncommon to find that the nonhandicapped person views that individual as having limited skills, emotions, and capacity to interact with others. These perceptual barriers have a much more significant effect upon the handicapped person than does the actual limitation itself.

Sometimes, when the external limiting factors are greater than the internal limiting factors, there is a need to either confront or educate the unenlightened that behavior of this nature is discriminatory and, for many, personally debilitating. In other instances, when perceived limitations exceed actual ones, the problem may relate to the handicapped individual's lack of acceptance and adjustment to his or her limitations. In either event, when perceived limitations exceed actual ones, the emotional adjustment of the handicapped individual and his or her capacity to deal with residential, vocational, educational, and recreational issues may be extremely limited. The level of general adjustment of the handicapped individual to society and society to the handicapped individual is directly related to capacity to address both the perceived and actual role one is to assume in society.

In some instances there is a need for an advocate, one who is able to speak up and address problems within the service system and the community, to intervene. There has been a great deal of discussion about advocacy during the past few years, particularly as a result of the citizen advocacy program of the NARC, the peer counseling programs of the Centers for Independent Living, and the recently established protection and advocacy systems that are part of the developmental disabilities legislation. Self-advocacy for many handicapped individuals is a long way off, while for others it is an unobtainable goal. The latter situation may result from the complexity of the handicap or because the service providers and other nonhandicapped persons are not listening to what the handicapped individual is saying. Too often there is a lack of recognition that the capacity to care and feel resides in all persons; what differs for the handicapped individual is the means of demonstrating and expressing those feelings (see Chapter 7).

At times it is not the system or the handicapping condition which is limiting, but rather the individual. In some cases this results from a lack of acceptance of one's limitations and, in others, from a lack of understanding of the nature of the handicap and its long range implications. The effect of the above-noted factors may have a more profound impact on the individual than the actual physical or intellectual limitations. In these instances it is important that efforts be directed toward helping handicapped individuals to begin to deal with their feelings so that some recognition and subsequent resolution or at least emotional stability can be achieved. Counseling or therapy on an individual basis may be helpful for some while for others group therapy may be the most useful.

Adjustment problems may be precipitated by the normal developmental process that all individuals experience, although for some handicapped individuals, this maturational period may be highly stressful. Typical adolescent adjustment issues dealing with independence versus dependence and sexuality are dealt with by the handicapped individual on a functional level with little recognition of the affective components of these issues. Maturational concerns and feelings associated with these concerns, if dealt with during the developmental years, will seldom emerge as adjustment problems in later years.

TRAINING NEEDS AND MANPOWER RESOURCES

Training activities have expanded considerably and reflect the changing scope of human services for all handicapped persons. At the university level specialty and generic training programs have begun to prepare individuals who can fill the gap in manpower at the service level. Preservice and inservice approaches to training can address the specific needs of agencies and vendors in orienting new staff and reorienting current staff to new technologies in the field of rehabilitation. Training is essential, not only for the direct care staff and professionals, but the researchers as well. Although without an immediate effect upon service delivery in most cases, research activity provides the building blocks of the future for the service provider. Training is multidimensional and multiphasic, addressing all groups of human service professionals, with the goal of increasing the quality and quantity of services provided to and for handicapped individuals.

As the range of rehabilitation options increases, so does the need for trained staff at all levels: the direct care, the supervisory, and the administrative levels. Manpower shortages are critical when program needs for the adult handicapped person are assessed. The problem is magnified by the rapidly changing patterns of service delivery to a community-based approach and the relative lack of interest to date among many professionals in getting involved with the handicapped adult. Historically, emphasis upon early intervention and educational services has generated a great deal of interest among universities in developing training programs in these areas. This university interest is reinforced by the federal system, where a large portion of the available training monies are directed at training personnel to provide services to handicapped children. Gradually, this trend has been changing, and there is now greater recognition of the needs of the handicapped adult.

Single disciplinary training has given way to an interdisciplinary approach as the scope of the need becomes more apparent. At both the graduate and undergraduate levels the emphasis upon cooperation, coordination, and total planning has played a significant role in creating a greater awareness of the life-long needs of some handicapped persons. Specific university training programs are now looking at the needs of the handicapped adult, not just from a vocational perspective, but from a social and emotional perspective as well. Emphasis on training at the community college level has provided some assistance in improved efficiency of the direct care staff as well.

The retraining of existing professionals and direct care staff is as important as the development of a new cadre of human service workers. The phenomena of staff burnout is all too apparent, particularly for direct care staff. Inservice and preservice training activities, providing both factual information and emotional supports, may delay the rate of staff burnout. There is clearly a need, however, to allow staff to have mobility and opportunity for advancement if career longevity in the human service field is to be encouraged.

Hand-in-hand with training goes the concept of competence on the job. In-service training activities with no recognition of the need to monitor both the quality of the training process and the capacity of the participants to apply this newly acquired knowledge will hardly resolve the need for development of quality programming. Issues such as licensure and certification at the professional level and some type of competency-based credentialing at the direct care level can address in a global fashion the question of staff abilities. The continual updating of skills and knowledge is essential for all staff if new and more advanced teaching and training technologies are to be incorporated into the day-to-day delivery of services to handicapped adults.

The need for training is major and one which in many ways will dictate the success of the community adjustment for handicapped persons. This rapidly changing field requires a continual upgrading of skills at all levels, while the phenomena of staff burnout necessitates a supportive and intellectually nurturing environment for the existing human service workers. The removal of more subtle stereotypic attitudes demonstrated by staff through statements such as "We have done it for years that way," or "in the past similar clients did it this way" may foster a more proactive rather than reactive approach to service delivery.

The training of staff will not alone resolve the manpower needs. There is a need to develop more advanced treatment and service technologies for the handicapped individual which will assist in social, vocational, and emotional adjustment. Research at both the pure and applied levels needs to be expanded so that less of a hit-or-miss approach to service delivery can be evolved. The recognition of priority of services for severely handicapped persons has served to highlight the need for development of more sophisticated strategies as well as a higher level of training for human service workers in the field.

The trend toward normalization, mainstreaming, integration, or whatever other term one wishes to use, is directed at the use of the community as the training and service milieu for the handicapped adult. Over the past several years the major thrust has been directed at the handicapped individual with little recognition of the needs and concerns of nonhandicapped persons. Some of the issues which have emerged under the banner of zoning in the development of community residence programs has shown that there is a great need for listening to the concerns of nonhandicapped persons. The initial responses at zoning hearings such as "What will it do to the value of my house," and "Are they dangerous?," have given way to the more sophisticated means of expressing apprehension such as "Is this the best neighborhood for them?," "Are there too many living in one house?," and "The public transportation system isn't as good here as it is on the East side." Although these are valid concerns when considering the establishment of a community residence program, they may also be symptomatic of a sophisticated discrimination system which is emerging. Much of the present and past effort has been on assisting the handicapped person to adjust to the nonhandicapped while almost no recognition of the adjustment of the nonhandicapped to the handicapped person has been made. In the development of a comprehensive approach to the determination of services for the handicapped adult, much of the training that is necessary is related to attitude change and the elimination or at least diminution of the belief structures that state that difference or deviance is dangerous.

Data questioning the relationship of expressed attitude and behavior show that this interaction at times is extremely complex. As community resources expand, approaches to attitude change (particularly toward handicapped individuals) need to be further studied with a close monitoring of the relationship of behavior to expressed attitudes. Attitude change is not only necessary in the community but among professionals as well. The move toward self-advocacy has shown that the professional often talks to and not with the handicapped individual. The conflicting message of encouragement to become an adult without allowing individuals to have control over the critical decisions which affect their future, seems only to frustrate and confuse and, in many ways, reinforce the dependency role for handicapped persons. If self-advocacy is to be a meaningful goal, professionals must allow the handicapped individual to have the right to choose, the opportunity to accept the responsibility of choice, to exercise the right to risk, and to develop an understanding of failure. The professional role is thus one which allows for the maximization of experience with the minimum level of support necessary to allow for the development of independence to the greatest extent possible.

ISSUES IN HUMAN SERVICES DELIVERY

As the needs of the handicapped individual and the range of services required become more apparent, a number of issues arise in the delivery of human services. Coordination and case management of the various components of the needed service play a key role in assuring that the handicapped individual receives the essential service in a timely and effective fashion. The emphasis upon generic as opposed to speciality services has required a shifting of the attitude and response of professionals to human service delivery. The advocacy movement, with the recognition of "not a privilege but a right" to service, has also created new demands upon the delivery of human services. Legislative, ethical, and fiscal mandates have placed greater stress upon the management and administration of a human service program. The concept of human services being "big business" has brought the world of services to people and industry closer together from both a management and administrative prospective. These issues face all individuals involved with either the provision or reception of services in the human service delivery system.

The recognition that certain handicapped individuals have life-long needs requires that there be a greater coordination of programs both from a cross-sectional and longitudinal perspective. The advocacy movement has pointed out that at times the reason for the lack of services is not due to the existence or non-existence of the resource or vendor but rather the lack of coordination and follow-through.

Development and monitoring of the individual service plan, individual written rehabilitation plan, or individual education plan often calls for an extensive coordination and facilitation mandating that a single source of accountability be established, a case manager. The interdisciplinary team approach to evaluation and service provides the framework from which the case manager approach can be initiated. The need for case managership is apparent, not solely for the purpose of gaining access to service but also for expanding and monitoring the appropriateness of the service for specific individuals. In some instances the case manager will serve primarily as an information and referral resource while at other times he or she will aggressively pursue services.

The case manager, functioning as a catalytic agent, can assure that the many recommendations are carried out in the proper sequence and intensity. The inherent problem of individuals falling through the service delivery cracks would be minimized since accountability would be clearly established. Legislative efforts have been directed at the establishment of coordinating and facilitating councils at the federal, state, and local levels. However, these efforts have looked less at the individual and more at agencies and/or organizations providing the services. The case manager would be addressing the need for a coordinated approach to individual services rather than systems coordination.

Compounding the problems of coordination and accountability, certain administrative dilemmas face the handicapped person. In some instances there is a financial disincentive to employment as the public assistance monies are directly related to expanded income levels. Trial work periods with a guarantee of continued eligibility for public medical coverage and rent subsidies may encourage some handicapped individuals to look more positively on the idea of employment. Stronger incentives toward the employment of handicapped individuals with tax credits or reimbursement for training may encourage industry to "take a chance" on the high risk handicapped worker. Effective implementation of equal rights and equal access legislation (Section 503 and Section 504) may provide further incentives to some public and private organizations to employ handicapped individuals. Government incentives to subcontract with rehabilitation facilities are providing a greater stability in subcontracted work in some of these facilities. To handicapped individuals in the working environment who have a reduced rate of productivity, similar encouragements or subsidy, integrated wtih federal sponsorship, may stimulate the development of "workshops without walls" or shelter enclaves in industry. The role of national health insurance may be a significant factor in encouraging industry to employ handicapped individuals who are covered in some fashion by such a health program. Although the details of any one of these proposals must be worked out, the role of the bureaucracy in expanding the options in the rehabilitation process of the severely handicapped individual is great.

As the portion of the tax dollar directed toward the provision of human services increases, the concept of a small, family-run business gives way to the realization that human services is in fact "big business." Over the past several decades the cost of providing care for those who are not able to care for themselves has escalated significantly. A number of issues emerge with this rapid growth. These pertain to the quality of service and the management of service, not only from the point of view of format or style but also from that of responsibility or accountability. Is it the responsibility of the public or private sector to manage such a service delivery system? In the past, almost by default, state and local governments have had the major share of the responsibility for providing most of the required services. The federal government has acted as the reimbursement agent and, to an extremely limited degree, monitoring agent. Private industry did not view this type of service as profitable or practical and thus was all too willing to allow the bureaucratic system to take on this responsibility.

The capacity of the public sector to provide the needed human services is highlighted by the multitude of large brick and mortar facilities known as institutions for the mentally retarded and mentally ill. Although it was clearly the trend of the past to use self-contained facilities, the concept of warehousing is not just a result of the facility but a staff attitude and perception as well. The recent decisions in the Pennhurst class action suit further verify that these facilities are inappropriate, inhuman, and unconstitutional. Not only was the facility unsafe but the programs provided to the residents were totally inadequate.

It would be easy to place all of the blame on the structure of this type of facility. However, a large portion of the blame belongs on the system, as well. The lack of prior training, the nonexistence of a career ladder, and the absence of material and training techniques all help to develop a lethargic, self-perpetuating, and self-serving attitude on the part of workers in such a service delivery system. New initiatives emerging from employee ranks are often met with limited or no support from the administration, while legislative bodies are more often than not reluctant to appropriate the necessary expeditures to bring the level of service up to standard.

The lack of incentive for involvement of the private sector has emanated from the lack of financing and reimbursement, inadequate monitoring, inefficient administration, and general disinterest in providing this type of service. Certain advocacy and consumer organizations have become involved out of a sense of personal commitment and have conducted business out of the "milk of human kindness" rather than from sound administrative or programmatic beliefs. Within the last decade as the community movement has expanded and private vendors have become more interested in working with state government in providing the full range of service options for the developmentally disabled. Much of this effort has been prompted by a willingness on the part of the bureaucratic system to reimburse costs of programs and spell out program goals and objectives. Class action suits during the past few years have also been a stimulus to vendors to engage in the development of comprehensive services at all levels. For example, the private sector, through federal supports such as Housing and Urban Development, Urban Mass Transportation Authorities, and Title XIX and XX of the Social Security Amendments, is finding sufficient fiscal incentive in the form of cash grants and subsidies to engage in providing services.

The public sector's past problems in providing comprehensive services raises serious concerns about the continuation of this model of service delivery. In many ways the utilization of "pass through" monies, as in the case of education, may be the mechanism which would provide fiscal stability in a wide range of treatment and service programs. The incentive for private vendor involvement is greatly enhanced as the expense and reimbursement procedures are clarified. It would seem that the flexibility of the private sector around the control of staff and program would indicate that this mechanism of direct service delivery could be much more responsive than the large and generally inflexible public agency approach. If one looks at the model of health care delivery, the use of the private insurer has met with noteworthy success. That is not to say that the private sector would be without its difficulties, but that the management structure in a private sector is often more responsive and capable of change.

The use of the private vendor in many states has shown that on a fee-for-service basis human services can be provided in a more effective and efficient fashion. The more recent approach of block funding and contracting has added a new degree of flexibility to funding services through the private vendor sector. As the use of the private sector has increased, it has become apparent that there is not a need for a dual public and private delivery system and that, in fact, such a dual system may lead to ambiguity of roles and inefficiency of operation. The public sector has more recently assumed the role of a regulatory agency in monitoring and evaluating existing programs in many instances. This role seems, in many ways, highly suited to it. Such a function creates an automatic check and balance; the private vendor has the capacity to engage in services and the public sector monitors the services.

The scope of the need and the degree of coordination necessary in providing services to handicapped persons, particularly severely handicapped adults, mandates a more sophisticated approach to rendering services by both the public and private sector. Bake sales can no longer support the community residences nor can token subcontract work from industry maintain a rehabilitation facility. Community apathy is changing to apprehension and resistance as more and more handicapped individuals are entering local neighborhoods, businesses, and recreational programs. Small business mentalities and economic inefficiencies must give way to more sound, fiscal approaches in human services. In addition to the professional trained in providing services directly to the handicapped adult, professionals with business expertise as well as those with competence in public relations need to be considered not as ancillary team members but full time members. The proliferation of the small, emotionally invested service vendors such as the various advocacy groups encourages fiscal inefficiency, a wide discrepancy in the quality of programming, and perpetuation of the "reinvention of the wheel" phenomena. On the other hand, massive service vendor systems such as those in the public sector are no more cost effective, the quality of the service is seldom monitored, and the opportunity for getting lost in the system is high.

Smaller, more well defined vendors with the capacity to address the broad range of service needs for both the community and the handicapped individual are necessary. Vendors who are able to provide a wide variety of residential options, day treatment programs, and recreational activities are necessary. In addition, these vendors must have the capacity to look at and control costs, recruit high quality and well trained staff, and deal with community concerns and needs. Such a vendor system can relate to both the community and the handicapped individual in the community through direct service and technical assistance. Emphasis placed upon community awareness and utilization of community health, educational, and social resources may provide a means through which the attitudinal barriers can be resolved. The smaller, more localized vendor system can provide technical assistance to the neighborhood resources as the assimilation of the handicapped person into the community progresses.

Much of this latter section has advocated for a more decentralized approach with recognition of the need for a broad-based and sophisticated service delivery system. The present public human service system is inflexible and, in many ways, unresponsive to change. However, it has the capacity to monitor, evaluate, and finance smaller, more adaptable units on a contract or fee-for-service basis. These smaller units of service are hardly the panacea, running the risk of encouraging duplication and possibly fragmenting research and training efforts. A totally private vendor model runs as many risks of insensitivity, unresponsiveness, and rigidity as the large public sector. What is necessary is a combination of both public and private services creating a system which has the capacity to change as the needs of the handicapped individual change, respond to the needs of both nonhandicapped and handicapped persons, provide a wide range of direct services, support pure and applied research and training at all levels, and, finally, be responsible and accountable financially and programmatically. The market approach of the private sector in combination with the bureaucratic or systems approach of the public sector seems to have a great deal of potential as the move towards the development of a comprehensive service system proceeds.

SUMMARY

Rehabilitation planning is complex, requiring more sophisticated data collection, a clearer identification of the needs of the service recipients, and greater accountability. The range of service needs as well as the magnitude of needs has yet to be clearly established; however, most professionals now realize that rehabilitation planning is an interdisciplinary process. For many handicapped people, particularly severely handicapped individuals, the need for services is life long although the nature of the need and the intensity of the need are variable. Programs must be responsive to individual differences and individual needs. Professionals must not only have skills in their own disciplines but be cognizant of the role of other disciplines as well. Business practices must be more systematically applied to the provision of human services and greater attention must be paid to the feelings of both handicapped and nonhandicapped individuals in the community.

Not only is the service delivery system changing but the nature of the service recipient is likewise changing. Self-advocacy and peer counseling have encouraged the handicapped individual to become an active participant rather than a passive recipient in the rehabilitation process. Greater awareness and sensitivity for those not able to advocate for themselves has been magnified by the expanded role of the citizen advocacy movement and the development of protection and advocacy projects at the local, state, and national level. Federal courts through the medium of consent decrees have required the system to be more flexible, responsive, and accountable whereas the advocacy movement has required that the system and the professionals in the system develop a capacity to attend to and respond to the request of the handicapped individual. The rehabilitation process is one which requires involvement on an active basis and working together of handicapped individuals and professionals directed at maximizing the strengths vocationally, socially, residentially, and recreationally. For the handicapped adult rehabilitation is an active rather than passive process; for the professional, an interdisciplinary process; for the nonhandicapped person, an acceptance process.

REFERENCES

National Association for Retarded Citizens. October 1973. The Right to Choose: Achieving Residential Status in the Community. NARC, Arlington, TX.

The President's Committee on Employment of the Handicapped. 1970. One in Eleven: Handicapped Adults in America. U.S. Government Printing Office, Washington, DC.

Halderman v. *Pennhurst State School and Hospital,* No. 74–1345 (E.D. PA 1977)

RELATED READINGS

Abeson, A. July 1977. The Educational Least Restrictive Alternative, pp. 23–26. National Center for Law and The Handicapped, South Bend, IN.

Baker, B., Seltzer, G., and Seltzer, M. 1974. As Close as Possible: A Study of Community Residences for Retarded Adults. Read House, Harvard University, Boston.

Cobb, H. 1976. Menatal Retardation: Trends in State Services. The President's Committee on Mental Retardation, U.S. Government Printing Office, Washington, DC.

Daniels, L. (Ed.), 1974. Vocational Rehabilitation of the Mentally Retarded. Charles C Thomas, Publishers, Springfield, IL.

Department of Health, Education and Welfare. May 1975. A Summary of Selected Legislation Relating to the Handicapped 1974. Department of Health, Education and Welfare, U.S. Government Printing Office, Washington, DC.

Department of Health, Education and Welfare. September 1977. Key Federal Regulations Affecting the Handicapped 1975–76. Department of Health, Education and Welfare, U.S. Government Printing Office, Washington, DC.

Gordon, J. (Ed.) 1975. Developmental Disabilities: An Orientation to Epilepsy, Cerebral Palsy and Mental Retardation. Temple University, Philadelphia.

Hull, K. January/February 1978. Advocates as Amicus Curiae: Friends of the Court Effecting Change, pp. 27–30. National Center for Law and The Handicapped, Division of Legal Services, South Bend, IN.

Implementing P.L. 94–142: Gearing up—consumer concerns. October 1976. *Closer Look.*

Kindred, M., Cohen, J., Penrod, D., and Shaffer, T. 1976. The Mentally Retarded Citizens and the Law. The Free Press, Macmillan Publishing Co., New York.

Office of the Handicapped Individuals. March 1977. Instructional Support System for Special Education. Programs for the Handicapped, Office of the Handicapped Individuals, U.S. Government Printing Office, Washington, DC.

Peterson, R., and Mitchell, D. May 1978. Orientation to the Process. National Association for Retarded Citizens, Federal Programs Information and Assistance Project, U.S. Government Printing Office, Washington, DC.

Rosen, M., Clark, G., and Kivitz, M. 1977. Habilitation of the Handicapped. University Park Press, Baltimore, MD.

Stahlecker, L. V. (Ed.) Occupational Information for the Mentally Retarded: Selected Readings. Charles C Thomas, Publishers, Springfield, IL.

The Commission for the Control of Epilepsy and Its Consequences. August 1977. Plan for Nationwide Action on Epilepsy. The Commission for the Control of Epilepsy and Its Consequences, Bethesda, MD.

Thompson, M. March 1977. Housing for the Handicapped and Disabled: A Guide for Local Action. The National Association of Housing and Development Office, U.S. Government Printing Office, Washington, DC.

Thurlow, M., Bruininks, R., Williams, S., and Morreau, L. January 1978. Deinstitutionalization and Residential Services: A Literature Survey. Information and Technical Assistance Project on Deinstitutionalization, Minneapolis, MN.

Waldman, S. 1976. National Health and Insurance Proposals: Provisions of Bills Introduced in the 94th Congress as of February 1976. Department of Health, Education and Welfare, Social Security Administration, Office of Research and Statistics, U.S. Government Printing Office, Washington, DC.

Wortis, J. (Ed.) 1975. Mental Retardation and Developmental Disabilities. Brunner/ Mazel Publishing Co., New York.

Chapter 7
Advocacy

Marianne Bennett & Robert P. Mc Neill

As advocacy systems more frequently appear across the spectrum of service delivery, the word "advocacy" risks becoming overused and misused. It may well be that more already has been said on the topic than many want to hear or can usefully interpret. In keeping with this concern, this chapter will not exhaustively review all the various advocacy models or types of advocates, nor will it systematically review the litigation of the past few years which has established (arguably) rights to treatment, habilitation in the least restrictive setting, education, and so forth. Rather, it will define some of the advocates and advocacy systems, identify problems for planners of such services, and suggest areas where advocates are most needed.

Many groups present a need for advocacy. It is in this broader context, *i.e.,* on behalf of children, the elderly, the environment, responsive government, etc., that the word advocacy is generally used. Persons with severely handicapping conditions, and in particular, those with impairment of intellect and adaptive behavior, have perhaps the greatest need for advocacy. They lack the ability to self-advocate, and they require an unusually complex array of services that only rarely is readily available.

AN OVERVIEW OF ADVOCACY

Advocacy, quite simply, means to plead the cause of another. In defining what special meaning the term has in the field of developmental disabilities or severely handicapping conditions, it is necessary to examine what benefits the advocate can provide and explore the types of problems the advocate is expected to solve.

For the severely handicapped, the concept of advocacy goes far beyond the narrow role of attorney or legal advocate. Although a legal advocate is needed in some instances, the range of necessary advocacy services includes assistance in gaining access to services, aid in utilizing available resources, support and encouragement for the individuals to maximize their ability to advocate for themselves, changes in the service system to make it more accessible to, and usable by, the severely handicapped, and information and education to increase public awareness of the needs of severely handicapped citizens.

Individual advocacy is the necessary link between a handicapped person's particular needs and the actual provision of services required, or the enforcement of certain rights through resort to a lawyer. *Collective advocacy* is the essential link in the process which begins with a recognition of inadequacy or injustice, leads to official change in policy, and, ultimately, to the provision of new services for groups of individuals.

Indeed, the successes of recent years in terms of court decisions and Congressional enactments have been occasioned by the advocacy of a few individuals and organizations. Such efforts themselves have led to greater demands for advocates and advocacy systems. The recognition by the courts over the past several years of the rights of the mentally retarded and subsequent efforts to implement those rights by Congress and state legislatures has led to a need to focus more attention on implementation of official rulings and new laws. Implementation of court decrees and new legislation is always more difficult than it is assumed will be the case beforehand; the actual provision of promised services, or services to which an individual is in theory entitled, becomes a problem requiring advocates or an advocacy system for resolution. A court order reciting certain minimum standards for institutional care for the retarded, or a state law promising ''appropriate habilitation'' will not lead to such standards or treatment unless and until someone's advocacy efforts result in actual implementation.

Important lawsuits and court decisions affecting the severely handicapped have marked the 1970s. The rights of severely handicapped persons in civil commitment proceedings, rights to a free, appropriate education, protections of important civil liberties, and the right to treatment for persons involuntarily confined to institutions have all been addressed by judicial decree.[1]

Although litigation is, and will continue to be, a major impetus for needed change, considerable attention has been directed to nonlegal advocacy. The basis for nonlegal advocacy systems is a recognition that the process of day-to-day existence can be quite difficult for the severely handicapped or developmentally disabled individual. Anyone who has ever applied

---

[1]Although a complete listing of landmark litigation is beyond the scope of this chapter, the following cases should be noted. *Dixon* v. *Attorney General* 325 F. Supp. 966 (M.D. Pa. 1971) (rights of mentally retarded persons in civil commitment); *Pennsylvania Association for Retarded Children* v. *Pennsylvania*, 334 F. Supp. 1257 (E.D. Pa. 1971); *Mills* v. *Board of Education*, 348 F. Supp. 866 (D.D.C. 1972) (right to public education); *Boyde* v. *Board of Registrars of Voters*, 334 N.E. 2d 629 (Mass. 1975) (right to vote); *Donaldson* v. *O'Connor* 493 F. 2d 507 (Cir. 1974) (right to treatment in institutions); *Halderman* v. *Pennhurst State School and Hospital* 446 F. Supp. 1295 (E.D. Pa. 1977) (right to habilitation).

for a driver's license, filled out insurance claims forms, or been a recipient of unemployment benefits or workman's compensation knows the complexities of the bureaucracy and the inherent insanity of the process. To expect a severely disabled person, particularly one whose mental capacity may be impaired, to navigate the bureaucracy unaided is to assure that the applicant will be unfairly treated, ignored, or abused. The intricacies of the Social Security Administration and the 20 titles that comprise the Social Security Act, a prime source of support for severely handicapped people, present a strong argument for the creation of capable advocacy systems.

A more serious problem than unfair treatment or abuse is *exclusion* from the service delivery system. Participation in various programs, services, and entitlements requires a fairly sophisticated degree of ability to understand the process by which application is made or entry is achieved. For the severely handicapped, an advocate may be needed simply to negotiate the application process.

Implicit in the idea that advocacy is an appropriate and, indeed, necessary component in the spectrum of services which should be available to the severely handicapped is a recognition of the validity of the concept of normalization. The principle of normalization derives from the field of mental retardation, but it certainly has applicability to other serious handicapping conditions. In essence, the principle holds that the retarded should live as normal a life as is possible, and that efforts on behalf of the retarded should be directed towards that goal.[2] To this end advocates help individuals obtain benefits to which they are entitled, assist in removing barriers which isolate severely handicapped persons from the rest of society, and attempt to expand the opportunities to participate equally as citizens.

A related concept which applies much more specifically to the problems of mental retardation and certain other developmental disorders than to serious physically handicapping conditions is the developmental model of programming. This concept rejects the notion that the retarded or otherwise developmentally disabled individual is incapable of growth and development. Rather, it asserts that each individual, regardless of the severity of the handicap, has potential for some growth, learning, and development.[3]

To enable severely handicapped individuals to live a life as normal as possible and to grow, develop, and learn to the extent their individual potential might permit requires a level of commitment not usually found in service systems. Programs and even attitudes of staff are "generic," and not usually designed for or sensitive to the severely impaired individual. Those who are able to seek assistance and maneuver their way through the system (and it

---

[2]For a helpful discussion of the principle of normalization, *see* Scheerenberger (1976), pp. 73–75.

[3]*See* Scheerenberger. (1976), p. 71.

helps if they can afford to hire a lawyer) will receive the rewards the system has to offer; those who fall between the cracks (*i.e.*, between the various generic service programs) or those who simply can not effectively gain access to the services theoretically available to them, are the unfortunate casualties of a large and complex system.

In short, both the developmental approach and the principle of normalization place significant demands on the service delivery system. Federal legislation and support from the Department of Health, Education and Welfare aimed at providing personnel trained in the interdisciplinary approach to services for the developmentally disabled and multiply handicapped have provided significant numbers of skilled, committed professionals in the field who have to some extent ameliorated past practices.[4] The demand for such trained workers still far exceeds the supply, however. For example, a major obstacle to reform in state institutions for the developmentally disabled remains the absence of qualified personnel in sufficient numbers to provide adequate habilitation for the residents.

Advocacy provides a mechanism of offsetting the major disadvantage a serious handicap poses when an impersonal, bureaucratic, and generic service system is confronted. To effectively carry out the needed functions, advocates must operate in a variety of forums and utilize a number of different mechanisms to plead the cause of their severely handicapped client.

Most of the nonlegal approaches to advocacy have roots in the Scandinavian "ombudsman" model. However, important adjustments were necessary to adapt that concept to the severely handicapped population which these systems serve. The traditional ombudsman serves a number of people in single problem situations. The consumer contacts the ombudsman and the description of the problem is provided by the client. Such an approach is not effective for most severely handicapped persons, who have a continuing need for advocacy, rather than an isolated need. The severely handicapped individual often cannot independently gain access to an advocacy system; therefore, the system needs to maintain an outreach effort. Finally, the handicapped person may be unable to articulate the problems which he or she is encountering. In some cases, the client, particularly one who has been institutionalized, may have had so little opportunity for normal experiences that the entire concept of choice and decision making is threatening and foreign.

Effective advocacy for the severely handicapped must be highly individualized, flexible in approach, and committed to maximizing the potential for self-advocacy. A variety of models are being tried. The following is a summary of systems most frequently encountered.

---

[4]Section 511, Social Security Act, administered by the Office for Maternal and Child Health, DHEW; PL 88-164 and subsequent amendments (The Developmental Disabilities Acts), administered by the Bureau of Developmental Disabilities, Office of Human Development Services, DHEW.

ADVOCACY MODELS

Citizen Advocates

Citizen advocacy is a method of providing advocates for the severely handicapped through the use of volunteers trained and committed to assisting the handicapped person in a one-to-one relationship. The model for citizen advocacy originated with parents' organizations in the field of mental retardation. Parents are usually primary advocates for their severely handicapped children (Turnbull and Turnbull, 1975). Most notably in the field of mental retardation, parents organized to provide mutual support to each other in coping with the problems and pressures of raising a severely handicapped child. As these parent organizations became involved in pleading for changes in the systems of service delivery to the severely handicapped, parents realized they could often press more effectively for children of others because such efforts were not impeded by the emotional constraints that attended advocating for their own child. This approach to effective advocacy led to the formation of citizen advocacy systems. The National Association for Retarded Citizens (NARC) has provided funding for national citizen advocacy. This definition has been adopted:

> Citizen Advocacy for mentally retarded persons is basically a one-to-one relationship between a capable volunteer ("advocate") and a mentally retarded person ("protege") in which the advocate defends the rights and interest of the protege and provides practical or emotional reinforcement (or a combination of both) for him. All of this occurs within the framework of a structured advocacy system. (NARC, 1974)

Under this definition the citizen advocate performs a variety of tasks. For example, the advocate may assist the protégé in applying for social security benefits and then also assist the protégé in learning how to shop for food and clothing, how to budget for rent and utilities, and how to save for major expenditures. The citizen advocate may investigate programs or services which might benefit the protégé, then will encourage the protégé to participate and will assist in problem solving as difficulties arise. The citizen advocate must be responsible for becoming knowledgeable about legal rights and then assist the protégé to obtain legal services when such intervention is necessary. Clearly, the citizen advocate must be a capable individual with a variety of practical skills.

The most important advantage for the protégé of having a citizen advocate is the availability of on-going assistance in a variety of areas affecting day-to-day needs and rights. The citizen advocate can develop a sensitivity to the particular needs of the protégé and a facility in advocating vigorously for that individual's particular needs. In addition the citizen advocate and the protégé develop mutual support and respect for the complementary efforts of each other and can work effectively as a team.

Problems with citizen advocacy efforts that have been encountered include turnover among the volunteer advocates, a lack of accountability by the advocate to the protégé, and, occasionally, an insufficient understanding of the particular needs of a protégé. Citizen advocacy coordinators have attempted to establish on-going back-up services for the volunteer advocate. Support for the volunteers must be specialized, organized, and well managed or the system becomes fragmented and paternalistic. Handbooks, films, and training sessions have been developed to assist citizen advocate planners in establishing effective networks of advocacy services.[5]

Case Manager Advocates

Case manager advocates may be defined as professionals trained to represent an individual's needs and rights. Case manager advocates may be found within service systems or independent of service providers. Frustration over the performance of governmental agencies has led to experimentation with in-house advocates—agency persons trained to represent consumers who have complaints against the agency. One model for this type of advocacy is the Client Assistance Project (CAP) of Vocational Rehabilitation. CAP components have been instituted on an experimental basis in a number of cities across the country. These projects provide in-house ombudsmen who advocate for vocational rehabilitation clients to the division of vocational rehabilitation as an agency. The units are autonomous from local project offices and are usually responsible to the state directors of vocational rehabilitation. Although these projects are relatively new, the early experiences have demonstrated that they provide a valuable mechanism for access to services.

The most important advantage of a professional, in-house advocate is the ability of the case manager advocate to be extremely knowledgeable about the rules, regulations and procedures of his agency. An effective case manager advocate can significantly enhance the accessibility and program compatibility for the benefit of the client.

An obvious problem with this approach to advocacy exists. The advocate is only nominally independent of the service provider, and a conflict of interest situation is inherent in the position. Ultimately, the advocate must choose between the interests of the client and the system of which he or she is part. The pressures on the advocate within the system will more than likely lead to a point of diminished effectiveness from the standpoint of the client. Notwithstanding the limitations, the in-house advocate is in a unique position to act favorably on behalf of the disabled client, and should be considered an important component of the agency or service provider. Ideally, a case man-

---

[5]The National Association for Retarded Citizens, PO Box 6109 Arlington, TX 76011 is an excellent resource for advocacy materials. In addition the Kansas University Affiliated Facility (Bureau of Child Research), Lawrence, KS 66045 has prepared materials which are helpful to the planner.

ager advocate and citizen advocate working cooperatively should be able to provide complementary components of advocacy services to the client experiencing problems with a particular service agency.

Case manager advocates can perhaps function most effectively when they are independent of service providers. The concept of professional, full time advocates received a boost from Congress through passage of Public Law 94–103 and subsequent amendments in PL 95–602. This law, the Developmental Disabilities Act, mandates Protection and Advocacy (P & A) systems for the developmentally disabled in each state and territory. In addition, the 1978 amendments to the Rehabilitation Act authorize P & A systems in each of the states for the severely handicapped, a population which admittedly overlaps with the developmentally disabled. The P & A systems are organized in a variety of ways and utilize a broad spectrum of advocacy models. However, in essence, each system can be categorized as an independent professional advocacy system. The availability of such systems across the country emphasizes the importance of advocacy services for the severely handicapped and should provide important information about where advocates can be most effective.

Systems Advocacy

Systems advocacy has been defined as "the process of influencing social and political systems to bring about change for groups of people" (Eklund, 1976).

This broad definition would cover most activities aimed at benefiting groups, as opposed to particular individuals, which are carried out in direct relation to social institutions and government. Lobbying by the NARC, for example, would clearly qualify as systems advocacy. Why then is a separate definition of this sort of activity as a category of advocacy needed?

The severely handicapped, and particularly mentally retarded individuals, are at greater risk than other groups in our society because of their disabling condition. Thus, the advocate is an indispensable party to the process of securing basic rights and services for this group. Other interest groups find it much easier to influence the system because they can themselves participate, frequently with great effectiveness, in the process. Thus, although the oil and gas industry may be ably represented in Washington, the industry also effectively represents itself through individual members of the interest group. Even the poor, who lack the economic power that makes the greatest difference in terms of influencing official policy, are able to organize, attend meetings, and plead their own cause. Evidence of this can be found at state Title XX planning meetings when eligible parent recipients of child day care services speak for themselves.

The process of influencing social and political systems is a different kind of activity when the group to be assisted cannot effectively participate in the effort. Systems advocacy, in the context of planning services to the severely handicapped, is therefore more than lobbying or traditional social activism. The process recognizes that systems need to be addressed in the broad sense, not just to benefit one individual, but to change policies, laws, and traditions that affect groups which are similarly situated. Moreover, systems advocacy (and all forms of advocacy) recognizes the special problem posed by the likelihood that the beneficiary of such activity will not be an effective participant in such effort.

Legal Advocacy

Despite the recent attention directed at new advocacy models, the backbone of advocacy services is still the legal advocate. In some advocacy systems a legal component is treated as the stick in the closet; in other systems legal advocates occupy a front line position. However, the importance of the legal advocate is underscored by the regulations for the Federal Developmental Disabilities Protection and Advocacy Systems which mandate a capability to pursue remedies through the legal process.[6]

Legal advocates for severely handicapped persons can be categorized into three models. The first is the *public interest law center*. The second is the *ombudsman*. The third is the *private bar,* providing services either through contract with P & A systems or other advocacy systems for the severely handicapped. Each of these models has its own strengths and each presents particular pitfalls for advocacy planners. In addition, there are a number of serious, unresolved ethical questions which arise in any legal representation of clients with diminished capacity.

Public Interest Law Center   A public interest law center may be defined as a law firm, usually structured as a nonprofit corporation, supported in whole or in part by public or philanthropic funding sources, which provides a broad range of legal services for a particular special interest consumer group. The centers may provide legal services within a particular state or region,[7] or they may be national in service delivery.[8] Some centers provide legal services to a broadly defined population,[9] whereas others have defined their client group

---

[6]Interim Guidelines for Development and Implementation of a System for Protection of the Individual Rights of and Advocacy for Persons with Developmental Disabilities under the Developmental Disabilities Services and Facilities Construction Act as amended by Section 113 of PL 94–103 for fiscal year 1978 (Revised November 1, 1976).

[7]The regional focus is exemplified by the Louisiana Center for the Public Interest, 700 Maison Blanche Building, New Orleans, LA 70112 which provides direct and indirect legal assistance to advocates in Louisiana, Texas, Arkansas, Oklahoma, and New Mexico. The Nevada Center for Law and the Rights of the Mentally Retarded, 700 Sutro Street, Reno, NE 89512 is primarily a Nevada resource.

[8]The Public Interest Law Center of Philadelphia 1315 Walnut Street, Philadelphia, PA 19107; the National Center for Law and the Handicapped, 1235 North Eddy Street, South Bend, IN 46617; and The Mental Health Law Project, 1220 19th Street, NW, Washington, DC 20036 are just a few of the national legal centers for the severely handicapped.

[9]The National Center for Law and the Handicapped, for example, lists its eligibility criteria as "all handicapping conditions."

narrowly and specifically. Some centers provide representation to individual clients as well as to clients representative of a class;[10] others select their clients primarily on the basis of the potential impact on the population as a whole.[11] All of the public interest law centers devote some of their resources to training and technical assistance either of the private bar, consumers, legislators, or administrative agencies. Many centers appear regularly as *amicus curiae* in cases which have a potentially significant impact in this developing area of the law.

The important contributions of the public interest law centers cannot be disputed. It is undoubtedly true that many of the landmark cases in developmental disabilities law would never have been brought without the availability of full time counsel, and the needed lawyers have frequently been provided by such public interest law groups. Because the centers have full time staff attorneys specializing in various legal issues affecting the severely handicapped and developmentally disabled, they have acquired a high level of expertise in particular fields. In addition, the centers have utilized interdisciplinary staffing patterns and have thereby expanded their capability to deal with complex issues.

These centers serve as national resources for other advocates and disseminate information through periodicals,[12] training packages,[13] conferences,[14] and workshops.[15] The importance of these outreach service capabilities has recently been underscored by Department of Health, Education and Welfare, which has provided funding specifically for such tasks.

---

[10]The Developmental Disabilities Law Project, University of Maryland Law School, 500 West Baltimore Street, Baltimore, MD 21201, provides both individual legal assistance through their clinical law office and intervention in class actions or impact litigation through the staff attorneys who have recognized expertise in mental disabilities law. Two projects which provide legal services to the severely handicapped in institutions are the Comserv Center for Legal Representation, PO Box 1269, Los Lunas, NM 87031 (the writers are both associated with this project) and the Institutional Legal Services Project, Easter State Hospital, Medical Lake, WA 99022.

[11]The most common vehicle for impact litigation is a class action in which several plaintiffs bring suit on behalf of themselves and all others similarly situated. However, individual cases can also be of genuine significance for the severely handicapped if they articulate new rights, particularly under federal law.

[12]Two publications which are of particular value to the legal advocate are *The Mental Disability Law Reporter,* ABA Commission on the Mentally Disabled, 1800 M Street, NW, Washington, DC 20036 and *Amicus,* National Center for Law and the Handicapped, *see* Footnote 8.

[13]The Public Interest Law Center of Philadelphia (*see* Footnote 8) has developed a training package on Section 504 of the Rehabilitation Act of 1973 designed for lay advocates in the community.

[14]The results of a series of regional conferences on advocacy under PL 94–103 have been published. The publications are available from Research and Training Center in Mental Retardation, Texas Tech University, Lubbock, TX 79409.

[15]National organizations such as the American Association on Mental Deficiency and the American Association for the Education of the Severely and Profoundly Handicapped regularly invite legal advocates to participate in their annual meetings and address legal concerns affecting the severely handicapped.

Advocacy planners should also be aware of certain drawbacks to the public interest law center approach when considering models of advocacy services for implementation in a particular area. The first problem is funding. As was noted above, these centers rely heavily on public monies. Although recent changes in legislation have made recovery of legal fees a more realistic possibility, no legal center has yet generated sufficient fees to be self-supporting. Therefore, a significant percentage of somebody's time will have to be devoted to fund raising. Not only does the task of proposal writing, reporting, and monitoring consume resources of a legal center, the activities of a publicly supported project are dictated to an extent by the types of tasks for which funds are available. Priorities are, in effect, set not by the advocates but by Congress and the executive agencies. Thus the emphasis in a particular legal center may shift from mental illness, to mental retardation, to special education, and then to employment as priorities for funding shift and change at the national level. Consumers may come to rely on the availability of a particular service only to find it discontinued in a succeeding fiscal year.

A second problem is the availability of legal counsel through public interest law centers for individual, nonrepresentative clients. The recognition that severely handicapped persons are entitled to individual representation in commitment, habilitation, education, and legal services has come about primarily through judicial decrees which have been followed by legislation at both the state and national level. However, the advocates who were instrumental in establishing these rights have not, as a rule, been available for the second generation implementation which must follow. Primarily, this lack of availability is a resource allocation problem. Even the largest and best supported public interest law centers rarely have available more than a handful of staff attorneys. Unlike their legal services counterparts, legal advocates for the severely handicapped face a 100-percent utilization figure among their client population. Even doubling the available attorneys in any existing center would not provide sufficient legal counsel to represent every institutionalized person, every school child, etc. Difficult decisions have had to be made and they generally have been to represent those cases which present legal issues with broad impact.

Finally, there is a federal forum preference among the public interest law centers which arises from a constitutional law orientation as a basis for their litigation choices, the practical concerns of bar admission, familiarity with procedural requirements, and general higher level of trust in the federal court system over state courts. This preference is not a drawback except to the extent that it has limited the reliance on state court remedies in suits brought by national legal centers. As state legislatures provide for remedies within their own court systems, there will have to be an increased emphasis on the procedures in each of the state court systems. Lawyers who practice in the state courts will need to develop the capability to pursue change through their state court systems. Moreover, it is important that a body of law at the state level be developed to complement and support decisions in the federal courts.

Ombudsman Lawyers The lack of sufficient funds to support an extensive legal staff has led to utilization of the legal advocate as a general ombudsman in many advocacy systems. The tasks of the lawyer/ombudsman vary but the following description is illustrative.

The lawyer may choose a particular issue and provide representation to clients with a problem in that area: for example, special education, accessibility to public buildings, access to community services for training, transportation and employment, are all issues which need to be addressed by a legal advocate. In some systems there may be multiple priorities and the lawyer carries a diverse caseload. The advocate in such a system is not the last resort for advocacy services, but often the first, and may handle the case from intake through resolution utilizing whatever remedies are appropriate.

For advocacy planners there are several important considerations to weigh in utilization of this model. First of all, an ombudsman can be a powerful political persuader as well as an effective advocate in individual cases. If a particular state is not complying with special education requirements, for example, the well publicized fact that due process education hearings will be vigorously pursued by a legal advocate with the capability and the resources to exhaust all available remedies may have a chilling effect on a recalcitrant state education department. It is generally true that a school board is less apt to disregard complaints about inadequate education programs when the parent is represented vigorously by counsel.

There needs to be a careful analysis of the most effective use of the lawyer/ombudsman. It is important that a state P & A system or an advocacy planner establish priorities within which the ombudsman will operate. It is also important that other types of advocacy services be available to supplement the efforts of the legal advocate. This may occur through training of lay advocates who will handle cases through the administrative stage with the lawyer available for consultation during the administrative process to insure an adequate record for a subsequent appeal.[16] Or it may be more effective to have all cases handled initially by the legal advocate and to phase in paralegal or lay advocates as the process becomes established and regularized. A system may choose a combination of these approaches and have most of the reviews handled by lay advocates and involve the legal advocate only in difficult or potentially precedent-setting cases. In order for such cooperative advocacy to be effective, there must be a constant interchange between lay advocates and the lawyer/ombudsman. The responsibilities for case selection, methods of case management, and the criteria for mandatory legal consultation must be

---

[16]One model for such cooperative efforts is the Colorado Association for Retarded Citizens, which trains advocates in cooperation with Colorado Legal Services which provides legal back-up when necessary.

clearly established. Although there is genuine respect among advocates for the varying capabilities of each type of advocacy, there has also been confusion over the extent of the advocacy responsibilities of each.

An additional consideration for advocacy planners in utilizing legal/ombudsman advocates is case selection and access by the disabled client to the legal advocate. Because the emphasis in this model is individual case representation, it is important to develop mechanisms which will avoid merely responding to the "squeaky wheel" consumer. The nature of the disabilities affecting this class of consumers means that the client most in need of a legal advocate is usually least able to gain access to those services. Mechanisms for making services available to the institutionalized developmentally disabled, the severely handicapped homebound, and the severely disabled person who is also an ethnic minority must be developed. A legal ombudsman should develop creative mechanisms for reaching those members of the client class most in need of an advocate.

Finally, a back-up system of legal support for lawyers serving in this capacity is needed. As was mentioned above, many advocacy systems have opted to use lawyers in an advocate/ombudsman role because of limited resources to support an extensive legal component. In some states this may mean employment of a single lawyer. The nature of the practice often means that the legal advocate will be isolated from the private bar and will find professional support sparse or nonexistent. The Legal Services Corporation has concluded that single-lawyer offices in the field of poverty law place an unmanageable strain on the lawyer involved. Advocacy systems should be aware of the long term detrimental effects of professional isolation and provide the resources for an attorney/advocate to establish ties with other legal advocates, public interest law centers, and national resource centers. In addition, strong efforts should be made to involve the private bars both to expand available services and also to decrease the isolation of the attorney/ombudsman.

Private Bar Advocacy Services   Although the response of the private bar has not been overwhelming, there are some discernible benchmarks that indicate a growing awareness of bar associations of the need for legal advocates in the field of severely handicapping conditions. The most obvious is the creation of bar committees concerned with mental disabilities.[17] Generally, these committees provide an educational service to the bar association as a whole, either through special continuing legal education programs or presentations at regularly scheduled bar conventions. The scope, caliber, and sophisti-

---

[17]The ABA Commission on the Mentally Disabled has provided funding for local bar-sponsored projects to expand the involvement of bar associations into this area of the law.

cation of these committee efforts vary widely but their existence is, itself, progress. Advocacy planners should become familiar with these committees and should not discount their impact.

Some advocacy systems contract with private attorneys for their necessary legal component. Although this approach probably is less costly than employing a full time lawyer, there are problems as well. The first is the problem of expertise. Representing severely handicapped and, particularly, developmentally disabled individuals is a unique experience for most lawyers. The usual principles which apply to the lawyer-client relationship are frequently absent in this case. Instead there is a requirement that the lawyer have a philosophical commitment to the client's maximum participation in and control over his own case. Although curriculum changes in law schools are beginning to address the problems of representing mentally disabled persons and other handicapped groups, most attorneys have had no particular training in this field. In addition, a lawyer in private practice may not be aware of what resources are available and may not have access to the most current information in legal concerns of the severely handicapped. Advocacy planners should, themselves, be knowledgeable of legal resources in their region and make such information available to contracting attorneys in order to maximize the attorneys' effectiveness. Utilizing private bar committees may be an effective mechanism of making available this information.

A few law firms have traditionally committeed a limited part of their resources to public interest work, performed without charge, in certain subject areas. Such *pro bono* services, as they are called, do not constitute a major source of legal work on behalf of severely handicapped individuals, but some increased attention to this population by law firms has been evidenced. Many law firms have adopted a fairly traditional approach to their *pro bono* files, however, and it will probably be difficult to encourage expansion into a new area of the law, particularly since *pro bono* efforts are not increasing in general. Education of the private bar as to the needs of severely handicapped persons with respect to legal services is an important step towards greater public interest work in this area by law firms.

An effective system of legal advocacy for severely handicapped persons should have components of all of the models. Full time legal advocates who have the capability of pursuing specific issues to achieve change are needed. There must be legal back-up of lay advocate efforts to provide the muscle of litigation where necessary and to assure that all remedies are adequately pursued. Furthermore, there must be a commitment on the part of the private bar to represent the unique needs of the severely handicapped client. Finally, there must be cooperation among all the legal advocates and between the lawyers and the nonlawyer advocates to provide effective services to the clients which the system serves.

ADVOCACY IN INSTITUTIONS

Large, institutionalized populations present a long list of problems requiring both individual advocacy efforts and legal representation of individual clients. Persons residing in institutions for the developmentally disabled are usually the least able to protect their own rights and act in their own self-interests. In addition, many of the residents of such institutions have minimal contact with family or friends and little or no opportunity to develop resources on the "outside" to assist them.

Class action lawsuits filed on behalf of entire populations of some of the more dehumanizing institutions have met with notable success and media coverage, but less than adequate attention has been directed to the chronic problems found in the more "acceptable" institutions. Aside from the question whether any institution can be an appropriate environment, every institutional setting gives rise to questions of regimentation, sterility of environment, and adequacy of habilitation plus problems of maximizing individual growth, learning, and development.

The unique problems which arise in institutional advocacy are illustrated by some of the problems which the authors have encountered in providing representation to severely handicapped clients in an institution in New Mexico.[18] Under New Mexico law a person may be civilly committed to residential habilitation for a developmental disability only upon a judicial finding by clear and convincing evidence that the individual is so greatly disabled that he needs the habilitation proposed and that the proposed commitment is consistent with the least drastic means principle.[19] Civil commitments may not exceed 6 months and a resident is entitled to a hearing to review his commitment at the end of every commitment period.

Two questions are presented in an extended commitment hearing in these circumstances. The first is whether the proposed commitment is consistent with the least drastic means principle or whether the individual could more appropriately be served in a less restrictive setting such as a community group home, companion home, foster home, or his own home. The second question is whether the habilitation which the institution is proposing meets the needs of the individual client. The first question relates clearly to deinstitutionalization, the second to institutional reform.

In theory, every client could reside in a less restrictive setting, either one presently available in the state or one which could be and needs to be made available. However, as a practical matter, there must be an alternative *immediately* available or the individual remains in the institution.

With very few exceptions, the clients represented are not capable of

[18]This project, the Comserv Center for Legal Representation, is supported by the Developmental Disabilities Office of HEW; Grant no. 50–p–30544/6–01 (03).
[19]43–1–1 - 43–1–23 NMSA 1978 Comp.

packing their bags and leaving the institution for independent living in their community. In many instances, staff at the institution will testify on behalf of an individual resident's discharge. However, without a comprehensive and adequate system of community care, judicial findings that a proposed commitment is not consistent with the least drastic means principle constitute a Pyrrhic victory. The legal project has determined such findings to be most helpful to its class of clients as a record upon which to base affirmative litigation efforts or as a mechanism to influence the political process which ultimately must provide the fiscal support for community care. However, it does not appear that periodic review of commitment will, of itself, provide the impetus for deinstitutionalization without an extensive system of community alternatives.

The second issue during a periodic review of commitment is the adequacy of the proposed habilitation plan. Although a detailed analysis of particular habilitation proposals requires review by an independent developmental disabilities professional, the initial review can be completed by project staff. This type of in-house review focuses on determining whether the recommendations of the institution staff are being implemented, whether the client is receiving a minimum number of hours of habilitation, whether there are gross deficiencies in the plan on its face (*i.e.,* a blind resident having movies designated as his recreation or a client with no teeth being on a toothbrushing program), whether the treatment of the resident contains any components for moving him or her closer to deinstitutionalization, and whether there are any forms of treatment (*i.e.,* aversive stimuli or psychotrophic medications) being administered which automatically raise issues of consent.

During the initial year of reviewing individual commitments, the legal project raised objections to most of the proposed habilitation plans because they were void of any substantive or meaningful planning or content. Institution staff would often provide testimony in support of the position being adopted by the legal advocate but profess their inability to provide the necessary services because of inadequate staff or resources. After a court hearing on an individual's program deficiencies the court usually adopted findings that the habilitation being provided was inadequate, and issued an order directing the provision of such services. Such court findings and orders do not themselves provide the trained staff needed, of course, and are not self-executing.

In summary, without the availability of a professionally adequate system of care within the institution, court orders which recognize the rights of institutionalized persons have limited value to the individual resident. How best to utilize such court orders to force the provision of more adequate appropriations for the total system of care is the fundamental issue any such legal project will ultimately face.

With respect to the fact-finding necessary to represent clients, the lawyers must develop mechanisms for cooperative efforts with the institution and its staff in order to obtain information on the client's behalf. This is often difficult because the relationship between the lawyer and the staff is technically adversarial and in a court proceeding is strictly adversarial. There are also ethical constraints on the lawyer in general practice which forbid communications with an opposing party who is represented by counsel. However, the attorney for the state is not in a position to be knowledgeable about individual residents at the state institution. In addition, the majority of the clients are unable to adequately communicate with their lawyer because of the severity of their disability. The legal project has had to tread carefully in its dealings with the institution staff while still vigorously pursuing the information which is needed to adequately represent the client. In general, the solution has been to make full disclosure to the staff at the institution concerning why information is being sought, disclose to the state that project staff receive information from the institution staff, and finally, maintain confidentiality concerning the source of particular client information when such confidence is requested.

Institutional advocates must also resist being drawn into purely intrainstitutional disputes where the client needs are not at issue. The position of the institutional legal advocate always remains one of creative tension as it relates to the institution. It is the opinion of the authors that this area of legal ethics warrants considerably more attention than it has received.

A similar problem arises in the relationship between the legal advocate and the parents of institutionalized clients. As was noted earlier, parents usually are the primary advocate for their severely handicapped child. However, it is also possible for serious conflicts of interest to arise between parents and children, particularly when the child has been institutionalized for a long period of time. Parents are sometimes uninformed concerning the available alternatives for community care, fearful of their child leaving a familiar institution, or afraid of reprisals against their child should they become vigorous advocates for improved services within the institution. In a few cases parents are actually antagonistic toward any efforts on behalf of their child and actively oppose advocacy for the child. The institutional advocate must seek to solicit the support of parents for advocacy efforts and must also make full disclosure to the parent about whom the advocate represents in the case of a conflict of interest. Such disclosure is crucial to protect the integrity of the legal representative and to guard against claims of misrepresentation by a parent.

It is also advisable for institutional advocacy projects to be available to parent organizations to assist them in undertaking collective advocacy on behalf of their child. Such availability has a dual benefit. It keeps the advocate sensitive to the position of parents and in addition can diffuse the negative impact of an advocate taking a position on behalf of a client which is in opposition to the wishes of a particular parent. Although the genuine conflict cannot be avoided, institutional advocates should always remember that the client in an institution needs all the support he or she can get. Therefore, much time and effort should be expended in conciliation of parent/child conflicts before the advocate adopts an adversarial posture.

The heavy political overlay of an institutional advocacy project is another area of concern for the institutional advocate. By its nature, institutional advocacy is directed at the long term goals of deinstitutionalization and institutional reform. Such goals involve political questions of a state's allocation of resources, redirection of systems of care, and changes in the methods of service delivery. Although political constraints should not influence the advocate's efforts on behalf of a particular client, the climate of opinion toward the class of clients is affected by the actions of an institutional advocacy staff. As with each of the conflict situations inherent in institutional advocacy, it is important that the advocates be aware of the pressures which may arise and delineate guidelines which serve to underscore the independence of the advocate's position and duties.

As with any advocacy system, the institutional advocate must establish priorities for advocacy. The problems which arise in representing an institutionalized population of severely handicapped clients are so numerous that the advocates can easily be overwhelmed and consequently ineffective. The authors have found in their own experience that the areas of concentration for advocacy have evolved from an initial posture of defending persons in civil commitment and review to a more affirmative position of advocacy on behalf of generic groupings for necessary changes in service systems. In addition, for legal advocates, appellate procedures are a valuable mechanism for binding determinations on the scope of statutory rights. The institutional advocate must recognize that the benefit to the client will not be measured in immediate successes or failures, wins or losses, but in the long process of changing the service system to meet the unique needs of the severely handicapped client.

ETHICAL CONSIDERATIONS

Certain principles should be kept in mind when planning advocacy services lest the advocacy become more of a burden than benefit to the severely handicapped person (Scheerenberger, 1976). First, it is undesirable to overprotect the individual and thus decrease the likelihood that the person will somehow manage on his own. A normal existence assumes certain risks and failures. Not every risk of failure should be avoided. Substituting the decision-making authority of a third person for that of a severely handicapped person, whether by formal guardianship or by informal individual advocacy, is a serious step and one which by definition reduces personal freedoms. The question to ask in each case is whether the advocacy is essential or paternalistic. Advocacy should not be permitted to limit appropriate self-determination.

Second, every effort should be made to limit the authority granted the advocate, whether by legal guardianship or informal advocacy, to those areas where the client is clearly incapable of exercising his or her own judgment. Obviously, in some cases, the severity of the disability (for example, profound retardation), offers slight opportunity for a limited guardianship or advocate with a limited function. However, in many instances personal civil rights have been abrogated by well-intended efforts to protect or help. In every case a careful evaluation of the client's capabilities should precede the decision to substitute an advocate's decision-making for the client's. This caveat is particularly important when the decision is to request that a court appoint a guardian because of the legal stigma of incompetence which attaches in such proceedings.

Care should always be exercised to avoid conflict of interest situations between advocate and client. The most common example of such conflict would be the advocate representing an agency which is a potential adversary of the handicapped person. This is not to say that advocates are not needed within the service system; such persons are in a unique position to help and their importance should not be discounted. It is unlikely, however, that such an advocate will find it possible to assist the handicapped person to exercise his or her rights when they go against the interests of the advocate's employer or organization. Advocates within the potential adversary organization must have carefully defined roles.

Finally, when the client has a severe mental incapacity, the legal advocate has a special responsibility. In such an instance, there is risk that the client's identity will be lost. Clients usually give direction to their attorney, at least in the initial stages of any legal work. Although the attorney usually has ample opportunity to persuade the client to consider various options, the client's wishes always remain a factor.

The proper role or conduct of an attorney who is representing a person with limited mental capacity is difficult to prescribe. Obviously, the usual canons of ethics apply. The problem is that they do not cover such situations very well. The lawyer in such cases should always ask whether the distinction between lawyer and client is being maintained and whether the lawyer's posture serves the client (or the class of clients) rather than the interests of the individual lawyer or the law firm.

PROBLEMS IN ADVOCACY

Much attention has been directed to the myriad components of an effective advocacy system. Different types of advocacy have been described. However, although there has been some preliminary consensus among the advocates concerning their roles and responsibilities, there has been less than adequate attention paid to how the advocate is viewed by third parties. Some advocates, particularly legal advocates, have relied on the traditional attorney/client relationship in dealing with third parties on behalf of their client. (For the legal advocate the problems are much more with the internal operation of the attorney/client relationship rather than how that relationship is perceived by third parties.) However, for the lay advocate operating in whatever role has been defined, there are serious problems encountered in dealing with third parties. The first and most obvious is *standing,* that is, the right of the advocate to speak for the client.

> **Example:** A lay advocate is representing a developmentally disabled client who has been denied benefits to which the advocate believes the client is entitled. The client is unable to speak for himself. The advocate decides to call the local office and request the file. Should the benefits office release information of this type to someone other than the client? What steps can or should the advocate take to obtain the information needed?

This problem has been resolved to some degree in the developmental disabilities program through utilization of P & A systems as umbrella agencies for advocates. These systems must have an executive order from the governor of the state and, as part of this order, the systems are given standing. In theory, this order establishes the legitimacy of the advocacy system. In fact, there remain conflicts with confidentiality requirements imposed on service providers and agencies by law.

A related problem is that certain information obtained by an attorney from a client is "privileged," that is, not available to third parties from the attorney. However, although the attorney-client privilege is well established, the extent to which the underlying principles apply to lay advocacy is much less clear. Suppose the client is sued by the same public benefits office for recoupment of funds allegedly overpaid. Can the advocate be compelled to testify concerning information gathered as an advocate? Suppose the advocate passes on information about the client to service providers in an attempt to obtain services for the client. Can the client sue the advocate for unauthorized disclosure? The best answer to these questions is that a lawyer should review, whenever possible, the facts of the situation in advance and the advocate be given some guidelines to follow.

REFERENCES

Eklund, E. 1976. Systems Advocacy. Kansas University Affiliated Facility, University of Kansas, Lawrence.

National Association for Retarded Citizens. 1974. Citizen Advocacy for Mentally Retarded Children: An Introduction. Washington, DC.

Scheerenberger, R. C. 1976. Deinstitutionalization and Institutional Reform, pp. 153–154. Charles C Thomas, Publishers, Springfield, IL.

Turnbull, A., and Turnbull, H. R. (Eds.) 1978. Parents Speak Out: Views from the Other Side of the Two Way Mirror. Charles E. Merrill, Columbus, OH.

Chapter 8

Coordination of Service Delivery Systems

Jerry O. Elder

As anyone who works in any of the human service delivery systems knows, the issue of coordination is an exceedingly complex one. In addition, the strategies for creating coordination are as difficult as the concept itself. The problems of handicapped individuals are so multifaceted that they require services from a variety of agencies and resources. This book has identified the major service delivery systems which provide services to handicapped individuals. Even within each of these systems, the subject of coordinating the various elements of a service delivery system is perplexing. However, when the subject of coordinating services between delivery systems is addressed, these problems are multiplied by the number of service delivery systems to which the client must have access. In delivering care to handicapped individuals it is necessary to consider all of the delivery systems identified in this book. The handicapped individual cannot receive all of the services he requires in any one of these systems.

In their book on coordinating human services, Aiken *et al.* (1975) identify four key elements requiring coordination in a fully integrated service delivery system: 1) programs and services, 2) resources, 3) clients, and 4) information. A number of mechanisms exist to facilitate coordination of these four elements. Aiken *et al.* (1975) proposed one such structure for a coordinated delivery system. However, this ideal service delivery system is based on three assumptions, one of which is that the system will work only in an urban setting. Their proposed structure contains three major components: a unit to coordinate cases, a coalition of organizations, and a community board. Assuming that the change required to create such a structure can be accomplished, this appears to be a very workable structure for creating a coordinated delivery system in an urban setting.

This chapter will discuss two other more simplistic approaches to facilitating coordination of service delivery to handicapped individuals. These are applicable to either an urban or a rural setting. The first of these approaches, the use of *interdisciplinary teams* to meet the needs of the handicapped individual, has been in existence for a number of years, particularly in University Affiliated Facilities for the developmentally disabled. A brief explanation of how these teams operate is essential in the sense that it is a major mechanism for service delivery to the handicapped.

The other approach, *interagency coordination,* is not a new concept, but is emerging as a solution to eliminating some of the duplication and gaps in services that currently exist across the many service delivery systems providing services to the handicapped. Interagency coordination involves collaboration by two or more agencies or programs in working together to integrate their separate activities for the purpose of improving services to the handicapped.

INTERDISCIPLINARY TEAMS

Many handicapped persons have multiple impairments; therefore, one professional discipline alone cannot really address the total needs of these individuals in order to provide comprehensive care for the total handicap. Numerous models of service delivery have evolved to meet the needs of handicapped individuals when more than one professional discipline is involved with their care. Such approaches include the multidisciplinary team, in which more than one discipline addresses the needs of the handicapped individual but in which there is very little communication and interchange of ideas and values in arriving at a proposed treatment plan. A second approach, often used by outreach teams, is a transdiscipline approach whereby members of a team are familiar with the skills and knowledge of other team members. This enables one team member to act and speak for the whole team when visiting with the client during a home or school visit.

The interdisciplinary approach, however, is the most widely used mechanism in evaluating and treating the multiple impairments of a handicapped individual. This approach has been used successfully in both service provision and in training of team members in University Affiliated Facilities over the past 15 years. Much has been written about the value of the interdisciplinary team approach to service delivery and, therefore, only a few of the salient points will be mentioned here. The use of interdisciplinary teams as a valuable tool in providing services to the developmentally disabled is discussed in both Elder and Magrab (1979) and Johnston and Magrab (1976).

Valletutti and Christoplos (1977) in their book, *Interdisciplinary Approaches to Human Services,* point out that interdisciplinary communication is a prerequisite to the interdisciplinary cooperation needed to identify goals for clients and to prescribe treatment, priorities, sequences, strategies, implementation processes, materials, and evaluation procedures. The importance of sharing interdisciplinary information in an open and honest fashion cannot be stressed enough in developing a successful interdisciplinary team.

An effective approach for developing communication and other skills and knowledge needed for effective teamwork has been developed by Ruben, Plovnick, and Fry (1975) in a two-phase, self-instructional health team development program. Phase one, or the core work, consists of seven 3-hour sessions or modules; this is the basic team development package. These modules focus on the most essential elements of team effectiveness such as self-assessment, goal setting, role negotiations, role definitions, and decision making. The second phase of the health team development program consists of six optional resource modules, each directed at specific problem areas that a developing team may encounter. The health team development program focuses on the most essential task-related elements of team effectiveness: goals, roles, and procedures. Each session deals directly with a specific task-related problem known to be draining the team's energy which must be solved to deliver better care. An added advantage of the health team development program is that it can be used successfully without the need for any third party's or outside consultant's assistance. Contained within each participant's workbook are materials, guidelines, and detailed instructions needed to implement the program. Anyone who is truly interested in developing a workable interdisciplinary team is strongly urged to invest in this self-instructional health team development program or some similar program that focuses on task-related elements of team effectiveness.

Interdisciplinary coordination through the use of interdisciplinary teams is one answer to sorting out the many varieties of services delivered, often simultaneously, by numerous agencies. As Valletutti and Christoplos (1975) point out, when interdisciplinary cooperation is lacking, the needs of the individual are invariably separated into portions shaped to fit the organizational needs and biases of the various agencies providing services to handicapped persons. As bureaucratic specialization supersedes integration, the separate needs of the person become more important than the whole self. Therefore, without interdisciplinary teams, services will overlap and confusion will arise as to responsibility for particular specialized services.

INTERAGENCY COORDINATION

The term "interagency coordination" is used frequently in current literature on human services. It can be broadly defined as an attempt by two or more agencies or programs to work together to integrate their separate activities for the purpose of improving services for a defined population. This coordination can include cooperative efforts in planning, budgeting, services delivered to a common clientele, or any functions common to participating agencies. These cooperative efforts are, then, usually spelled out in written interagency collaborative agreements.

Interagency coordination can operate at either the client, program, or system level. System-level interagency coordination involves collaborative efforts that look beyond the administrative constraints of individual agencies. Instead it focuses on the system of services required to meet client needs. The role of a state Developmental Disabilities Planning Council as a coordinating body for the total service network with an impact on developmentally disabled individuals is an example of system-level coordination. Program-level coordination results when various agencies integrate their efforts around administrative functions, organizational structures, or their individual programmatic thrusts and modify them as needed to ensure more coordination between their separate operations. Coordination of early identification and screening procedures for the birth to 5-year age group among all agencies who have responsibility in this area would be an example of program-level coordination. Client-level interagency coordination is evidenced when various program or agency representatives work together at the local level to integrate the separate services they provide to an individual client in a manner which emphasizes the client's total spectrum of needs and avoids duplication and fragmentation. An agreement between a local school district and a crippled children's agency to avoid duplication of the evaluation of a client for which both agencies have responsibility would be an example of client-level interagency coordination.

The idea of "interagency coordination," "interagency cooperative arrangements," or the latest phrase, "interagency collaborative agreements," in serving the handicapped persons and their families is not new. The cooperative approach to serving persons with handicaps has been tried many times and many ways. Unfortunately, the success stories are too few and the instances of "paper cooperation" too many. Many of these agreements are referred to as "warm fuzzies," which are simply promises to cooperate. Cooperation, however, has not necessarily resulted in implementation of more or better services. In many instances, the spirit of cooperation has *not* been supplemented with the concepts and procedures necessary to overcome the many governmental, organizational, and functional barriers which characterize all levels of bureaucracy.

Roadblocks to Developing Interagency Agreements

A number of roadblocks exist which inhibit the development of interagency cooperative agreements. One of the biggest of these is the existence of the *status quo,* that is, "we've gotten along so far without cooperating with someone else, why do we have to do it now?" There is a lack of willingness on the part of many bureaucrats to cooperate with other agencies for a variety of reasons. These might include the resistance to more work, an attempt to protect their own "turf," and the fear of having to change the way they are doing things. This last factor, that of resistance to change, is a great inhibitor. People become comfortable in the way things are done and are very resistant to any type of change in their work methods or procedures. It is very difficult to overcome years and years of tradition in an existing service delivery system. However, bureaucrats must be convinced that the changes being proposed are for the good of the client population and they must set aside their own individual and agency biases. They must be convinced that, for the benefit of the client, agency regulations may have to be changed to accommodate some of the interagency collaborative systems.

Another roadblock has to do with variations in client eligibility criteria. Although this is not as much of a problem as it used to be since the passage of the 1978 Amendments to the Rehabilitation Act, which made the definition of a developmental disability much more broadly based, there are still times when a child eligible under PL 94-142 is not eligible under other federal legislation such as the Crippled Children's and Developmental Disabilities programs.

Overcoming the problem of confidentiality of information is another major constraint. Without the necessary signed releases, it is impossible to transfer information about clients from one agency to the next. One exception to this is under the Supplemental Security Income Program whereby clients, in accepting assistance through this program, give their permission for exchange of information between agencies. This approach could also be applied to other programs at the state level.

Another roadblock deals with professional jargon used by different agencies. An evaluation by educational people is somewhat different from what a physician might describe as an evaluation.

One more major roadblock is the existence of segregated and fragmented service delivery systems. This has resulted from piecemeal additions to various programs which were formed without any long range plan centered on the care of the handicapped child. The lack of communication and coordination among and across various federal and state agencies also adds to this confusion. Increasing numbers of free-standing programs have meant a duplication of effort in some respects and gaps in others, as well as confusion for consumers. There also has been ambiguity in the roles and functions of multiple agencies involved at all levels. The dispersion of authority and responsibility has meant that no one person or agency interprets overall needs, develops priorities, monitors progress, presents achievements, etc., for services to the handicapped. PL 94-142 comes close to filling this role for handicapped children for the majority of services. However, as experience with this law has proven, responsibility for coordinating care of handicapped children does not ensure its provision.

Overcoming Roadblocks

How can the obstacles in developing interagency agreements be overcome? No one person has all the answers to this dilemma. Some answers can be found, however, in looking at some concepts and ideas behind the development of interagency collaboration agreements. The most basic concept in developing interagency collaborative agreements is that, in order for interagency coordination to work at all, it must come from and be worked out at the lowest programmatic level possible. It does little good for those in the "ivory towers" of the university or administrators in the central office of a human service or educational agency to work up a grandiose plan for coordination with some other agency or agencies and then try to impose that plan at the local program level. Past experiences have proven that unless the program people at the working level are involved in the thinking and the planning for interagency coordination or for any new or changed service or program, the chances of its succeeding are severely lessened.

Role of Facilitator In order to develop the necessary working relationships between agencies at the local level, a *facilitator* must be available to work with program and administrative staff to develop the best possible collaborative effort for the benefit of the handicapped individual. A facilitator is an essential element in developing any interagency collaborative agreement, and ideally is assigned full time to that job function. If that is not feasible, it should be at least a major function of the individual's responsibility. It does little good to add this responsibility to someone in an agency who already has a full time job without taking other job responsibilities away so this person can devote the proper amount of time and effort to acting as a facilitator for interagency collaborative agreements. The person filling the role of facilitator should be sensitive to the needs of the clients of each agency and of the agency staff themselves. The subject of interagency agreements must be approached lightly on the basis of a "soft-sell," not a "hard come-on." The attitudes of many bureaucrats in agencies will have to be changed because one of the biggest obstacles to overcome is that of the bureaucrats' protection of their own "turf." The facilitator must also be knowledgeable about the total service delivery system.

Effective Communication Probably the biggest factor in overcoming roadblocks to interagency agreements is something that is too often taken for granted, and that is effective communication. It has to begin between the client and professional provider, then up through the professional and supervisor to the department head, then to the state level administrator, and then across and down agencies at all levels. Effective communication is an important facet to all stages in developing interagency collaborative agreements. The role of each of the parties involved in interagency collaborative agreements must be established and determined in the beginning. It is especially important for the people who will be working together to get to know each other, even though some may be adversaries. In dealing with complex human beings, it is essential to recognize that each plays a different role, and to determine what role each is playing.

Understanding the Dynamics of Change   Resistance to change on the part of almost everyone was one of the obstacles listed to developing interagency agreements. In order to overcome this, it is helpful to understand some of the dynamics of change. It is not really accurate to say that people resist change. It is true, however, that people resist *being* changed. If a change is implemented without obtaining input from staff, it is certain to be met with all sorts of resistance. On the other hand, if program staff suggest or work out the change, then it will almost certainly be implemented. Although "people resist being changed," "people don't resist the changes they choose." (Main Event Management Corp., 1972).

Any time a change is made in an organization, it is also important to recognize that this change is accompanied by a drop in both production and positive attitude on the part of staff. After a period of time, however, staff usually adjust to the new circumstances. When this occurs, a gradual increase in production and positive attitude of staff should be evident; this will probably result in a higher level of output than before the change took place.

Another factor to remember about change is there are four methods that can be used to reduce the adverse impact of change on people (Main Event Management Corp., 1972). The first is to *ceremonialize* a major change. Schedule a news conference or special staff meeting, etc., to identify the end of one era and the beginning of another, *i.e.,* a change of director, a new building, a new program. A second method is to *form groups* to deal with change. Small employer task forces should be made to feel part of the change both before, in planning for a change, and afterward, in dealing with problems relating to the change. A third method to reduce the impact of change is to *control the rate* of change. There is a certain level beyond which people cannot tolerate change. It therefore must be controlled so that it evolves a little at a time. For example, avoid hiring a new director, firing key supervisors, and introducing new policies all at once. If all three must be done, phase each change in over a period of time. A final method is related to the previous suggestion. *Make short term, low profile goals* whenever possible. This can be summed up by a little rhyme, "Life by the inch is a cinch, but life by the yard is hard." Although long term goals are planned, they should be implemented, whenever feasible, in short term intervals, a step at a time.

Secure Commitment from Agency Heads   Another key element in overcoming roadblocks is to first obtain commitment from agency heads toward the concept and philosophy of interagency collaboration. Although working from the lowest possible program level in negotiating these agreements is advocated, a facilitator's job is much easier if agency heads have already committed themselves to the importance of establishing interagency collaborative agreements between their agencies for the common goal of better service to the handicapped person.

Importance of In-Service Training Another factor in overcoming road-blocks to interagency collaboration is to stress the importance of in-service training to teachers and professionals in the field. A lot of the resistance on the part of teachers to attending to the special needs of the handicapped child or adult is not because they do not want to, but because they do not have the training and skills to know how to teach, let alone handle the special needs of this person. This is where in-service education becomes a key factor in training teachers to be able to deal with the special needs of the handicapped person.

Premises of Interagency Collaboration

Resources Will Be Minimal One of the basic premises behind developing interagency collaboration is that resources in terms of dollars for future increases in human services will be minimal, if existing at all. Taxpayers have spoken through Proposition 13 in California and ballot measures in other states. The legislative and executive branches of the government at both the state and federal levels appear to be responding to this message with fiscal restraint. The President's Fiscal Year 1980 Budget contained very small increases for human services. Many human service training programs were cut severely and the fate of these programs was in the hands of Congress via the fiscal year 1980 appropriations.

Systems Are Duplicative and May be Improved Another basic premise is that human service delivery systems are duplicated and can be improved. This is primarily true in urban areas. Many cases can be cited where handicapped clients have been shifted from agency to agency trying to find the necessary components in the health, educational, social, or vocational delivery systems. In this process of being shifted from agency to agency, numerous services are duplicated because each agency has set procedures which were designed with the concept that only that particular agency would provide a given service. The formation of human service delivery umbrella organizations at the state level was the first step in reorganizing these separate and fragmented delivery systems into a coherent human services delivery system. Those exercises were painful and troublesome and disrupted a number of efforts and activities. Unfortunately, it was basically just a reshuffling of boxes on an organizational chart and juggling of various programs that were somehow related on a functional basis. This reorganization did not, by and large, meet with the approval of program staff at the local level and has not been very successful.

Collaborative agreements between components of human service delivery systems can eliminate much of the duplication that currently exists. Eliminating this duplication can increase the efficiency and effectiveness of the various components of the delivery system. This, in turn, will bring about a more equitable utilization of existing resources. Agencies working together can mutually develop savings in each of their programs and also enhance the quality of the service being provided. However, there are problems and inhibitors to establishing interagency agreements which can and must be resolved. One of the basic problems is legislative constraints that provide little incentive or even discourage two agencies from working cooperatively together. However, this can be overcome inasmuch as legislators are more and more attuned to listening to proposals that will create savings and provide services more effectively to a particular client population.

Joint Policy Will Be Mandated by Legislation   Another basic premise is that new legislation and regulations will mandate interagency efforts. Joint policy statements have been developed by the Bureau of Education for the Handicapped to coordinate health services with the Bureau of Community Health Services and educational services with the Rehabilitation Services Administration. Similar joint policy statements are being developed between other federal agencies at the urging of the Secretary of Health, Education and Welfare. Furthermore, the Rehabilitation Comprehensive Services and Developmental Disabilities Act of 1978 created a National Institute of Handicapped Research which has, as one of its major responsibilities, coordination through an interagency committee of all federal programs and policies relating to research in rehabilitation. As many of these federal programs come up for renewal, more and more of this writing in of an interagency collaborative effort will be seen.

Mandating cooperation through regulation or legislation is not sufficient to ensure that agencies will work together in a coordinated effort. There must be a "payoff" for either the client population or the agency itself. In other words, some benefit must be gained from this exercise that will promote and encourage agency staff to work together, *i.e.*, cost benefit, better services, etc. In addition, it is best in initial stages to involve as many agencies as possible in planning for interagency collaborative agreements. When a particular agency is left out of the initial planning effort, their cooperation is inhibited further down the line. It is helpful also to have the collection and analysis of the data needed to establish interagency agreements gathered and tabulated by a third party. Data gathered by one agency from another agency is suspect by the other agency staff, whereas an impartial third party tabulating this information is not as threatening to either agency. Unfortunately, in some situations, resources are not sufficient to hire a third party to gather such data.

There must also be indications that these agreements, when written, will improve the system and not just increase the level of services. It is not a matter of just being bigger; it is also necessary to be better in providing services to the client population. Also, it is helpful if there is cost savings for more than one agency. Savings must be demonstrated in either personnel time or dollars expended by at least one of the agencies involved, but it is helpful if this can be demonstrated for multiple agencies.

The final basic premise of interagency cooperative efforts is that it just makes good common sense. It is unproductive and a waste of human resources to duplicate services that can be coordinated by working cooperatively together.

Goals of Interagency Collaboration

What are some of the goals or outcomes that interagency collaboration should be working towards? Probably the most basic of these is to coordinate the various human service delivery systems towards a common program goal of high quality care for handicapped individuals. In order to accomplish this, there must be comprehensive and coordinated planning to develop a service delivery model to achieve the desired result. With the innumerable agencies and separate programs involved in delivering care to the handicapped, the only conceivable way this can be accomplished is through collaborative interagency agreements. Items which need to be addressed in planning a service delivery model for the handicapped which would work toward a nonfragmented effort of meeting the needs of the whole person are: 1) development of common program standards, 2) agreement on determining the agency or person responsible for individual case management, 3) cooperative identification procedures, 4) reducing duplication of certain services, 5) a better knowledge of services available, 6) facilitation of financial assistance for these services to assure that the handicapped will have access to the necessary services with the minimum amount of duplication and red tape, and 7) providing uniform methods of accounting.

Common Program Standards A major deterrent to interagency collaboration is the differing standards used by various programs. A desirable outcome would be the development of program standards that are appropriate for multiple delivery systems and which carry the commitment of all service providers. In order to accomplish this difficult and global goal, there has to be a large amount of "give and take" by all agencies involved. It requires considerable negotiation, but the result of common program standards is well worth the extra effort.

Determining Responsibility for Individual Case Management The problem of duplicating individualized service planning under various federal programs should be addressed in interagency collaborative agreements. PL 94–142 requires an Individual Education Plan (IEP). The Supplemental Security Income for children requires an Individual Service Plan (ISP). Most Crippled Children's state agencies require an individual management plan. Similar individualized plans are mandated for ICF/MR patients and Vocational Rehabilitation clients. By developing a management plan jointly through an interagency agreement, such information could be accessible to all agencies, thus facilitating a timely and free exchange of information. Formats could be developed that would focus on client needs and outcome of services to meet the requirements of all agencies involved.

Cooperative Identification Procedures Cooperative identification procedures are a critical element for those agencies which have a responsibility for early identification and screening of handicapped children. If agencies responsible for such programs as Crippled Children's Services, Supplemental Security Income, Head Start, Early Childhood Education, Early Periodic Screening Diagnosis and Treatment, and Maternal and Child Health Services could coordinate their separate identification, screening, and evaluation functions, handicapped children could be served earlier and more effectively.

Reducing Duplicative Services Another goal to work toward in interagency collaboration would be the elimination of, as much as possible, duplicated services provided to specific populations. An example of this can be found in the evaluation of children under various federal programs. A yearly evaluation is required for a handicapped child under numerous programs. Currently, some of these children are seen under more than one of these programs and receive a separate evaluation by each agency. The following federal programs require a multidisciplinary team evaluation: PL 94-142, Supplemental Security Income, Developmental Disabilities, Vocational Rehabilitation, Maternal and Child Health Services, and Title XIX for institutionalized mentally retarded persons. Through interagency agreements the duplication that now exists could be eliminated or severely reduced.

Inventory of Service Programs In order to determine which agencies affect which services for handicapped persons, it is first necessary to determine what those programs are and what services they provide. Since most of these programs are federally funded, a beginning point would be to inventory federal programs which potentially have an impact upon services for persons with handicaps. Source documents for this search include the *Catalog of Federal Domestic Assistance* (1977), *Federal Assistance Programs Serving the Handicapped* (1976), *Guide to Federal Resources for the Developmentally Disabled* (Russem, 1978), and others published by special interest groups.

Determining Responsibility in Funding Another goal is the facilitation of joint funding by various agencies for the care of the handicapped. There is a large amount of confusion on the part of both the handicapped and agency staff who serve them as to which programs have first or last dollar responsibility in making payment for services. For example, in their implementing regulations, PL 94-142 and Section 504 of the Rehabilitation Act of 1973 require that each handicapped child must be provided all services necessary to meet his or her special education and related needs. If this statement were read as mandating that schools must assume all costs, it would place an impossible financial burden on school districts to pay for services they have never before provided and can ill afford. However, there is no requirement in any of the legislation that schools can plan only services in the IEP which the schools pay for. That is, nothing in law or regulations prohibit schools from meeting IEP requirements by utilizing other nonschool community services and funding where they are available. Arrangements with other sources of funds at any level, cost-sharing across agencies, and even tapping the too often overlooked insurance benefits which pay for needed services should be worked toward in developing interagency collaborative agreements. By developing joint funding in interagency agreements, resources can be maximized and the question of which agency provides the first dollar for services can be resolved.

Providing Uniform Methods of Accounting Another goal to be worked toward in developing interagency collaborative agreements is to provide uniform methods of accounting for and reporting of expenditure of funds among the many service providers. In the absence of such a uniform accounting system, the cost of providing services can only be estimated.

Process of Developing Interagency Agreements

Commitment of the Agency The first step in developing interagency collaboration agreements is to gain the approval and commitment of the agency or organization administrators who will be providing services to the targeted handicapped population. Without this commitment, all the negotiation and work carried out at the local level may go for naught.

Inventory of Programs The next step is to develop an inventory of programs available in the state providing services to handicapped children. This would include conducting an analysis of policies, laws, and regulations affecting services for handicapped children within the state. An analysis of this information can then be summarized on a two-dimensional matrix with federal and state programs identified along one axis and client-centered services categories along the other.

Analysis of Organizational Relationships After this, an analysis of organizational and governmental relationships among state, county, and local agencies providing services for the handicapped within a given state should be conducted. By utilizing the information from the matrix, organizational and governmental relationships can be identified. The impact of these relationships on programs for the handicapped can then be determined. From the results of this analysis, a list of agencies which need to formulate interagency agreements can be developed. A complete inventory of services, functions, and payment mechanisms for each of these agencies should then be made. Not only does the information from this inventory provide a useful directory and overview of federal and state programs, but it also allows participating agencies to determine which type of agreements should be negotiated for sharing and expanding resources.

Reasons for Failure of Interagency Agreements (Smith, 1978)

Written interagency agreements are generally expected to facilitate the coordination of planning and service provision across diverse types of programs at various administrative levels. However, they seldom function at the level originally anticipated. Some of the reasons for these failures can be examined, and ways can be found to prevent them from happening in future agreements.

Response to External Pressure The first reason for failure is that agreements are often developed in response to external pressures, that is, from federal level initiatives, legislative mandates, consumer groups, and public relation efforts with other programs. Agreements are much more effective if they are developed in response to an identified need, common to two or more agencies, that can be addressed more effectively in a combined effort. Unfortunately, most interagency agreements developed to date have been in response to external pressures. The only thing that can be said in defense of this is the mandate to develop interagency agreements is becoming the norm rather than the exception, and agency staff are going to have to become used to living under and working with interagency agreements. For example, the 1978 amendments to the Rehabilitation Act contain several references to interagency agreements which are mandated in this piece of legislation.

Lack of Specific Accountability A second reason for failure deals with the fact that interagency agreements often fail to specify particular programs, services, tasks, roles, and responsibilities of each of the parties involved to encourage accountability. Instead, these agreements often contain only broad statements relative to coordination. This can easily be overcome by being more specific in addressing these particular areas.

Lack of Designated Monitor The third reason for failure is that no responsible party is designated to assure implementation of the agreement and to regularly monitor progress in implementation. This can be overcome by specifying a person within each agency who is responsible for insuring that the agreement is carried out and monitors its progress.

Inadequate Distribution and/or Explanation Another reason is that administrators of programs in agencies often sign the agreement without insuring adequate distribution and clarification of the agreement to staff affected by its implementation. This seems extremely short sighted on behalf of the administrators, but it occurs more often than not. Obviously, procedures have to be developed for distributing copies of the agreement to the people who are working in the program through either interoffice memos or procedural manuals relating to the program. If major changes are made in working procedures, then attention also should be given to in-service training to properly prepare staff for these new working relationships.

Disregard by Staff Failure is also evident because interagency agreements have historically been viewed by many as ineffective for coordination and have therefore been ignored. This is an effect of imposing such agreements on staff. (They feel that if they agree to it, they can just ignore it later, after it is signed.) The solution to this relates back to the need for a designated party to ensure implementation of the agreement and monitoring of its progress.

Insufficient Rapport   A final problem in developing these agreements relates to spending insufficient time in developing rapport and in getting the trust needed to assure the full cooperation and vested interest of staff before entering into the agreement. Individuals who develop the interagency agreement need to get to know the persons they are dealing with well enough to determine whether they can be trusted or not. (It needs to be ferreted out whether people are just being courteous and will do just as they please after the agreement is signed or whether they will abide by the provisions in the agreement.)

Levels of Interagency Agreements

There are basically two levels of interagency agreements which need to be developed. The first of these, which should be a prerequisite to the second, is a broad, almost philosophical type of agreement, usually written between state-wide agencies which will specify each state agency's legal requirement for providing services to a defined handicapped population. It then should go on to specify what services each provides and what services they are obligated to provide funding. The type of service delivery and place where these services are to be delivered should also be specified in this level of agreement.

The second level of agreement is client oriented and is worked out at the lowest possible program level. These agreements might be between individual school districts or an educational service district and one or more state agencies or private agencies. They are based on the premises spelled out in the state-wide agency (first level) agreements, but are more detailed in that they spell out exactly what agency is to provide what type of services for which type of handicaps and are even more specific in payment and funding mechanisms.

Elements of Interagency Agreements

Whatever form or format is used in developing interagency agreements is of no real concern as long as the basic components are included. Interagency agreements can be designed in many ways. The primary rule is to keep them as simple as possible and in easily understood language. The language of the legal profession should be avoided whenever possible. Numerous elements can be included in an interagency agreement, but not all are applicable or required in every type of agreement. A developmental disabilities consortium at the Ohio State University University Affiliated Facility (Smith, 1975) developed a list of critical elements of interagency agreements. This list of criteria, which I have expanded, is reproduced here. It can be used as a checklist for developing both levels of agreements mentioned in the previous section.

1. Statement of clear purpose of agreement between parties with delineation of goals and measurable objectives for the terms of the agreement
2. Definition of any terms that could be ambiguous between the parties
3. Clear delineation of specific program, service, or focus for the agreement to facilitate clear communication of the need for and intent of the agreement
4. Designation of the agency which has first dollar responsibility for payment of services and specification of other financial or funding arrangement for payment of services
5. Designation of specific actions, roles, and responsibilities of each party within the agreement as well as mutual responsibilities
6. Designation of staff position(s) within each agency responsible for:
   a. Implementing the agreement as specified
   b. Monitoring the implementation
   c. Negotiating change when necessary to update agreement
7. Specification of general administrative procedures for parties affected by the agreement (*i.e.*, specified time period for agreement, mechanism for updating/revising, scheduling of meetings set for parties to agreement, confidentiality safeguards, referral mechanisms, information sharing, other assurances)
8. Evaluation design specified and agreed upon by all parties to be used in monitoring implementation of agreement; identification of person(s) responsible for evaluating and sanctions agreed upon to assure its implementation.

In itself, the process of developing agreements can be very rewarding. If all parties to the agreement begin with the assumption that all agencies have a legitimate and important role in that there is a shared and genuine concern for persons with handicaps as well as their families, then promises should be able to be made to provide programs in cooperation with and jointly funded by both public and private agencies (Audette, 1978).

CONCLUSION

The main issue in any agency or organizational structure is the integration of activities in a manner most appropriate to that agency's or organization's goals. Each of the hundreds of public and private agencies and organizations serving the handicapped have differing goals, but they are all involved in the common issue of service integration. The integration of these services provided through various agencies has been the subject of this chapter and in more general terms, the theme for this book. The system or systems in existence today for delivery of services to the handicapped are so large and complicated that the only logical and rational way to straighten out all of the confusion is to concentrate on providing these services at the lowest possible program level, *i.e.*, the individual client or group of clients with similar handicaps. Programs and service delivery systems are already in place. What is needed is a mechanism for sorting out the multitude of services into a coordinated system that will fit the individual client's needs. Such a mechanism has been described in this chapter.

Services coordination at the local level through a facilitator acting independently from all the agencies involved appears to be the rational remedy to the present fragmented services delivery system for the immediate future. Over a period of time it may be possible to change the delivery systems, if that is what is required, to meet the needs of handicapped individuals. Changes in legislation, regulation, and funding authority which will facilitate a more coherent service delivery system take time. A change in attitudes of those responsible for and those actually providing services to handicapped people also requires time. As referenced in the chapter on Community Service Planning (Chapter 1), the age of specialization has reached its cyclical peak. Each of the specialty disciplines serving handicapped persons must realize it cannot be all things to all people but must instead work as part of an interdisciplinary team. At the same time, each must come to the realization that the use of interdisciplinary teams and interagency collaboration efforts are not threats that will take away professional roles. Quite to the contrary, interagency agreements are designed to enhance specialized roles of disciplines in working together toward meeting the unique needs of handicapped individuals.

REFERENCES

Aiken, M., Dewar, R., Titomaso, N., Hage, J., and Zeitz, G. 1975. Coordinating Human Services. Jossey-Bass, San Francisco.

Audette, R. 1978. Interagency agreements to support programs for persons with handicaps—A manual for establishing program relationships in the State of Washington. Unpublished report.

Elder, J. O., and Magrab, P. R. 1979. Administration of Special Facilities. In P. J. Valletutti, F. Christoplos (eds.), Prevention of Developmental Disabilities. University Park Press, Baltimore.

Johnston, R. B., and Magrab, P. R. 1976. Developmental Disorders: Assessment, Treatment, Education. University Park Press, Baltimore.

Main Event Management Corp. 1972. Main event management. In Model-Netics Coursebook. Main Event Management Corp., Sacramento, CA.

Ruben, I. W., Plovnick, M. S., and Fry, R. E. 1975. Improving the Coordination of Care: A Program for Health Team Development. Ballinger Publishing Co., Cambridge, MA.

Russem, W. 1978. Guide to Federal Resources for the Developmentally Disabled. Federal Programs Information and Assistance Project, Washington, DC.

Smith, C. B. 1978. Interagency agreements as a mechanism for coordination. Unpublished manuscript.

U. S. Department of Health, Education and Welfare. 1976. Federal Assistance Programs Serving the Handicapped. DHEW Office of Handicapped Individuals, Washington, DC.
U. S. Office of Management and Budget. 1977. Catalog of Federal Domestic Assistance. U.S. Government Printing Office, Washington, DC.
Valletutti, P., and Christoplos, F., Interdisciplinary Approaches to Human Services. University Park Press, Baltimore.

Chapter 9

Case Study for Planning Coordinated Services

Elynor Kazuk, Lorna Greene & Phyllis R. Magrab

After a need for change has been perceived in a community and interagency collaboration is accepted as a way to effect the change, participating agencies must begin to develop specific plans for accomplishing their mutual goals. Knowing exactly where and how to initiate this process may be problematic to many communities. This chapter describes one method for developing specific plans for an interagency project that is intended to reflect comprehensive and coordinated planning. The method is a systematic approach to collecting and summarizing information in order to develop plans that are based on an accurate assessment of community needs. It represents a process that can be applied or adapted to numerous service delivery questions.

The goal, in this particular case, was to develop a community-based, interagency delivery system for preschool, handicapped children that would provide every child diagnosed as handicapped with a written and operational individualized plan based on both a health and an educational assessment. The task faced by the participating community agencies was twofold: 1) to determine the extent of the need in the community and the resources available to meet that need and 2) to develop plans for filling the gaps through interagency coordination and through requests for funding of resources not available in the community.

The Workbook presented on the following pages represents a format for the systematic collection of data in response to the tasks stated above. It was originally designed as a method for communities to request funding from a federal-level Interagency Task Force comprised of agencies serving preschool handicapped children.* The lead agency, in this case, was the Administration for Children, Youth and Families/Head Start Handicapped Effort.

---

*Interagency Task Force members include Ray Collins, Administration for Children, Youth and Families (ACYF); Pam Coughlin (ACYF), Linda Randolph (ACYF); Doris Haar, Developmental Disabilities Office, Rehabilitation Services Administration; Jane DeWeerd, Bureau of

Although the Workbook is designed for planning a system to serve the handicapped preschool populations, it is an approach that is adapted easily to other target groups. Primarily, it suggests a concrete method for agencies to use in developing interagency plans and gives one example of how a group of agencies can gather information on the current status of a problem, determine the resources available to solve the problem, and plan around existing gaps that need to be filled in order to accomplish whatever goals the group may establish. Once the Workbook has been completed, it provides a baseline for evaluating the project activities. In addition, the worksheets can be used periodically to record the progress of the project, to make revisions in the plans, and to share changes with participating agencies.

The Workbook that follows is divided into five sections:

I.   Participating Agencies
II. Demographic Data
III. Resource Utilization
IV. Grant Objectives and Strategies
V.   Evaluations

Part I (Participating Agencies) requires a description of current interagency efforts in the community, both formal and informal, including active documentation by the agencies of these efforts and their plans to expand. Part II (Demographic Data) requires the collection of baseline information about the target population in the catchment area. Part III (Resource Utilization) assists in defining the resources currently available, the gaps in services that exist, and the ways in which better utilization can occur through collaboration. Part IV (Grant Objectives and Strategies) assists in detailing planned activities to meet the overall goals and to determine the fiscal support needed. Part V (Evaluation) raises the issue of evaluation, in this case by a third party, but does not address the planning for it. For this particular project this was accomplished through a separate contract. The Workbook is accompanied by definitions of terms used in the preparation of the application.

Education for the Handicapped; Vince Hutchins, Bureau of Community Health Services (BCHS); Merl McPherson (BCHS); Marion Slatin (ACYF); Helen Martz, Office of Child Health, Medicaid/EPSDT. The Task Force was staffed by the American Association of University-Affiliated Programs (AAUAP), Phyllis Magrab and Elynor Kazuk under Grant No. 54-P-71476/3-01 from the Developmental Disabilities Office. Lorna Greene served as a consultant to AAUAP in the development of the Workbook.

WORKBOOK

INTRODUCTION

In order to achieve the primary goal of this project, which is to provide and to implement a comprehensive individualized plan* for all preschool handicapped children in your area, it will be necessary for you to do the following:

A. Determine how many handicapped children there are in the area and how many of these children need comprehensive individualized plans.

B. Determine the extent to which the catchment area can fulfill this goal and the gaps that would need to be filled through additional funding.

C. Design and implement an interagency system which incorporates all the activities leading to the successful accomplishment of the goal.

This workbook is designed to assist you in carrying out the above tasks. It is divided into five major sections: 1) Participating agencies; II) Demographic Data; III) Resource Utilization; IV) Grant Objectives and Strategies; and V) Evaluation. In the workbook there are mandatory worksheets for collecting necessary information from various agencies, definitions of terms which are used throughout the project, and pages on which to summarize the information collected from all of the agencies. These summaries will be useful in determining the progress of the project throughout the funding period and will be useful to the reviewers in evaluating and comparing the proposals from all of the applicants. If you have any questions, please call your Resource Access Project (RAP) representative or the Administration for Children, Youth and Families Regional Office.

---

*A *written* plan which includes long term goals, short term objectives, activities, and persons responsible, which is based on health and educational assessments of the child by qualified professionals and which is accepted by the parents for implementation.

ૃ. PARTICIPATING AGENCIES

In order to better serve the target population, a major aspect of this proposal is to promote interagency collaborative efforts. In seeking to identify sites which will become final candidates for this grant, reviewers will pay close attention to existing interagency efforts as well as to plans for the development and expansion of such efforts. It is *mandatory* that the following agencies/programs serving your catchment area are members of such an effort and are participants in the planning of this proposal:

1. Head Start
2. Resource Access Project (RAP)
3. Local Department of Education; Division of Special Education
4. Title V programs (*i.e.,* Maternal and Child Health programs, Crippled Children's Services)
5. Local Title XIX (Medicaid/EPSDT) and Title XX programs
6. HEW agency serving developmental disabilities.

We suggest that you additionally seek support from the following:

1. Mental Health Centers
2. University Affiliated Facilities (UAF)
3. Preschools and day care centers, including handicapped children's early education projects
4. Parent, foster parent, and citizen organizations
5. Local providers and other referral sources.

A letter of active support is mandatory from each agency/program or individual that you include as participating in this proposal. The letter must include a statement of support, the specific activities the member will contribute to the project, and the signature of an authorized representative of the agency/program. (See *Worksheet A* in the back of the Workbook for example.)

Make every attempt to seek the recognition and support of the state or regional persons comparable to the local representatives of agencies/ programs you have in your group. The Resource Access Project (RAP) in your area is an excellent source for the names of county or state persons in administrative positions at various agencies whom you should contact for support or guidance. In addition, do not neglect individual professionals and consumers in mounting your interagency effort or in enlarging the membership of the group.

Participating Agencies Summary

1. Detail below the agencies/programs participating in the planning of this proposal. Please indicate Original (O) members, New (N) members, and Anticipated (A) members in the "duration of membership" column.

Agency/Program	Individual	Title	County or State Contact	Duration of Membership O-N-A

2. Please show by an asterisk (*) on the list above those state persons/agency/programs who have provided support in writing to this effort.

    Indicate the reasons for a lack of response from any agency/program.

    Would you like assistance in contacting a state representative?

    Please specify which state representatives (agencies/programs) you would like assistance in contacting.

3. In the space below briefly describe any organized interagency effort(s) on behalf of preschool handicapped children which currently exist in the catchment area. Include in the description the *type* of interagency effort (for example, Task Force, Interagency Council, Lead Agency), membership, guidelines for activities (formal or informal agreements, contracts, etc.), and frequency of meetings. Submit contract, minutes of meetings, newspaper articles, etc., which show evidence of the existence of this interagency effort.

4. Often, collaborative activities occur among agencies which are not part of an organized effort. Use *Worksheet B* in the back of the Workbook to collect information from participating and other appropriate agencies about these collaborative activities. Copies of all completed worksheets should be submitted with the proposal.

II. DEMOGRAPHIC DATA

The demographic data requested will be time consuming to collect. All agencies participating in this project should contribute this information as well as any other agency/program or individual willing to do so. It is of utmost importance that it be as accurate as possible to provide a base line of information for your community in planning the project and evaluating its progress. It will also be used for later evaluation and comparison studies.

To collect this statistical information use the Worksheets provided in this Workbook (*Worksheet C*). All competing applicants are required to use the same Worksheets in order to facilitate the initial comparisons of the information and to give appropriate objective weight to the information. Make every effort to *count each child only once.* Along with a copy of the Worksheet for the statistical information, provide each of your sources with a copy of the diagnostic criteria and definitions included in the Workbook. It is essential that all parties participating in this effort work from the same definitions in providing responses.

After you have collected the information on the required Worksheets be sure to submit the originals of them and a signed Letter of Understanding (*Worksheet C*) for each agency/program or individual from whom you have collected data.

Demographic Description of Catchment Area Summary

(Summary of *Worksheet C* information)
1. Total Population   _____
    Total Number of Children, Birth to 3 Years   _____
    Total Number of Children, 3 to 6 Years   _____

    Total Number of Children Professionally Diagnosed as Handicapped as Shown by Major Disability and Age. (You must use the Head Start diagnostic criteria and definition of "professionally diagnosed" as shown in the back of the Workbook). Enter each child only once. *Do not* include children *believed* to have a handicap, but who have *not* been professionally diagnosed.

Disability	Birth to 3 Years	3 to 6 Years
Blindness	_____	_____
Visual Impairment	_____	_____
Deafness	_____	_____
Hearing Impairment	_____	_____
Physical Handicap (Orthopedic)	_____	_____
Speech Impairment	_____	_____
Health Impairment	_____	_____
Mental Retardation	_____	_____
Serious Emotional Disturbance	_____	_____
Specific Learning Disabilities	_____	_____
Total Number of Children Professionally Diagnosed as Handicapped:	_____	_____

Demographic Description Summary, *continued*

2. Total Number of Professional Diagnoses Performed by Head Start Diagnostic Team or Other Diagnostic Team: _____

3. Estimated Number of Handicapped Children in Catchment Area:

	Birth to 3 Years	**3 to 6 Years**
Not *Professionally* Diagnosed	_____	_____
Not Identified	_____	_____
Basis and source for above estimate:	_____	_____

4. Problems with Securing Professional Diagnosis: (Rank in order of frequency of problem*)

Problem	Frequency Rank
Time Lag between Referral and Diagnosis	
Lack of Available Diagnostic Resources in Community	
Lack of Responsiveness by Resource Agencies	
Fear of Labeling Children	
Diagnosticians Lack of Understanding of Categorical Descriptions	
Lack of Money to Pay for Diagnosis	
Other	

*Adapted from Table 58 of Report of Services to Handicapped in Head Start.

Demographic Description Summary, *continued*

5. Total Number of Children Professionally Diagnosed as Handicapped (same as #2): Birth to 3 Years____ 3 to 6 Years____

	Birth to 3 Years	**3 to 6 Years**
Number Professionally Diagnosed by Head Start	_____	_____
Number Professionally Diagnosed by Public Schools	_____	_____
Number Professionally Diagnosed by Other Programs	_____	_____

(If estimates, please indicate)

6. Of Those Children Professionally Diagnosed as Handicapped:

	Birth to 3 Years	**3 to 6 Years**
Total Number of Children for Whom: a) A Comprehensive Individualized Plan* Has Been Completed b) A Partial Individualized Plan Has Been Completed	_____	_____
Total Number of Children Currently Receiving Treatment/Intervention as Recommended by: a) Any Type of Written Individualized Plan b) An Unwritten (Informal) Plan	_____	_____
Total Number of Children Pending Treatment/Intervention	_____	_____
Total Number of Children for Whom Treatment/Intervention is Inadequate or Unavailable (please indicate if an estimate)	_____	_____

*In this proposal a comprehensive individualized plan is a written plan based on both an educational and a health assessment. A partial individualized plan would be a written plan based on either one or the other.

7. Problems with Securing a Comprehensive Individualized Plan (Rank in Order of Frequency of Problem):

Problem	Frequency Rank
Time Lag between Diagnosis and Completion of Appropriate Plan	
Lack of Professional Persons Who Have Been Identified as Planning Team	
Lack of Functional Assessment	
Reluctance or Refusal of Family to Accept Plan	
Lack of Resources to Carry Out Plan	
Professional's Lack of Understanding of a Comprehensive Individualized Plan	
Use of a Partial Individualized Plan Not Based on Both an Educational and Health Assessment	
Other	

III. RESOURCE UTILIZATION

When you complete this section of the Workbook you will have described the resources currently available in your area, the extent to which they are used, and what gaps in services exist. The Matrix provided in the Workbook will summarize the data collected through *Worksheet D.* Use the Worksheet as follows:

1. Gather information from all providers of service to preschool handicapped children in your area whether or not they are listed as participants in this proposal.
2. Assign a code number to each agency/program or individual. On *Worksheet D* and on the *Resource Summary* pages enter the code number.
3. Submit (with the final proposal) all pages of *Worksheet D* for each agency/program or individual.

4. When you have the Worksheets completed, enter on the *Summary Matrix of Community Resources,* the number of each program/ agency/individual for *each* service they deliver for each of the handicapping conditions.

It is our intention that the collection and review of this information will provide a basis for an internal evaluation by each community of its current capabilities and an insight into methods and means for improvement or expansion whether or not that community becomes a final project site. The Worksheets from each provider and the completed *Matrix* will be rewarding information to all participants.

Resource Utilization Summary List

1. *Worksheet D* is to gather data for completing the list below and the *Matrix* on the following page. Please fill out the *Matrix* and also submit the completed Worksheets as a separate attachment.

Assigned Program Number	Program/Agency Name	Assigned Program Number	Program/Agency Name
List all agencies that have been included in this survey, and the assigned program number.		List all agencies that have been included in this survey, and the assigned program number.	

Enter the program number of the above providers in the appropriate category on the following pages. Some categories may have several providers whereas others have none.

SUMMARY MATRIX OF COMMUNITY RESOURCES

Services	Handicapping Conditions									
	Blindness	Visual Impairment	Deafness	Hearing Impairment	Physical Handicap (Orthopedic)	Speech Impairment	Health Impairment	Mental Retardation	Serious Emotional Disturbance	Specific Learning Disability
1. Counseling										
2. Screening										
3. Diagnosis										
4. Evaluation										
5. Education (classroom or home based)										
6. Follow-up										
7. Referral										
8. Personal Care										
9. Legal (protective/advocate)										
10. Recreation										
11. Staff Training										
12. Transporation										
13. Treatment (specify: PT/ OT/speech)										

222

14. Equipment															
15. Instructional Materials															
16. Day Care															
17. Foster Care															
18. Parent Training															
19. Case Management															
20. IEP as in PL 94-142															
21. Comprehensive Individualized Planning															
22. Financial Assistance															
23. Health Services															
24. Public Education															
25. Homemaker Service															
26. Home Nursing															
27. Preventive Services															
28. Other															

2. Briefly describe below a way in which better utilization of *existing* resources can occur through collaboration in order to fill the gaps and eliminate unnecessary duplication of service in the *Matrix* and to provide a comprehensive individualized plan to all children professionally diagnosed as handicapped. If no provider of a particular service is shown on the *Matrix* and your community does not currently need that service (and does not anticipate need of it) please explain. Furthermore, if a variety of providers are shown for a particular service but for some reason the service is still inadequate, explain how collaboration will assist in meeting that need. In addition, describe how actual gaps will be filled by your collaborative efforts.

3. Please indicate any barriers you perceive to interagency collaboration in your area, such as conflicting agency regulations, constraints from local and state statutes, or unclear funding formulas.

4. From the information collected through the *Matrix* complete the chart below regarding needs for services to preschool handicapped children in your area which are necessary for providing a comprehensive individualized plan to all children professionally diagnosed as handicapped.

Identified Need for Service (list in order of priority)	Reason Need Exists	Resources Necessary to Fill Need	Estimated Cost of Resources for 1 Year

Total Estimated Cost $_____

IV. GRANT OBJECTIVES AND STRATEGIES

1. Using the outline on the following page briefly describe how you will carry out the activities necessary to meet the overall goal of increasing the number of children professionally diagnosed as handicapped for whom a written comprehensive individualized plan has been completed. Estimated costs for these activities should be used for planning purposes only and do not constitute a budget.

2. Provide a diagram (attach flow chart) of how the preceding activities will be carried out in a collaborative, nonduplicating manner by the agencies participating in the effort.

3. How does your entire plan meet the specific needs of the severely or hard to serve handicapped preschool children in your area?

SUMMARY PLAN   *(Do not detach)*

Objective	Method/ Activity	Who Will Accomplish?	Where Will It Take Place?	When Will It Take Place?	Are Resources Currently Available to Carry Out?		Estimated Cost of Method/Activity
					Yes	No	
To educate parents regarding the importance of screening for handicapping conditions and to encourage them to have their preschool children screened							
To screen for possible educational, medical, and health problems							
To diagnose and assess problems suspected from screening							
To develop comprehensive, individualized plans for each child and his or her family							
To follow the progress of the child in accomplishing the objectives stated in the individualized plan							
To determine appropriate placement among all available community programs							
To maximize interagency coordination in delivery of service							
To encourage parent involvement and training							
To provide continuity of care after the child reaches school							
To link this project with existing preventive services							

V. EVALUATION

Evaluation of the project will be conducted throughout the funding period by an independent contractor. Part of the evaluation will include the impact of the project activities on the kindergarten and first grade population. Specific details of the evaluation will be provided to the sites later. At this point all that is necessary from the competing sites is a letter from the authorized agent(s) of the school district(s) in your catchment area indicating that demographic data (Section II) on the kindergarten and first grade population will be made available to the evaluator if your area is selected as a final project site.

PROJECT DEFINITIONS
AND
WORKSHEETS FOR PARTICIPATING AGENCIES

DEFINITION OF TERMS (as used in this project)

Case Management

Assuming the responsibility for the coordinating of all aspects of a child's progress through the process of screening, diagnosis, and treatment, including but not limited to client contact, resource contact, referral, and follow-up.

Comprehensive Individualized Plan

A *written* plan which includes long term goals, short term objectives, activities, and persons responsible, which is based on health and educational assessments of the child by qualified professionals and which is accepted by the parents for implementation.

Counseling

The provision of advice, direction, or reassurance to a handicapped child or his/her family on a one-to-one basis or in a group.

Day Care

Care in a licensed facility for less than 24 hours.

Diagnosis

The professional judgment made regarding a condition based on the symptoms and providing, as a result, a categorical definition of the condition.

Diagnostic Team

A group of persons representing at least three areas of expertise who perform a diagnosis to determine a handicapping condition.

Education

Instruction or training primarily in all areas of cognitive development.

Equipment/Materials

Books, teaching devices, audiovisual equipment, or other purchases except for orthopedic or prosthetic devices, eyeglasses, or expenditures for capital improvement.

Financial Assistance

Direct provision of money.

Follow-Up

The reexamination of a child's progress, on a regular basis, to determine whether appropriate recommendations are being carried out.

Foster Care Placement

Placement of a child in a family home, licensed to provide 24-hour care on a continuing basis for children awaiting other placement or service.

Functional Assessment

The process whereby a categorical diagnostic definition is related to a functional or working definition which describes the limitations or needs imposed by the condition, and identifies the areas that require special education and related services.

Health Services

Provision of medical, nursing, dental, clinic, or hospital services.

Home Nursing Service

The services of an RN or LPN provided to the child in his or her home or in a foster home.

Homemaker Service

Assistance in the care of the home and the family.

Individualized Educational Planning

The development of an Individualized Educational Plan (IEP) as defined in PL 94-142.

Instructional Materials

Any materials for the education of a child, a service provider, the parent of a child, or the public if it relates to their understanding of or assistance to handicapped preschool children.

Interagency

A collection of individuals, agencies, or programs, representing a variety of services, who function as a group to eliminate duplication to fill service gaps and to increase service to preschool handicapped children.

Intervention

A prescribed method for remediation or rehabilitation which may or may not involve therapy, medication, or a prosthesis.

Legal Service

Any service of a protective or advocacy nature performed by a professional or paraprofessional legal person.

Major Disability

That condition which has the greatest deterrent to the individual's normal growth or development.

Nonprofessional

A person performing a duty which requires no specialized education or training.

Paraprofessional

A person performing a duty requiring some specialized training or education.

Parent Training

Formal or informal sessions planned for and delivered to parents of handicapped children on subjects specifically related to the condition of the child or the family.

Personal Care

Individualized care of a personal nature delivered by a nonprofessional in such areas as dressing, feeding, grooming, etc.

Preventive Services

Genetic counseling, immunization, and other services provided prior to the onset of a handicapping condition.

Professional

A person having achieved at least a Bachelor's Degree from an accredited college or university, or certified or licensed in their field of expertise, *e.g.*, M.D., psychologist, speech therapist, osteopath, special educator, teacher.

Professional Diagnosis

A diagnosis performed by individuals or groups who are defined as professionals and whose field of expertise is directly related to the condition being diagnosed.

Public Education

The provision of information on or about conditions or services aimed at improving public awareness and public understanding of the conditions and the service.

Recreation

Activities primarily of a social nature for handicapped children and/or their families.

Referral

Directing a child to another agency, program, individual, or department for appropriate specific service.

Screening

The use of quick and simple procedures to detect those who have a high probability of having the problem in question.

Staff Training

Training for professional or paraprofessional persons to improve their expertise in any area of service to handicapped children and/or their families.

Transportation

Provision of direct transportation with agency, public, or private vehicles.

Treatment

The direct provision of therapy, medication, or a prosthesis.

CATEGORICAL DEFINITIONS OF HANDICAPPING CONDITIONS

The following categorical definitions of handicapping conditions shall be used for the purpose of this grant:

Blindness

A child shall be reported as blind when any one of the following exist: a) the child is sightless or has such limited vision that he/she must rely on hearing and touch as his/her chief means of learning; b) a determination of legal blindness in the state of residence has been made; c) central acuity does not exceed 20/200 in the better eye, with correcting lenses, or visual acuity which is greater than 20/200, but is accompanied by a limitation in the field of vision such that the widest diameter of the visual field subtends an angle of no greater than 20 degrees.

Deafness

A child shall be reported as deaf when any one of the following exist: a) his/her hearing is extremely defective so as to be essentially nonfunctional for the ordinary purposes of life; b) hearing loss is greater than 92 decibels (ANSI 1969) in the better ear; c) a legal determination of deafness in the state of residence has been made.

Hearing Impairment (Handicap)

A child shall be reported as hearing impaired when any one of the following exist: a) the child has slightly to severely defective hearing, as determined by his/her ability to use residual hearing in daily life, sometimes with the use of a hearing aid; b) there is hearing loss from 26 to 92 decibels (ANSI 1969) in the better ear.

Physical Handicap (Orthopedic Handicap)

A child shall be reported as crippled or with an orthopedic handicap who has a condition which prohibits or impedes normal development of gross or fine motor abilities. Such functioning is impaired as a result of conditions associated with congenital anomalies, accidents, or diseases; these conditions include, for example, spina bifida, loss of or deformed limbs, burns which cause contractures, cerebral palsy.

Speech Impairment (Communication Disorder)

A child shall be reported as speech impaired with such identifiable disorders as receptive and/or expressive language impairment, stuttering, chronic voice disorders, and serious articulation problems affecting social, emotional, and/or educational achievement; and speech and language disorders accompanying conditions of hearing loss, cleft palate, cerebral palsy, mental retardation, emotional disturbance, multiple handicapping conditions, and other sensory and health impairments. This category excludes conditions of a transitional nature consequent to the early developmental processes of the child.

Health Impairment

These impairments refer to illnesses of a chronic nature or with prolonged convalescence including, but not limited to, epilepsy, hemophilia, severe asthma, severe cardiac conditions, severe anemia or malnutrition, diabetes, or neurological disorders.

Visual Impairment (Handicap)

A child shall be reported as visually impaired whose central acuity, with corrective lenses, does not exceed 20/70 in either eye, but who is not blind; or whose visual acuity is greater than 20/70, but is accompanied by a limitation in the field of vision such that the widest diameter of visual field subtends an angle of no greater than 140 degrees; or who suffers any other loss of visual function that will restrict learning processes, *e.g.,* faulty muscular action. Not to be included in this category are persons whose vision with eyeglasses is normal or nearly so.

Mental Retardation

A child shall be considered mentally retarded who, during the early developmental period, exhibits significant subaverage intellectual functioning accompanied by impairment in adaptive behavior. In any determination of intellectual functioning using standardized tests that lack adequate norms for all racial/ethnic groups at the preschool age, adequate consideration should be given to cultural influences as well as age and developmental level (*i.e.* finding of a low IQ is *never by itself sufficient* to make the diagnosis of mental retardation).

Serious Emotional Disturbance

A child shall be considered seriously emotionally disturbed who is identified by professionally qualified personnel (psychologist or psychiatrist) as requiring special services. This definition would include, but not be limited to, the following conditions: dangerously aggressive toward others, self-destructive, severely withdrawn and noncommunicative, hyperactive to the extent that it affects adaptive behavior, severely anxious, depressed or phobic, psychotic or autistic.

Specific Learning Disabilities

Children who have a disorder in one or more of the basic developmental processes involved in understanding or in using language, spoken or written, which disorder may manifest itself in imperfect ability to listen, think, speak, read, write, spell, or do mathematical calculations. Such disorders include such conditions as perceptual handicaps, brain injury, minimal brain dysfunction, dyslexia, and developmental aphasia. This definition does not include children who have learning problems which are primarily the result of visual, hearing, or motor handicaps, of mental retardation, of emotional disturbance, or of environmental disadvantage. For preschool children, precursor functions to understanding and using language, spoken or written, and computational or reasoning abilities are included. (Professionals considered qualified to make this diagnosis are physicians and psychologists with evidence of special training in the diagnosis of learning disabilities and at least Master's degree-level special educators with evidence of special training in the diagnosis of learning disabilities.)

WORKSHEET A
Sample Letter of Support

The _____ of _____
(Signature Agency)   (Catchment Area/Location)
declares its support for the _____ Interagency
(Group)
effort on behalf of preschool handicapped children in _____.
(Area)

Moreover, in pursuit of a more integrated approach to service for these children and their families, the _____
(Signature Agency)
will perform the following activities:
(Include the appropriate activities in which the members will participate such as those listed below.)

---

1. Send a qualified representative to the regular meetings of the _____.
   (Interagency Group)
2. Under appropriate guidelines, share information regarding screening, with _____.
   (Agency/Program)
3. Advise the Interagency group at least 30 days in advance of any screening activity.
4. Provide professional person, at least three times a year, to review and assist in the development of Comprehensive Individualized Plan for professionally diagnosed, handicapped preschoolers.

_____   _____
Signature of Authorized Representative   Date

WORKSHEET B
Collaborative Efforts*

(detach and duplicate for each participating agency and submit with final proposal)

Name of Agency Providing Information: _____

Areas of Handicapping Conditions Served: _____

X = A type of collaboration currently or previously used with this agency, either as a provider or receiver of service

O = Interested in using in the future

XO = Both

Agency Names	Consultation	Training	Direct Service	Information Exchange	Staff Sharing	Child Recruitment	Child Placement	Sharing Facilities	Joint Project	Membership in Interagency Group	Other
						Types of Collaboration					
1. Head Start											
2. Resource Access Project											

236

3. Local Department of Education										
4. Title V Program										
5. Local Title XIX and Title XX										
6. HEW Agency Serving DD Population										
7.										
8.										
9.										
10.										
11.										
12.										
etc.										

*Adapted from Service Integration Project: Final Report, Chapel Hill Training Outreach Project, Anne Sanford, Director.

Signature of Authorized Representative   Date

WORKSHEET C
Sample Letter of Understanding

Dear Community Provider,
Pursuant to a grant from _____, we are collecting
        (Granting Agency)
statistical data on handicapped children in _____.
        (Catchment Area)

Please review the enclosed worksheets, definitions, and diagnostic criteria attached.

After completing the worksheets to the best of your ability, please have them checked by an authorized representative and returned with the section below to _____ by _____.
    (Person/Agency)   (Date)

Figures in the attached pages were compiled by _____
        (Agency/Individual)
according to diagnostic criteria and definitions provided to our office.

It is agreed that this information is being provided to assist _____
_____ with the development of a proposal to assist
(Agency Applying for Grant)
preschool handicapped children and their families through the collaborative delivery of service in _____.
        (Catchment Area)

_____ /_____
Authorized Signature   Date

Demographic Data

Agency Providing Information _____

Date _____

Contact Person _____ Phone _____

Total Number of Children Professionally Diagnosed as Handicapped as Shown by Major Disability and Age. You must use the Head Start Categories and definition of "professionally diagnosed" as shown on the enclosed list of definitions and terms.

Do not include children believed to have a handicap but who have *not* had a professional diagnosis. Enter each child only once.

1. Disability	Birth to 3 Years	3 to 6 Years
Blindness	_____	_____
Visual Impairment	_____	_____
Deafness	_____	_____
Hearing Impairment	_____	_____
Physical Handicap (Orthopedic)	_____	_____
Speech Impairment	_____	_____
Health Impairment	_____	_____
Mental Retardation	_____	_____
Serious Emotional Disturbance	_____	_____
Specific Learning Disabilities	_____	_____
Total Number of Children Professionally Diagnosed as Handicapped	_____	_____

2. Total Number of Professional Diagnoses Performed by a Diagnostic Team: _____
   (Three or more professionals representing at least three different disciplines.)

3. Estimated Number of Children Assumed to Be Handicapped But Not Professionally Diagnosed:

                         Birth to 3 Years   **3 to 6 Years**

                         _____   _____

Basis and source for above estimate:

4. Problems in Securing Professional Diagnosis (rank in order of frequency of problem)*:

Problem	Frequency Rank
Time Lag between Referral and Diagnosis	
Lack of Available Diagnostic Resources in Community	
Lack of Responsiveness by Resource Agencies	
Fear of Labeling Children	
Diagnosticians Lack of Understanding of Categorial Descriptions	
Lack of Money to Pay for Diagnosis	
Other	

5. Total Number of Children Professionally Diagnosed as Handicapped Who Are Currently Receiving Service from Your Program (same as total of #1):

                         Birth to 3 Years   **3 to 6 Years**

                         _____   _____

---

*Adapted from Tables 58 and 59, Report of Services to Handicapped in Head Start. 1978.

6. Of Those Children Professionally Diagnosed as Handicapped and
Served by Your Program:

	Birth to 3 Years	3 to 6 Years
Total Number of Children for Whom: a) A Comprehensive Individualized Plan* Has Been Completed	_____	_____
b) A Partial Individualized Plan Has Been Completed	_____	_____
Total Number of Children *Currently Receiving* Treatment/Intervention as Recommended by: a) Any Type of Written Individualized Plan	_____	_____
b) An Unwritten or Informal Plan	_____	_____
Total Number of Children Pending Treatment/Intervention	_____	_____
Total Number of Children for Whom Treatment/Intervention Is Inadequate or Unavailable (please indicate if an estimate)	_____	_____

---

*In this proposal, a comprehensive individualized plan is a written plan based on an educational and a health assessment. A partial individualized plan would be based on either one or the other.

7. Problems in Securing a Comprehensive Individualized Plan (rank in order of frequency of problem):

Problem	Frequency Rank
Time Lag between Diagnosis and Completion of Appropriate Plan	
Lack of Professional Persons Who Have Been Identified as Planning Team	
Lack of Functional Assessment	
Reluctance or Refusal of Family to Accept Plan	
Lack of Resources to Carry Out Plan	
Professionals' Lack of Understanding of a Comprehensive Individualized Plan	
Use of a Partial Individualized Plan Not Based on Both an Educational and Health Assessment	
Other	

*(MANDATORY: duplicate for each
contributing provider and submit
with final proposal)*

WORKSHEET D
Resource Utilization Data
Collection Worksheet

This information may be gathered by phone or detached and duplicated for each provider of information. Submit with final proposal.

Program Number _____
(Assigned by Interviewer)

Name of Program or Agency _____

Address _____

Contact Person _____ Phone _____

1. Handicapping Conditions Served—check all applicable.
   Blindness   _____
   Visual Impairment   _____
   Deafness   _____
   Hearing Impairment   _____
   Physical Handicap (Orthopedic)   _____
   Speech Impairment   _____
   Health Impairment   _____
   Mental Retardation   _____
   Serious Emotional Disturbance   _____
   Specific Learning Disabilities   _____

2. Ages Served (circle all applicable)
   0 - 1 - 2 - 3 - 4 - 5 - 6 - 7 + Adult _____

3. What types of professionals deliver services (psychologist, physician, audiologist, special educator)?

4. What types of paraprofessionals or nonprofessionals deliver service?

5. What are eligibility requirements for clients?

6. What fees do clients pay?

7. What are the procedures for securing service for clients?

8. What instrument and/or procedures are used in identifying and assessing handicapping conditions?

9. What is the approximate number of clients from birth to 6 years served annually? _____

10. Are your services utilized fully _____, moderately _____, minimally _____?

11. Is service initiated by:
    _____ Parents _____ Advocate _____ Referral _____
    Case Manager _____ Agency _____ Other

12. Are the services authorized by (check)
    _____ State legislation _____ Federal legislation
    _____ State agency policy _____ Federal agency policy
    _____ Other (specify) _____
    _____

Program Number _____

Please check the appropriate columns below regarding the services you provide handicapped children. A definition of each of the services is provided with this Workbook.

	Services You Offer (Mark X)	Ages Served 0/3 3/6	Services You Would Like to Offer (Mark O)	If "O," Why Do You Not Currently Offer?
1. Counseling				
2. Screening				
3. Diagnosis				
4. Evaluation				
5. Education (classroom or home based)				
6. Follow-up				
7. Referral				
8. Personal Care				
9. Legal (protective/advocate)				
10. Recreation				
11. Staff Training				
12. Transportation				
13. Treatment (specify: PT/OT/speech)				
14. Equipment				
15. Instructional Materials				
16. Day Care				
17. Foster Care				
18. Parent Training				
19. Case Management				
20. IEP in PL 94-142				
21. Comprehensive Individualized Planning				
22. Financial Assistance				
23. Health Service				
24. Public Education				
25. Homemaker Service				
26. Home Nursing				
27. Preventive Services				
28. Other				

Index

Action plans, in educational planning design, 68
Acute illness, management in residential facility, 123
Adult education programs, 157
Advocacy, 173-191
  and ethical considerations, 189-190
  collective, 174
  efforts of public and private sectors, 22-23
  individual, 174
  in institutions, 186-189
  models, 177-183
  overview, 173-176
  problems in, 190-191
  systems, 179
Advocates
  case manager, 178
  citizen, 177
Amicus curiae, 181
Amino acid metabolism disorders, and mental retardation, 85
Ashkenazic Jews, screening for lipidoses, 83

Bar, private, and legal advocacy, 184-185
Bar committees, 184
Behavioral modification techniques, and behavior problems, 102
Behavior problems, of severely disabled people, 100
Blindness
  and lobbying, 23
  categorical definition, 232
  problems in detection and programming, 105

Carbohydrate metabolism disorders, and mental retardation, 84-85
Case management
  definition, 228

determining responsibility for, 202
Case manager, as coordinator of service delivery, 164
Case manager advocates, 178
Case study for planning coordinated services, 211-245
Categorical definitions of handicapping conditions, 232-234
Cerebral palsy, 103
Change, minimizing adverse impact of, 199
Chicago study, 95-96, 107, 108
Child Development Consultant, in special education, 60
Child find, in needs assessment, 56-57
Child Health and Planning (CHAP), 106
Chronic illness, management in residential facility, 123
Citizen advocates, 177
Class action lawsuits, 186
Clinics, as providers of outpatient services, 97
Collaborative Efforts (Worksheet B), 236-237
Commitment, and least drastic means principle, 186
Communication, role in coordination planning, 7, 113, 198
Communication disorder (speech impairment), categorical definition, 233
Community, definition, 1
Community-based interagency delivery system for preschool, handicapped children, case study, 211-245
Community-level planning, 17-23, 25
Community-level services, and federal legislation, 30
Community medical centers, as adjuncts to residential facility care, 125
Community Mental Health Centers—Staffing and Construction Act (PL 94-63), 26
Community residences, as residential planning option, 151

Comprehensive individualized plan, definition, 228
Consulting teacher program, 60
Consumerism, as force in service delivery, 73-74, 107-108
Continuum of planning variables, in cyclical model, 10, 11, 14-17
Continuum of services
  and Early Periodic Screening Diagnosis and Treatment Program (EPSDT), 72
  in needs assessment, 59-60
Contractual arrangements, to serve developmentally disabled individuals, 113-114
Coordination of services
  barriers, 7-8
  health care, 105
Cost-efficiency
  as continuum in cyclical model, 16-17
  in human service delivery, 167
Costs, of service delivery, 61, 62
Counseling
  by Division of Vocational Rehabilitation, 156
  definition, 228
  for job placement assistance, 156
  genetic, 81
Cyclical model of service delivery
  and interdisciplinary team approach, 145-146
  application, 10-13
  continuum of planning variables, 10, 11, 14-17
  definition, 9-10
  impact of public and private sectors, 21-23
  implementation, 13-17
  list of planning options, 37

Data collection
  and difficulties in planning, 148
  for demographic data, 216-220
  for determining incidence of handicapped individuals, 143
  for needs assessment, 54
  for participating agencies, 214—216
  for planning health services in residential settings, 126-128
  value in planning, 27
Davis v. Watkins, 48
Day care
  definition, 228
  program options, 153-157

Deafness
  categorical definition, 233
  causes, 104
  screening for, 104
Deinstitutionalization
  and Willowbrook case, 132-134
  effect on composition of population in residential facilities, 126
Demographic data, collection in case study, 216-220
Demographic Description of Catchment Area Summary, 217
Deprivation, psychosocial, and mental retardation, 79-80
Developmental Disabilities Planning Councils, 34, 148
Developmental disability
  and specialized diagnostic services, 96-98
  definition within legislation, 35, 141-143
  determining frequency in population, 93
  history of federal legislation, 33-34
  needs assessment, 91-96
  screening for, 110-111
Developmental Disabilities Assistance and Bill of Rights Act (PL 94-103), 33
Developmental Disabilities Services and Facilities Construction Act (PL 91-517), 33
Developmental Disability Bill of Rights Act of 1978, 148
Diagnosis, definition, 228
Diagnostic clinics
  and developmental disability, 96-98
  as problem in service delivery, 112
Diagnostic team, definition, 228
Diana v. State Board of Education, 48
Division of Vocational Rehabilitation, and counseling, 156
Drugs (see Medications)
Duplication, of human service delivery systems, 200, 202, 203

Early intervention
  and physical disabilities, 104
  and psychosocial mental retardation, 79
  approaches for increased success, 111-112
Early Periodic Screening Diagnosis and Treatment Program (EPSDT), 72, 106
Education
  adult, 157
  definition, 228

higher, 158
issues in planning, 70–74
opportunities for, 157–159
public, definition, 232
right to, history of federal legislation, 32–33
Education Amendments of 1974 (PL 93-380), 157
Education for All Handicapped Children Act (PL 94-142)
and consumerism, 74
and mainstreaming, 41
and work/study programs, 154
as reflection of societal attitudes, 5
health service implications, 115
list of mandates, 49–51
provisions of, 32–33
Emotional disturbance, serious, categorical definition, 234
Employment
gainful, 156
residential planning options for, 153–157
transitional, 154
Environment, and residential planning, 149–162
Equal education, history of federal legislation, 32–33
Equal opportunities, history of federal legislation, 31–32
Equipment/materials, definition, 229
Ethical considerations, and advocacy, 189–190
Evaluation
of health care services, 108–117
of IEP impact, 68–70

Facilitator, role in interagency agreements, 198
Financial assistance, definition, 229
First Chance Centers (Handicapped Children's Early Education Program), 60, 74
Follow-up
definition, 229
of high risk infant, 109
Foster care placement, definition, 229
Funding
and educational budgets, 72
and fiscal restraint, 200
determining responsibility for, 203
estimating and strategy, 226–228

mechanisms for, impact on health care planning and coordination of services, 105–107

Genetic counseling services, 81
Genetic disease, prevention and role of law, 86–87
Goals, statement of, in plan design, 67
Grants, objectives and strategies, 226–228
Group homes, as residential planning option, 151
Gross national product (GNP), budget for education, 72
Guadalupe Organization v. *Tempe Elementary School District,* 48

Habilitation
definition, 137
plans, 187
Handicapped Children's Early Education Assistance Program (First Chance), 60, 74
Head Start, 72, 74
HBAg carrier state, in viral hepatitis, 133
Head counts, in needs assessments, 56
Health care
and federal legislation, 29–34
characteristics of available services, 91–93
coordination of services, 105–108
defining, 93
evaluation of services, 108–117
general, for developmentally disabled persons, 98
inpatient services, 99
outpatient services, 96–99
problematic areas in service delivery, 109–113
Health impairment, categorical definition, 233
Health services
and federal legislation, 114–115
and state and local legislation, 116
definition, 229
Health Systems Agencies (HSA's), and coordination of legislation affecting health services, 114
Hearing impairment (handicap), categorical definition, 233
(*see also* Deafness)
Higher education, and Rehabilitation Act Amendments of 1973 (Section 504), 158
High risk infant, follow-up as problem of service delivery, 109

High risk pregnancy, screening for, 84, 96
High risk registry, 109
Home, and residential planning, 150
Home care programs, as residential planning option, 151
Homemaker service, definition, 229
Home nursing services, definition, 229
Hospitals, as providers of inpatient services, 99
Hospital for the Ruptured and Crippled, 138
Housing, and federal legislation, 30–31
Housing and Community Development Act of 1974, Housing Assistance Payments Program, Section 8, 31
Housing Authorization Act (PL 94-375), 30, 31
Human service delivery systems
    definition, 2
    foundation principles, 4
    influence of community attitudes, 3–6
    issues, 164–169
    primary characteristics, 2–3
    problems of creation, 6–8
Hyperactive children, and medications, 101
Hypoglycemia, and mental retardation, 84

Immunization, for diseases causing mental retardation, 82
Improper classification, and litigation, 48
Incentive contracts, in special education, 62
Incidence data, for handicapped individuals, 143
Independent Living Program (1978 Amendments to Rehabilitation Act of 1973), 32
Individual Education Plan (IEP)
    evaluation of impact, 68–70
    in PL 94-142, 50
    objectives in planning, 53
    process for development of, 62–65
Individualized educational planning, definition, 229
Individualized plan, comprehensive, definition, 228
Inpatient services, 99
In-service training, 200
Institutional advocacy, 186–189
Institutions (see Residential Facilities)
Instructional materials, definition, 229
Intensive care facilities, in residential facilities, 125

Intensive care unit (ICU), and follow-up of high risk infants, 109, 110
Interagency
    agreements, 196–198, 204–207
    collaboration, 200–204
    communication, as problem in service delivery, 113
    coordination, 195–196
    definition, 229
Interagency agreements
    checklist, 207
    elements of, 206
    levels of, 206
    process of developing, 204–206
    overcoming roadblocks, 198
    reasons for failure, 205
    roadblocks to development, 196–198
Interdisciplinary teams
    and coordination of service delivery systems, 194–195
    and cyclical model of service delivery, 145–146
    function in IEP development, 62
Intermediate Care Facilities for the Mentally Retarded, 105
Intermediate care facilities (ICF)
    as residential planning option, 150
    for mentally retarded persons, 105
Inventory, of programs, 204
Intervention, definition, 230

Joint policy statements, 201

Larry P. v. Riles, 48
Learning disabilities, specific, categorical definition, 234
Least drastic means principle, and civil commitments, 186
Least-Restrictive Environment Decision-Making Model, 63, 64
Lebanks v. Spears, 48
Legal service, definition, 230
Legislation (see also specific law by title and PL number)
    and health services, 29–34, 114–116
    and planning health services in institutional settings, 130
    and training of service providers, 149
    as continuum in cyclical model, 15–16

effect on planning services, 28-34
federal, and community-level services, 30
federal housing, 30-31
mandating interagency efforts, 201
role in prevention of genetic disease, 86-87
Life cycle, and cyclical model of service delivery, 145-146
Litigation (*see also* specific case by title)
in special education planning, 46-51
role in planning health services in institutional settings, 131
right to education, 46-47
right to treatment, 47-48
Lipidoses, and menal retardation, 83-85
Lobbying, 23
Local Education Agency (LEA), 51

Mainstreaming concept, 33, 41, 72
Major disability, definition, 230
Manpower (*see* Personnel)
Maryland Association for Retarded Children v. State of Maryland, 47
Matching services, in needs assessment, 55
Maternal and Child Health and Mental Retardation Planning Amendments (PL 88-156), 106
Medicaid, 105
Medical services, 96-99
Medicare, 105
Medications
and hyperactive children, 101
and treatment of behavior problems, 100, 101, 102
checklist for improved follow-up, 101
Mental age scales, 42
Mental retardation
and inborn errors of metabolism, 83-85
and maternal-fetal blood incompatibilities, 82-83
categorical definition, 234
distribution frequency, 80
early detection, 81
elimination via immunization, 82
mechanisms causing, 78-79
psychosocial or polygenic sociocultural, 79-80
planning for prevention, 77-89
public attitude toward, 6
Mental Retardation Facilities and Community Mental Health Centers Construction Act of 1963 (PL 88-164), 26

Mills v. *Board of Education of District of Columbia,* 47
Mission statements, in plan design, 66
Motor disabilities (*see* Physical disabilities)
Multiply handicapped persons, as "problem cases," 99, 100

National Association for Retarded Citizens (NARC), and residential planning, 151
National Commission on Architectural Barriers, 139
National Council on the Handicapped, 34
National Health Planning and Resources Development Act of 1974 (PL 77-157), 114
Needs assessment
for developmental disabilities, 91-96
in educational planning, 54-59
News Media, impact on public opinion, 132
New York State Association for Retarded Children v. *Carey* (Willowbrook Consent Decree), and deinstitutionalization, 93, 116
Nonprofessional, definition, 230
Normalization concept
and continuum of services, 59
and PL 94-142, 41
historical basis, 4

Office of Education, 42
Ombudsman lawyers, and legal advocacy, 183-184
On-the-job training (OJT), as residential planning option, 154
Orthopedic handicap (physical handicap), categorical definition, 233
Outpatient services, 96-99, 125

Parent training, definition, 230
Participating Areas Summary, 215
Pediatricians, and participation in PL 94-142, 115
Pennsylvania Association for Retarded Children v. *Commonwealth of Pennsylvania,* 46
Personal care, definition, 230
Personnel
and health care services, 116-117
distribution of resources in planning, 26-27
in diagnostic clinics, 97

Personnel (*cont.*)
in management of physical disabilities, 103
in planning groups, 65
in special education, 58-59
recruitment, 123
training, and legislation, 149
training needs, 162-164
Phenylketonuria (PKU), and mental retardation, 85
Physical disabilities, 103-104
and early intervention, 104
and predictability of test results, 104
personnel required for management, 103
treatment, 103
Physical handicap (orthopedic handicap), categorical definition, 233
Physicians
and Willowbrook Consent Decree, 132
difficulties in recruitment for residential settings, 123
Physician extenders, in residential facilities, 124
PL 77-157, 114
PL 78-113 (Vocational Rehabilitation Act of 1943), 139
PL 83-565 (Vocational Rehabilitation Amendments of 1954), 139
PL 88-156 (Maternal and Child Health and Mental Retardation Planning Amendments), 106
PL 88-164 (Mental Retardation Facilities and Community Mental Health Centers Construction Act), 26
PL 89-10, 106
PL 89-333 (Vocational Rehabilitation Act Amendments of 1965), 139
PL 91-517 (Developmental Disabilities Services and Facilities Construction Act), 33
PL 92-603, 106
PL 93-112 (Rehabilitation Act of 1973), 31
PL 93-380 (Educational Amendments of 1974), 157
PL 94-63 Community Mental Health Centers—Staffing and Construction Act), 26
PL 94-103 (Developmental Disabilities Assistance and Bill of Rights Act), 33, 179
PL 94-142 (Education for All Handicapped Children Act), 5, 32, 41, 56, 115, 197
PL 94-375 (Housing Authorization Act), 30, 31
PL 95-602 (Rehabilitation, Comprehensive

Services, and Developmental Disabilities Amendments of 1978), 33-34, 106, 179
Placement match, in IEP development, 63, 64
Planning services
community level, 25
for rehabilitation, range of options, 149-162
for special education, 70-76
general considerations, 23-28
residential options, 150-153
suggestions for design, 66-68
Planning variables, as continuum in cyclical model, 11
Polygenic sociocultural retardation, 79-80
Population estimates
in needs assessment, 55
in service planning, 24
Preventive services, definition, 230
Professional, definition, 230
Professional diagnosis, definition, 230
Program standards, and interagency collaboration, 202
Private bar
and legal advocacy, 184-185
and reluctance to serve handicapped population, 128-129
Private sector
function in community planning, 17-23
impact on cyclical model, 21-23
Pro bono services, of private bar, 185
Protection and Advocacy (P & A) systems, 179
Psychosocial mental retardation, 79-80
Psychiatrists, and treatment of behavior problems of severely disabled people, 100
Public attitude
and prevention of mental retardation, 80
historical role in shaping human service delivery systems, 3-6
impact on cyclical model, 21-23
impact of news media, 132
toward handicapped individuals, 161, 163, 164
Public education, definition, 232
Public interest law center, and legal advocacy, 180-183
Public sector
function in community planning, 17-23
impact on cyclical model, 21-23

Randolph Sheppard Act of 1936, 138
Recreation, 159-162
definition, 232

Recruitment, of physicians, 123
Referral, definition, 232
Rehabilitation
  definition, 137
  magnitude of the need, 143
  scope of the need, 144
Rehabilitation, Comprehensive Services and
  Developmental Disabilities Amendments
  of 1978 (PL 95-602), 33-34, 147
Rehabilitation Act of 1973 (PL 93-112), 31,
  32, 115
Rehabilitation planning, range of options,
  149-162
Residential facilities, and delivery of health
  services, 121-135
Residential planning options, 150-153
Resource room, in special education, 60
Resource utilization, data collection in case
  study, 220
Resource Utilization Data Collection Work-
  sheet (Worksheet D), 243-245
Resource Utilization Summary List, 221
Resources, community, summary matrix in
  case study, 222
Respite care, as residential planning option,
  151
Ricci v. Greenblatt, 48
Right to education
  history of federal legislation, 32-33
  litigation, 46-47
Right to treatment litigation, 47-48

Sample Letter of Support (Worksheet A), 235
Sample Letter of Understanding (Worksheet
  C), 238-242
Screening
  cooperative interagency procedures, 203
  definition, 232
  for deafness, 104
  for developmental disability, 96, 110-111
  for genetic disorders, 86, 87
  for phenylketonuria (PKU), 85
  for Tay-Sachs disease, 84
Segregation, as continuum in cyclical model,
  14
Seizures
  frequency distribution, 94, 102
  key elements in appropriate management,
    102-103
  refractory cases, 103
Self-contained classrooms, in special education, 59, 60

Self-determination, as continuum in cyclical
  model, 15
Self-regulation, as continuum in cyclical
  model, 17
Self-survival, as continuum in cyclical model,
  14-15
Serious emotional disturbance, categorical definition, 234
Service delivery
  case study, 211-245
  costs at elementary school level, 60
  cyclical model, 8-23, 145-146
  impediments to, 146-149
  problematic areas in health care, 109-113
Service linkages, as problem in service deliv-
  ery, 113
Service programs, inventory of, 203
Services, medical, 96-99
Severely and profoundly retarded persons,
  service requirements, 81
Sheltered workshops, as residential planning
  option, 153
Single port of entry, in needs assessment, 57
Skilled nursing facilities, as residential plan-
  ning option, 150
Smith Hughes Act, 138
Social factors, effect on planning services,
  34-36
Social Security Act, 105, 106
Socioeconomic status, and mental retardation,
  80
Soldiers Rehabilitation Act, 138
Special education planning
  historical overview, 42-46
  litigation, 46-51
  need for, 51-53
Special educators, needs assessment, 58
Special classes
  for exceptional children, 44-45
  improper procedures for placement and liti-
    gation, 48-49
Special Olympics, 159, 160
Specific learning disabilities, categorical defi-
  nition, 234
Specific objectives, in plan design, 67
Speech impairment (communication disorder),
  categorical definition, 233
Staff (see Personnel)
Staff burnout, 163
Staff training, definition, 232
State Education Agency (SEA), in PL 94-142,
  50, 51

State Plan, in PL 94-142, 50
Summary Matrix of Community Resources, 222
Systems advocacy, 179

Tay-Sachs disease
  frequency, 83
  screening for, 84
Technology, as continuum in cyclical model, 17
Terminology, definitions of, 228-234
The Futures of Children, 70
The Right to Choose, 157
Total care facility, as residential planning option, 152
Training
  for special educators, 43
  in-service, 200
  of service providers, 149, 162-164
  on-the-job, as residential planning option, 154-155
  parent, definition, 230
  staff, definition, 232
Training programs
  as residential planning option, 154
  for health care personnel, 117
Transitional employment programs (TEP), as residential planning option, 155
Transportation, definition, 232
Treacher-Collins syndrome, 104

University Affiliated Facilities (UAF's), 7, 127
Utilization Review and Independent Professional Review Programs, 130

Vendor model of human service delivery, 168
Viral hepatitis, as endemic disease at Willowbrook, 132-135
Vision (*see* Blindness)
Visual impairment (handicap), categorical definition, 233
Vocational/day programs, as residential planning options, 153-157
Vocational education, historical overview, 139-141
Vocational rehabilitation, historical overview, 137-139
Vocational Rehabilitation Act of 1943 (PL 78-113), 139
Vocational Rehabilitation Act Amendments of 1954 (PL 83-565), 139
Vocational Rehabilitation Act Amendments of 1965 (PL 89-333), 139

Welch v. *Likens,* 48
Willowbrook Consent Decree (*New York State Association for Retarded Children* v. *Carey*)
  and deinstitutionalization, 93, 116
  and impact of news media, 132
  specifications of the court, 131
Workbook, 213-245
Worksheet A (Sample Letter of Support), 235
Worksheet B (Collaborative Efforts), 236-237
Worksheet C (Sample Letter of Understanding), 238-242
Worksheet D (Resource Utilization Data Collection Worksheet), 243-245
"Workshop without walls," as residential planning option, 155
Work/study program, as residential planning option, 154
Wyatt v. *Aderhold,* 47